EU CITIES FACILITATING THE COMMONS

This book explores the role of cities in the EU in facilitating civic participation through the commons (CPC), through the prism of constitutional principles.

It fills a gap by providing a much-needed theoretical framework for commons-oriented initiatives. It focuses on democracy, participation, local governments and cities, by looking at the two legal orders of the European Union and the Council of Europe. At its core is the case study of Italy, where there is institutionalised collaboration between society and the State in over 320 cities. It shows that by leveraging the four key European constitutional principles of participation, local self-government, subsidiarity and solidarity, all EU cities can act as drivers of the commons. A fascinating and innovative exploration of civic participation through the commons that reinforces local democracy.

Volume 139 in the Series Modern Studies in European Law

Modern Studies in European Law

Recent titles in this series:

The Dynamics of Powers in the European Union
Edited by Christina Eckes, Päivi Leino-Sandberg and Anna W Ghavanin

The European Convention on Human Rights and Private Law:
Comparative Perspectives from South-Eastern Europe
Edited by Mateja Durovic and Cristina Poncibò

Judging Composite Decision-Making:
The Transformation of European Administrative Law
Filipe Brito Bastos

EU Diplomacy in Multilateral Fora
Edited by Christine Kaddous and Frank Hoffmeister

The Market Citizenship Illusion: Free Movement Rights for Atypical Workers
Alice Welsh

Actors and Roles in EU Disability Law
Edited by Delia Ferri and Eva S Krolla

The Impact of War (in Ukraine) on the EU
Edited by Inge Govaere, Sacha Garben and Eleanor Spaventa

The European Judiciary: A Community of Law and a Community of Judges
Edited by Alejandro Saiz Arnaiz and Joan Solanes Mullor

Dissensus over Liberal Democracy: Insights from European Judges
Edited by Ramona Coman, Viktor Kazai, Leonardo Puleo and Andrew Bradley

Structural Principles of EU Law
Marcus Klamert

Environmental NGOs and Access to Justice before the CJEU
Mario Pagano

Dealing with Rule of Law Crises in the European Union:
Challenges from a Comparative Federalism Perspective
Niels F Kirst

EU Citizenship and Responsibility:
The Evolving Roles of the Union, the Individual, and the Member States
Maria Haag

EU Cities Facilitating the Commons:
Building Blocks of European Constitutional Law for Local Democracy
Chiara Salati

For the complete list of titles in this series
see www.bloomsbury.com/uk/series/modern-studies-in-european-law/

EU Cities Facilitating the Commons

Building Blocks of European Constitutional Law for Local Democracy

Chiara Salati

•HART•

OXFORD • LONDON • NEW YORK • NEW DELHI • SYDNEY

HART PUBLISHING

Bloomsbury Publishing Plc

Kemp House, Chawley Park, Cumnor Hill, Oxford, OX2 9PH, UK

1385 Broadway, New York, NY 10018, USA

Bloomsbury Publishing Ireland Limited, 29 Earlsfort Terrace, Dublin 2, D02 AY28, Ireland

HART PUBLISHING, the Hart/Stag logo, BLOOMSBURY and the Diana logo are trademarks of Bloomsbury Publishing Plc

First published in Great Britain 2026

A catalogue record for this book is available from the British Library.

A catalogue record for this book is available from the Library of Congress.

ISBN: HB: 978-1-50998-966-9
ePDF: 978-1-50998-968-3
ePub: 978-1-50998-967-6

Typeset by Compuscript Ltd, Shannon

For product safety related questions contact productsafety@bloomsbury.com

To find out more about our authors and books visit www.hartpublishing.co.uk. Here you will find extracts, author information, details of forthcoming events and the option to sign up for our newsletters.

To Elmar

PREFACE

The origin of this book dates to 2018 during an internship at the NGO Labsus-Laboratorio per la sussidiarietà (Turin), where I wanted to learn how the principle of subsidiarity was driving public authorities to support a new form of civic participation through the commons in hundreds of Italian cities. This raised an urgent question: if this is possible in Italy, could this form of participation also find support in other EU cities through common European constitutional principles?

This journey continued at the University of Macerata with a fully funded three-year PhD scholarship for which I remain deeply grateful. This doctoral period was enriched by research stays at the University of Antwerp Government and Law research group (Antwerp), the Eurac Research Institute for Comparative Federalism (Bolzano/Bozen), and the FinEst Centre for Smart Cities (Tallinn). Insights from many conversations with scholars and preliminary presentations of this work became invaluable inspiration. I am indebted to the lessons learned, ideas shared, light bulb moments and future opportunities that opened up. The idea of this book later continued to develop in parallel with my work as a post-doc researcher at the Eurac Research Institute for Comparative Federalism and during research stays at the Council of Europe (Strasbourg) and Ximpulse GmbH (Bern), where it was also nurtured by these rich and stimulating environments for which I am sincerely grateful. Complementing these research contexts, my collaboration with the Labsus network across Italy over the years has been an invaluable opportunity to engage directly on the ground with practitioners, policymakers, and citizens.

All in all, this book is a derivative work of my doctoral thesis awarded by the University of Macerata in 2023 and deposited in its institutional repository. The thesis was rewritten and underwent considerable revision to become a book.

I am thankful to colleagues, friends and all those people who at different moments shared with me the fascinating research work for this book. From every encounter I learned something valuable that I carry with me and that contributed to my own search for understanding. This book is not the result of a single effort, but of a network of exchanges, questions, doubts, answers. A special thanks goes to Erika Arban, who became my supportive reference point in the long process of transforming my PhD work into a book. I am sincerely grateful to the entire Hart Publishing team for their trust in the potential of this book and for their guidance and support in shaping this book. Last but not least, I am deeply grateful to my family and to those people always on my side in every new life chapter.

I look with confidence at the future of EU cities, where the vision outlined in this book is more concrete and feasible than it might seem. Much remains to be done to transform our local – multi-level – democracy across the EU, and the journey is far from over: I look forward to continuing it.

CONTENTS

PART II
DEMOCRACY AT THE LOCAL LEVEL

PART III
CIVIC PARTICIPATION THROUGH THE COMMONS (CPC) IN THE CASE OF ITALIAN CITIES

LIST OF ILLUSTRATIONS

TABLE OF CASES, LEGISLATION AND OFFICIAL DOCUMENTS

Cases and Legislation from the Italian Case (Selection)

EU Sources (Selection)

International Sources (Selection)

Introduction

Local democracy is at the forefront of democracy thanks to local governments' innovation capacity and closeness to people. In the regional context of the European Union (EU), while democracy is often said to be in crisis, this mainly concerns its representative channels, whereas participatory forms are flourishing at different levels, especially the local one, offering additional tools for democratic legitimation. Civic participation through the commons (CPC) is an emerging form of participation that has recently taken root across the EU. It involves citizens not only in decision-making but also in practical actions of governance of commons. Their governance constitutes a challenge for our societies – 'the commons challenge' – in so far as they constitute all those tangible or intangible goods in our communities that questions traditional legal categories based on the public–private divide. To date, CPC remains largely non-institutionalised and experimental, except in Italy. There, since Bologna's pioneering step in 2014, CPC has spread to over 320 cities and other local authorities. The Italian case stands out for giving CPC a constitutional and legal framework, at first through Article 118(4) of the Constitution on subsidiarity in its horizontal (or social) dimension, and second through the model of shared administration, with municipal regulations on commons and collaboration pacts. In recent years, hundreds of thousands of citizens have engaged in such democratic exercises, reaching even those who distrust representative channels. The findings coming from the Italian case are thus crucial for the wider EU context, where CPC still lacks study from a European constitutional law perspective. This, in fact, is key to understanding the transformation of democracy within the EU – and beyond that.

Why this Book?

This book is about civic participation through the commons in EU cities. It addresses that from a European constitutional law perspective, which means looking at common European constitutional principles primarily belonging to the two legal orders of the EU and of the Council of Europe (CoE) in the context of the wider European legal space. The research context is the one of civic participation in local democracy, and the regional context is the one of the EU. That is why the book's main target is cities in the EU, in the acknowledgement of the many diverse legal orders having an impact on them. Moreover, the emerging role of the 'city' as an autonomous subject of research is identified when approaching local democracy and therefore constitutes an important part of the work. This reflects a worldwide phenomenon of urbanisation where cities are on the rise in claiming their role as protagonists of democratic innovation beyond states' borders and traditional administrative structures.

Within this topic, this book identified two major gaps in the literature. First, the lack of a common European theoretical framework on civic participation through the commons for all EU cities. This, in fact, could be beneficial for all those EU cities that are facing the commons challenge and need guidance and constitutional hooks upon which to frame their institutional support towards such new forms of civic participation. Second, the study of the Italian case in a wider European constitutional law perspective. The reasons for that could be diverse: its recency; its language barriers; its essential entrenchment in administrative law scholarship; and its focus on the Italian national context; its intrinsic connection with very concrete grass-roots practices that imply not only a theoretical, but also an empirical look by researchers.

The aim of the book is twofold: one external and one internal. On the external level, the book aims at identifying those common European constitutional principles that – on the basis of the case of Italian cities and a comparative overview of the broader European context – may constitute building blocks for a future theoretical framework also for all other EU cities facing the commons challenge. On the internal level, the research aims at linking the Italian case to the wider European public law context, specifically to European constitutional principles, so that the Italian case would have wider European cover. The overarching aspiration of the book is to contribute to the European legal debate on the commons.

The relevance of the overall contribution of the book is supported by many aspects. For example: (1) it presents an in-depth study of the Italian case of shared administration of the commons; (2) its findings contribute to shed new light on the potential application on the ground of the European constitutional principles of participation, subsidiarity, local self-government, solidarity; (3) it gives a general overview of what is happening around the EU on the commons; (4) it contributes to the growing literature on cities as autonomous subjects of study within a European public law perspective, drawing preliminary conclusions on their key role in experimenting with innovative forms of participation; and (5) it brings into the academic debate citizens' concrete practices that are currently happening across Italian and other European cities.

What this Book Offers

First and foremost, this book offers an answer to one overarching research question, that is: **how can EU cities facilitate civic participation through the commons by leveraging European constitutional principles?** To answer this question, the book research design has been divided into four parts, each one

addressing one key research sub-question derived as a need to unpack the overall one: how is democracy in the EU undergoing transformation, and what role does the principle of participation play in redefining its frontiers? (Part I); what are the key constitutional principles governing local democracy, and to what extent are cities playing a role in that? (Part II); why is the Italian case of civic participation through the commons relevant for local democracy, and what lessons can be drawn for the broader European context? (Part III); how are EU cities addressing the commons challenge, and which European constitutional principles can serve as building blocks for a shared theoretical framework? (Part IV).

Overall, this book argues that EU cities can facilitate and support emerging forms of civic participation through the commons thanks to some common European constitutional principles, which constitute what all EU cities have in common being immersed in the wider European legal space and not only subject to national legal orders. It does so by offering some primary building blocks of European principles that EU cities can use, aware that they only constitute a first step for the development of a common theoretical framework that as a work-in-progress will need to be continued. Its originality lies in bringing together various research streams under a broad umbrella of European constitutional law, with the aim of combining a theoretical approach with a practical action-oriented perspective for EU cities.

Of course, limitations exist. First, the difficulty in translating from both a terminological and conceptual perspective for a non-Italian readership a specific case of democratic innovation deeply rooted in the Italian legal order. Being obviously context related, some concepts explained in Part III on the Italian case may not be easily understood because of the different cultural backgrounds of the readers. Second is the difficulty in analysing the discourse on the commons, because of the challenges that a researcher faces when approaching this topic. Not only does it lie at the intersection between different disciplines, but it also generates the interests of both academic scholars as well as citizens and public institutions, providing for elements for both abstract academic debates and concrete grass-root initiatives. The conclusion outlines future research directions to bridge this limitation. All in all, also on the basis of these considerations, it is possible to state what this book surely is not: namely, a book fully devoted to the Italian case, nor a comparative work on the commons in the EU. These limitations emphasise the need for more future research.

Methodology and Essential Definitions

Situated within a European constitutional law perspective, the book adopted a methodology with doctrinal legal research as the primary research method used. This means using traditional sources like legal literature, case law and legislation coming from European constitutional law, Italian constitutional and administrative law, EU law, local government law. In particular, doctrinal legal research was used for analysing concepts such as democracy, participation, subsidiarity, local self-government, cities, shared administration. However, there were certain limitations in using only this research method, since it was not enough for dealing with certain transversal phenomena and concepts like the emerging phenomena of soft law, governance and the rising role of cities, which all present new challenges to legal scholars for their capacity to undermine traditional legal concepts like the hierarchy of sources, democratic legitimation, state theory. Since traditional doctrinal legal research seemed not to be fully equipped to properly understand these concepts according to traditional state-related categories, this implied a need for thinking outside state concepts and looking at non-state acts produced by non-state actors (like, for example, citizens or NGOs).

As a consequence, the book combines a doctrinal research method with elements of interdisciplinarity as well as transdisciplinarity. Interdisciplinarity is used to borrow concepts from other fields to enrich the legal analysis. Transdisciplinarity is used to integrate societal practice insights from grass-roots communities/activists, going beyond traditional legal research. Doctrinal legal research, indeed, needed to be enriched at many points by additional disciplinary perspectives to better understand concepts, and to answer the central research question of legal nature. The study, in fact, builds on literature coming from different auxiliary disciplines including political science, public administration, urban studies, economic theory. Incursions into other fields were made necessary by the particular nature of the subject matter, which is in constant flux, and difficult to frame exhaustively in a single discipline. In fact, concepts such as democracy, participation, the commons can all be studied from many different perspectives. To this end, concepts outside the purely legal debate such as governance, democratic innovations and polycentricity were useful to explain central legal concepts such as democracy, participation and local government, and therefore were integrated into the book. Additionally, another example is the contribution of the statistical criteria developed by the EU for classifying urban settlements which, together with EU urban policies, were useful for understanding what a city is in the context of the EU. All these cases demonstrate that if researchers want to look at certain phenomena that are crossing disciplinary boundaries, then they have to equip themselves with insights also coming from other disciplines, from professional knowledge (for example, institutional reports, policy documents, or civil society organisations' studies), as well as from societal grass-roots practices that are already contributing to their understanding. All in all, this work also constitutes an invitation to approach legal phenomena not only from a traditional doctrinal legal research perspective, but also from a wider one, understanding law as a social science. In this way, the role of legal scholars to create order and provide meaning through their theoretical reconstructions would not cease, but on the contrary, it would be enriched by additional perspectives giving originality to their work.

In conclusion, in light of this methodological premise, this introduction would like to equip the reader with some basic coordinates about terminology, as this may be of use from a conceptual perspective. Precise definitions are given throughout the whole work when needed: these here, however, are the essential ones. Such essential definitions are valid for the purpose of this book and should not always be considered as such beyond this work and in different disciplinary contexts.

- **European legal space** = the wider legal space of Europe, where different legal orders coexist, namely the EU legal order, the CoE legal order, the national legal orders.
- **City/cities** = emergent concept of public law that aims at recognising autonomous significance to the city in relation to other local governments, willing to capture the *civitas* in its original significance beyond the mere administrative borders of the *urbs* as defined by state structures. It is the place where transformations of democracy are concretely taking place from the perspective of both government and governance.
- **Civic participation through the commons (CPC)** = innovative type of action-oriented form of civic participation taking place through the commons.
- **Commons (or 'common goods')** = goods whose governance can be conflictual or collaborative. A collaborative governance of the commons occurs when it is shared by a community that – often thanks to institutional support from public authorities – gets organised according to a set of rules at the intersection between the public and private dichotomy.
- **Commons challenge** = the emerging challenge faced by different levels of government – and especially cities – in dealing with grass-roots initiatives claiming to be commons-oriented in the absence of legislation or constitutional and legal reference frameworks to that.
- **Democracy in the EU** = an integrated system of government and governance, characterised by multiple forms – representative and participatory – and multiple levels – EU, national, regional, local – which are driving democratic transformation by recognising both institutional and societal pluralism.
- **Forgotten meaning of subsidiarity** = is the horizontal (or social) dimension of the principle of subsidiarity, which foresees the institutional support by public authorities – usually the local level – towards individuals' spontaneous initiatives of general interest. This dimension has been forgotten almost everywhere in Europe, where the vertical understanding of this principle is largely predominant, except in the Italian case, where it is outlined at Article 118(4) of the Constitution.
- **Shared administration of the commons** = organisational model adopted by over 320 Italian cities and local governments in order to face the commons challenge, which comprises a prototype of municipal regulation and the collaboration pact legal tool.

- **The Italian case (or the case of Italian cities)** = experience of over 320 cities and other local authorities in Italy that, starting from the pioneering contribution of Bologna in 2014, to date have adopted – although to different extents – the organisational model of shared administration of the commons, in this way institutionalising CPC by legal means.

Structure

Based on the four parts into which the book is divided as a reflection of the research question and sub-questions, the work comprises eight chapters, in addition to this introduction and an overall conclusion at the end. Part I (chapters one and two) sets the scene by depicting the frontiers of two consolidated concepts: democracy and participation. After having scrutinised the current state of democracy in the EU context, the principle of participation is presented with reference to its contribution to the transformation of democracy through democratic innovations. Local level participation, in fact, is presented as the forefront of democracy in the EU not only for its contribution to decision-making processes, but also to action-oriented civic initiatives. Part II (chapters three and four) explores the constitutional contribution of the principles of subsidiarity and local self-government to the local level of democracy. The rising role of cities as autonomous legal subjects receives a special focus in so far as it reflects wider urbanisation processes taking place not only around the EU, but at the global level. Part III (chapters five and six) looks at the pioneering Italian case, for its constitutional anchorage of a new form of civic participation in local democracy, namely civic participation through the commons (CPC). It does so by dissecting the principle of subsidiarity and its concrete expression through the shared administration of the commons organisational model, and draws some conclusions of European importance. Part IV (chapters seven and eight) provides an overview of the complex commons debates and practices across the EU, with a focus on the institutional experience of four EU cities. Ultimately, it outlines some building blocks of European constitutional law that constitute the contours of a work-in-progress European theoretical framework that all EU cities could use to face the commons challenge (see the key figure in chapter eight). The conclusion summarises the main findings and outlines a research agenda for follow-up research.

All of that has been pursued with the general conviction that European constitutional principles – which constitute the common thread of the whole book – are keepers of unexplored meanings from which implementation possibilities can still be created. Its findings are of European relevance but also beyond that.

PART I

Democracy and Participation in the EU

1

Setting the Scene: The Transformation of Democracy in the EU

I. What Democracy in the EU?

Considered as 'a mission – something to be made, created, … a labour that never ends, a challenge always still to be met in full, a prospect forever outstanding',[1] the idea of Europe resembles closely that of democracy. Resulting as the outcome of many crises in the historical development of the European Union (EU) and regarded as something never fully realised nor precisely defined, democracy is assumed as the most distinctive value of the common European identity, alongside the rule of law, human rights and the protection of minorities. Democracy is something we can all agree upon, as it has been implicit in the European integration process from the very beginning and constitutionalised with time through an ongoing process of adjustment and refinement.[2] Yet, a clear, shared and measurable definition of democracy as an EU constitutional principle has not been agreed upon so far, as the EU process of self-definition during the enlargement processes has shown.[3]

Democracy stands at the core of the broader European legal space, where national, EU, and Council of Europe (CoE) legal orders coexist.[4] These overlapping

[1] Z Bauman, *Europe: An Unfinished Adventure* (Polity 2004).

[2] The Union's first set of membership conditions was defined in 1978 (Declaration on Democracy, Copenhagen European Council, 7–8 April 1978, Bull EC 3/78, 6). In 1993 these became the 'Copenhagen political criteria', expanded to also include minority protection and applied in the 2004 enlargement. See further, C Hillion, 'The Copenhagen Criteria and their Progeny' in C Hillion (ed), *EU Enlargement: A Legal Approach* (Hart Publishing 2004).

[3] For a critical account on the failure of the EU to distinguish between the principles of rule of law and democracy, and to provide them with a shared understanding between EU countries, see D Kochenov, *EU Enlargement and the Failure of Conditionality: Pre-Accession Conditionality in the Fields of Democracy and the Rule of Law* (Kluwer Law International 2008). In contrast to democracy – the EU's understanding of the rule of law has been consolidating throughout years through various contributions from the EU Commission, the European Court of Justice, the European Parliament and the Council: see L Pech, 'The Rule of Law as a Well-Established and Well-Defined Principle of EU Law' (2022) 14 *Hague Journal on the Rule of Law* 107.

[4] A von Bogdandy, 'The Transformation of European Law: The Reformed Concept and Its Quest for Comparison' 2016-14 MPIL Research Paper Series 13. The European legal space is the space for European law to advance 'common aims under common values' (2). European law, on its side, 'identifies this puzzling complex of interdependent legal orders', and does not focus exclusively on EU law, but it is much wider. Similar to the idea of a European legal space is the concept of 'aree geo-giuridiche' proposed by Toniatti for referring to the three legal orders that contribute to define the European

orders define democracy as a shared principle rooted in centuries of European tradition. As a fundamental concept of constitutionalism[5] which lies at the intersection between political and legal theories, democracy is enshrined in national constitutions, EU primary law (founding Treaties and unwritten general principles of EU law), as well as in the Statute of the Council of Europe.[6] The complexity of this multitude of layers demands a shift away from national sovereignty towards a transnational law perspective, exemplified most clearly by the EU's supranational law.[7] The EU has pioneered a new form of legal and political authority,[8] where democratic principles take on distinct supranational meaning. Spanning through different legal orders, it can be said that democracy belongs to the constitutional identity of Europe and to European public law,[9] and more specifically of the EU. While its expression varies – from deeply embedded to merely symbolic,[10] or imposed as a precondition for membership[11] (as was the case for Central and

constitutional space: the EU, the CoE and the OECD (on this reference see F Palermo, *La forma di Stato dell'Unione Europea* (Cedam 2005) 9 and further references). Additionally, Italian scholarship has developed the idea of a *constitutional law of integration* ('diritto costituzionale dell'integrazione'), which can be traced back to the concept of European legal space as described here: Palermo in *La Forma di Stato* used it to describe the fragmentary discipline of constitutional relations between the EU and its Member States, interacting among each other as different complementary spheres.

[5] M Rosenfeld and A Sajó (eds), *The Oxford Handbook of Comparative Constitutional Law* (Oxford University Press 2012) 19. For an introduction on democracy within constitutional theory, see G Frankenberg, 'Democracy' in M Rosenfeld and A Sajó (eds), *The Oxford Handbook of Comparative Constitutional Law* (Oxford University Press 2012).

[6] The Statute of the CoE dates back to 1949 and mentions democracy in its preamble. Democracy as a principle was also affirmed later in other charters and international treaties of the CoE, such as the fundamental European Convention on Human Rights (1953), which refers generically to 'political democracy' and 'democratic society', or the European Charter of Local Self-Government (1985), which constitutes the reference point in the European legal space for local democracy.

[7] 'Transnational law' is the broad term used to define the types of legal phenomena that do not fit into the dichotomy of state law and international law and that transcend the limits of the State. 'Supranational law' is a sub-category of transnational law, and it refers to the case when an autonomous legal order is created by two or more states – the most developed and referred case being the EU. See, on this distinction, K Tuori, 'Transnational Law: On Legal Hybrids and Legal Perspectivism' in M Poiares Maduro, K Tuori and S Sankari (eds), *Transnational Law: Rethinking European Law and Legal Thinking* (Cambridge University Press 2014); and G Della Cananea, 'Transnational Public Law in Europe' in MP Maduro, Kaarlo Tuori and Suvi Sankari (eds), *Transnational Law: Rethinking European Law and Legal Thinking* (Cambridge University Press 2014). The supranational law of the EU is part of (public) transnational law, as it exists in a legal area outside the Member States. However, as Tuori claims, EU law could also be considered as 'the most advanced epitome of transnational law' (Tuori 'Transnational Law', ibid, 26). On the perspective of transnational law as an emerging system of law, see A Bostan, 'Transnational Law – A New System of Law?' (2021) 11 *Juridical Tribune* 332.

[8] A von Bogdandy and J Bast (eds), *Principles of European Constitutional Law* (Hart Publishing 2009) 12; M Klamert and D Kochenov, 'Article 2 TEU' in M Kellerbauer, M Klamert and J Tomkin (eds), *The EU Treaties and the Charter of Fundamental Rights: A Commentary* (Oxford University Press 2019) 24.

[9] The concept of European public law defines a legal field that addresses the transformation of public law in Europe, beyond the mere borders of EU law. The concept also aggregates phenomena of various legal orders with the purpose of European unity: see A von Bogdandy, 'The Idea of European Public Law Today' 2017-4 MPIL Research Paper Series 13.

[10] We refer to those EU countries that, despite declaring themselves democracies, are paving the way to the construction within the EU legal order of a model of so-called 'illiberal democracy', which is stepping back from some constitutional guarantees within national borders.

[11] See M Claes, 'How Common Are the Values of the European Union?' (2019) 15 *Croatian Yearbook of European Law & Policy* VII: she argues that the EU's 'common constitutional principles' and

Eastern European countries in order to guarantee their accession to the EU) – its central role is undeniable.

Within the EU legal order, the most important positive basis of democracy lies in Article 2 of the Treaty on European Union (TEU). Though it refers to 'values', legal scholars agree these are binding legal 'principles'.[12] Unlike values, which are ethical and subjective, principles are enforceable legal norms. More precisely, Article 2 principles must be seen as 'founding principles' – core norms of primary law that define the Union's constitutional foundation.[13] Since EU primary law is deeply connected with Member States' constitutions, it should be treated as constitutional law.[14] Democracy, therefore, can be equally defined and referred to as a 'founding principle' of the EU legal order, or as a 'European constitutional principle'.

Despite these doctrinal qualifications of democracy, the primary law of the EU carries no definition of what democracy is. In parallel to that, the Court of Justice of the European Union (CJEU) of the EU also started to use the concept of democracy as a legal principle in the 1980s[15] by drawing inspiration from national democracies, but still not contributing with a clear definition. The authors of the Treaties have been described as successful in freeing democracy from the framework of the nation states:[16] however, nowadays a general vagueness of democracy as a principle still remains, leaving space for national-level understanding and practices. A step forward was taken with the organisation of Title II TEU titled 'Provisions on democratic principles' in the Treaty of Lisbon. The four Articles of this Title (Articles 9, 10, 11, 12 TEU) refer to different aspects that have been qualified as expressions of democracy, namely the concept of EU citizenship, the functioning of the EU as a representative democracy, the open dialogue between citizens and EU institutions through participatory means (and instruments like the European citizens' initiative, ECI), and the role of national parliaments. As has

'European values' are based on Western European traditions, later imitated by new Member States. She questions whether the EU should allow diversity in applying these fundamental values. But since EU law rejects such diversity, the main challenge is defining clear standards – which still do not exist for democracy.

[12] A von Bogdandy, 'Founding Principles of EU Law: A Theoretical and Doctrinal Sketch' (2010) 16 *European Law Journal* 106; D Kochenov, 'The Acquis and Its Principles: The Enforcement of the "Law" versus the Enforcement of "Values" in the European Union' in A Jakab and D Kochenov (eds), *The Enforcement of EU Law and Values* (Oxford University Press 2017) 9. On the legal significance of European values and on their capacity to put in practice integration through (European) constitutional law, see C Calliess, 'Europe as Transnational Law – The Transnationalization of Values by European Law' (2009) 10 *German Law Journal* 1367.

[13] von Bogdandy and J Bast (eds), *Principles* (n 8) 12: 'founding principles [are] those norms of primary law which, in view of the need to legitimise the exercise of public authority, determine the general legitimatory foundations of the Union'.

[14] von Bogdandy 'Founding Principles of EU Law' (n 12) 16.

[15] See von Bogdandy and Bast (eds), *Principles* (n 8) 47 for a list of case law. In a similar vein, worth mentioning is the contribution of the CJEU to the definition of another European constitutional principle – namely the rule of law – while its recognition was still not included in the EU Treaties: see Case 294/83 *Parti Ecologiste Les Verts v. Parliament* [1986] ECR 1339, para 23.

[16] A von Bogdandy, 'European Democracy: A Reconstruction through Dismantling Misconceptions' (2022) MPIL Research Paper Series 1.

been observed[17] and as we will see later in this work (chapter two), the complexity of interdisciplinary discussions on the principle of democracy finds a reference point in this Title.

This book defines democracy as the distribution of power within society. From its Greek origin – *dēmos* (people) and *kratos* (power) – it signifies government of people, whether directly or indirectly. After centuries of development in the relationship between individuals and a public authority, democracy has emerged as the most enduring and desirable system of government.[18] That is why today's debate no longer contrasts democracy with other regimes but examines its internal diversity.[19] This shift is especially visible in Western legal tradition,[20] and in Europe in particular. Since the rise of modern constitutionalism,[21] and throughout the development of different forms of constitutional states in continental Europe,[22] states have predominantly embraced constitutional democracy grounded in the supremacy of the constitution. This model adapts liberal constitutional principles to new realities, evolving into pluralist democracy for its promotion of social, political and institutional pluralism.[23] Today, democracy in the EU is grounded in

[17] In von Bogdandy and Bast (eds), *Principles* (n 8) 48 the authors recognise the interdisciplinarity surrounding the concept of democracy. As we will see, this is the same for the concept of participation.

[18] On democracy as the most developed form of government, see A Lijphart, *Patterns of Democracy: Government Forms and Performance in Thirty-Six Countries* (Yale University Press 2012). Well known is the observation of Winston Churchill concerning democracy, when on 11 November 1947 he said: 'Many forms of Government have been tried and will be tried in this world of sin and woe. No one pretends that democracy is perfect or all-wise. Indeed, it has been said that democracy is the worst form of Government except for all those other forms that have been tried from time to time' (quote reported from 'The International Churchill Society' (ICS) at winstonchurchill.org).

[19] See M Luciani, 'Forme di governo' (2010) *Enciclopedia del Diritto*. It is interesting to note that 'even dictators try to legitimize their rule by invoking democratic principles': K-P Sommermann, 'Citizen Participation in Multi-Level Democracies: An Introduction' in C Fraenkel-Haeberle et al (eds), *Citizen Participation in Multi-Level Democracies* (Brill-Nijhoff 2015) 2.

[20] The concept of 'Western legal tradition' includes together in a single term the legal traditions of the common law and the civil law, and it refers to the common heritage of values that both legal traditions share and have been built upon throughout centuries of evolution and revolutions. Democracy is, specifically, one of those values considered at the core of the Western legal tradition, being a founding value of both civil law and common law legal traditions. The reference is HJ Berman, 'The Western Legal Tradition in a Millennial Perspective: Past and Future' (2000) 60 *Louisiana Law Review* 739. For further reading see HJ Berman, *Law and Revolution, II: The Impact of the Protestant Reformations on the Western Legal Tradition* (Belknap Press 2006).

[21] Which is usually traced back to the entry into force of the US Constitution in 1789: see further, M Rosenfeld, 'Comparative Constitutional Analysis in United States Adjudication and Scholarship' in M Rosenfeld and A Sajó (eds), *The Oxford Handbook of Comparative Constitutional Law* (Oxford University Press 2012) 46.

[22] As a starting point, see Dieter Grimm, 'Types of Constitutions' in M Rosenfeld and A Sajó (eds), *The Oxford Handbook of Comparative Constitutional Law* (Oxford University Press 2012).

[23] In contrast to the current predominant model of constitutional democracy among European states, and in the light of the emergence of states advocating for a model of 'illiberal democracy', the liberal tradition has been recently pointed out for its fundamental contribution to democracy in G Halmai, 'Does Illiberal Democracy Exist?' in G Amato, B Barbisan and C Pinelli (eds), *Rule of Law vs Majoritarian Democracy* (Hart Publishing 2021). While reflecting on the concept of 'illiberal democracy' the author states 'that there is no democracy without liberalism, and there also cannot be liberal rights without democracy' (171).

pluralism, openness, diversity and liberty. This vision echoes the Roman *civitas* – the complexity of all its inhabitants living together in the city under the same legal order despite their religion, ethnicity, language – rather than the exclusive Greek *polis* built on strict inclusion of only people sharing the same origin.[24] Modern European constitutional democracy has moved from unity to difference. The EU embodies this shift as a 'demoicracy': a government of people – both states and citizens – that govern together, not as one.[25] EU democracy exists without a unique *demos*,[26] encompassing multiple peoples (*demoi*). As a *demoicracy*, the EU is neither a union of national democracies nor a unified democracy: it is a sui generis type of democracy that does not replicate the nation states one, but that is actually inventing a new concept of post-national democracy.[27] Terms like *demoicracy* and *transnational democracy*[28] reflect this shift. The latter describes a legal order rooted in both states and citizens, where democracy functions in a union beyond a Westphalian system of international relations.[29]

The EU, as a legal and political community, is built on shared values, projects, goals – not a single identity like nation states. This challenges the historical evolution of the concept of democracy – the 'transformations of democracy'[30] – that from ancient direct democracy in the Greek city states, developed into modern representative systems with the nation states' era, and that is now entering a third phase shaped by transnational governance and the erosion of states' autonomy.[31] In this evolving order, the key question is what form of democracy can address the

[24] U Curi, 'Alle radici dell'idea di città' in F Pizzolato et al (eds), *La città e la partecipazione tra diritto e politica* (Giappichelli 2019); M Cacciari, *La città* (Pazzini Editore 2021). As Cacciari observes, the contemporary European law is rooted on ancient Roman law in so far as it conceives the city as the space where people accept to be subjected to the same law, despite their diversities. European cities are therefore rooted not in the ancient Greek *polis*, but in the ancient Roman *civitas*.

[25] K Nicolaïdis, 'European Demoicracy and its Crisis' (2013) 51 *Journal of Common Market Studies* 351, 352. The idea of *demoicracy* was first articulated in K Nicolaïdis, 'The New Constitution as European "Demoi-Cracy"?' (2004) 7(1) *Critical Review of International Social and Political Philosophy* 76. See also F Cheneval and F Schimmelfennig, 'The Case for Demoicracy in the European Union' (2013) 51 *Journal of Common Market Studies* 334, 340.

[26] von Bogdandy 'European Democracy' (n 16); JHH Weiler et al, 'European Democracy and its Critique' (1995) 18(3) *West European Politics* 4, 5.

[27] On this point, K Nicolaïdis, 'The Idea of European Demoicracy' in J Dickson and P Eleftheriadis (eds), *Philosophical Foundations of European Union Law* (Oxford University Press 2012) 251; Y Mény, 'De La Démocratie En Europe: Old Concepts and New Challenges' (2003) 41 *Journal of Common Market Studies* 1, 13.

[28] Nicolaïdis 'European Demoicracy and its Crisis' (n 25) 353.

[29] J Hoeksma, 'Replacing the Westphalian System' (2020) *The Federal Trust*, available at: fedtrust.co.uk/wp-content/uploads/2020/10/Replacing-the-Westphalian-system.pdf.

[30] RA Dahl, 'A Democratic Dilemma: System Effectiveness versus Citizen Participation' (1994) 109 *Political Science Quarterly* 23; RA Dahl, *Democracy and Its Critics* (Yale University Press 1989).

[31] The concept of 'transformation of democracy' dates back to Dahl, who described democracy as having gone through these three major transformations: Dahl 'A Democratic Dilemma' (n 30). Also in SP Huntington, 'Democracy's Third Wave' (1991) 2 *Journal of Democracy* 12, the author defines three waves of democratisation, referring to the major surges of democracy in history: the first beginning in the 19th century; the second after the Second World War; and the third since the mid-1970s.

complexity of the European expanding legal space, which is developing alongside the 'widening and deepening'[32] process of the EU integration.

Despite the absence of a shared definition of democracy within the EU legal order and the broader European legal space, and despite the lack of a common index for measuring democracy among EU Member States,[33] this book treats democracy as a core concept of the Western legal tradition and, more precisely, of European constitutionalism. Democracy constitutes a system of government that is based on the recognition of societal pluralism (*demoi*) as well as institutional pluralism. At its heart is the recognition of diversity and pluralism among peoples (*demoi*), who do not form a single *demos* as in nation states. Beyond being a value, democracy is a founding principle of the EU legal order and a European constitutional principle, which must therefore be safeguarded, with sanctions for its breach or backsliding.[34] In this definitional void, and based on the EU Treaties, this book examines democracy in its multi-form (representative and participatory) and multi-level (EU, national, regional, local) dimensions. These two dimensions of forms and levels frame our approach to democracy. In this sense, this book's working definition of democracy in the EU is an integrated system of government and governance characterised by multiple forms – representative and participatory – and multiple levels – EU, national, regional, local – which are driving democratic transformation by recognising both institutional and societal pluralism.

II. Forms and Levels of Democracy

On the basis of EU Treaties, the multi-form dimension of democracy refers to its actual forms used for including society in the exercise of power: they are representative and participatory forms. The multi-level dimension refers, instead, to democracy as a system of government that is used at all levels (EU, national, regional, local) for the exercise of power. The two dimensions are undoubtedly

[32] F Cameron, 'Widening and Deepening' in F Cameron (ed), *The Future of European Integration and Enlargement* (Routledge 2004).

[33] There are many international democracy indexes and databases whose aim is a quantitative measurement of democracy. Each one uses their own conceptual understanding of democracy, their own categories, indicators, regional areas of interest. They also come up with different working definitions of democracy, and this clearly shows the multitude of perspectives on a concept that is undoubtedly disputed and complex. Among the most recognised democracy measurements, we can list the *V-Dem* dataset and annual Report on the status of democracy in the world (www.v-dem.net/); the reports on freedom and democracy, as well as the democracy scores of the world countries made by the Freedom House (freedomhouse.org/); the Global State of Democracy Indices and the reports on the status of democracy elaborated by the International Institute for Democracy and Electoral Assistance (International IDEA, www.idea.int/); the Policy5 project (www.systemicpeace.org/csprandd.html); the democracy index of the Economist Intelligence Unit (EUI, www.eiu.com/n/).

[34] As an introduction on democracy – and rule of law and values – backsliding see Pech (n 3); KL Scheppele et al, 'EU Values Are Law, after All: Enforcing EU Values through Systemic Infringement Actions by the European Commission and the Member States of the European Union' (2021) 39 *Yearbook of European Law* 3; Kochenov, 'The Acquis and Its Principles' (n 12) 9; D Kochenov, 'Europe's Crisis of Values' (2014) 48 *Revista Catalana de Dret Públic* 106.

intertwined, but different combinations result in different ways of being for democracy.[35]

(a) Multi-form dimensions of democracy: representative democracy. The EU Treaties define two democratic forms:[36] representative and participatory. Article 10(1) TEU affirms that 'the functioning of the Union shall be founded on representative democracy', confirming that citizens govern indirectly via elected delegates. Citizens' representation rests on dual legitimation:[37] citizens elect the European Parliament, while national representatives serve in the Council and European Council. As the foundation of modern democracies,[38] representative democracy allows citizens to enjoy rights while delegating civic duties to their representatives.[39] Despite critiques,[40] until today the method of representation has served the purpose of giving an institutional structure to democracy.[41] Today this is based upon the fundamental role of parliaments, with trust linking representatives and the represented. Yet representation also spans regional and local authorities' assemblies.[42] This diversity of public arenas is therefore represented by an institutional pluralism that aims at mirroring societal pluralism.[43] Still, this pluralism is incomplete. Citizens increasingly seek direct influence, not just

[35] This preliminary classification of democracy is necessary given the versatility of this long-standing and multifaceted concept. The book follows Dann's call to rethink broad notions such as democracy beyond the national level, framing them within European constitutional law as a new path for legal scholarship. See P Dann, 'Thoughts on a Methodology of European Constitutional Law' (2005) 6 *German Law Journal* 1453.

[36] Many more are the forms of democracy that have been defined in the literature: among the others, direct democracy, deliberative democracy, liberal democracy, constitutional democracy. They also refer to different disciplinary angles (mainly law and political sciences). As we will see in ch 2, the concept of 'participatory democracy' is wide enough so as to include other labels of democracy that have been considered as self-standing by some scholars.

[37] von Bogdandy and Bast (eds) *Principles* (n 8) 50. See the provision of Article 10(2) TEU.

[38] Dahl, *Democracy and Its Critics* (n 30) 215, where he refers to representation as an 'essential element of modern democracy'. See also Sommermann (n 19) 8, saying that 'representative democracy remains the basic structure of modern democracy and elections will, therefore, continue to be at the centre of democratic self-determination'.

[39] B Constant, *The Liberty of Ancients Compared with That of Moderns* (1819), originally delivered as a lecture at the Athénée Royal, Paris.

[40] B Manin, *The Principles of Representative Government* (Cambridge University Press 1997) is specifically worth mentioning for his interesting critical position. According to Manin, what he defines as 'representative government' is a perplexing phenomenon since it was originally conceived in explicit opposition to democracy. In fact, while nowadays we conceive the relationship between those who govern and those who are governed as democratic, that was originally seen as undemocratic. Representative government, indeed, 'includes both democratic and undemocratic features', and that explains why still nowadays we cannot consider as democracies many states that – however – are to be categorised as representative systems. All in all, Manin's position is interesting in so far as he was able to point out both the democratic and undemocratic dimensions of a representative government (or system).

[41] von Bogdandy and Bast (eds) *Principles* (n 8) 50.

[42] On the necessary distinction between 'representative democracy' and 'parliamentary state', see further the fundamental pages of N Bobbio, *Il futuro della democrazia* (Corriere della Sera 2010 reprint of 1984 edition) 42–44, where he criticises the false conviction that these two concepts have the same meaning, observing that in modern states representation does not refer to the mere role of parliaments.

[43] On the concept of societal pluralism: ibid 17–19.

through elected officials, but they are willing to contribute as private actors:[44] in this sense, the challenge of accommodating the contemporary pluralism of non-institutional actors is what has been lately defined as 'law of diversity' – for qualifying a conceptual category capable of accommodating more diverse non-state actors into decision-making processes.[45] As a result, participatory democracy is gaining ground – not replacing but complementing representative democracy to strengthen legitimacy.

(b) Participatory democracy. Alongside representative democracy, the EU Treaties also enshrine participatory democracy, recognising the need to combine both forms.[46] Article 10(3) TEU affirms the right to participate, while Article 11 TEU mandates open dialogue, consultations and the European Citizens' Initiative (ECI). These rights were foreshadowed in Article I-47 'the principle of participatory democracy' of the failed draft Treaty establishing a Constitution for Europe,[47] now embedded in Article 11 TEU. Participation is also reinforced by Article 15(1) of the Treaty on the Functioning of the European Union (TFEU), calling for openness to ensure civil society's participation and good governance. Participation, therefore, targets EU institutions directly by creating these opportunities for citizens to participate at the EU level. The Charter of Fundamental Rights of the European Union adds further references to participation in Article 25 (on the rights of the elderly) and Article 26 (on the integration of persons with disabilities).[48] In practice, however, participatory democracy already unfolds across all levels of government – and not only at the EU level – through a 'universe of practices'[49] that do not correspond to a unitary design, extending much beyond treaty provisions. The concept of 'participation', indeed, enables varied citizen-focused democratic practices (see further chapters two, five, six and seven). For now, EU law's recognition of participatory democracy marks a key step forward.

(c) Multi-level dimensions of democracy. Although the Treaties focus on representative and participatory democracy at the EU level, democracy operates across multiple levels. Articles 4 and 5 TEU affirm this: Article 4(2) refers to Member States' national identity 'inclusive of regional and local self-government', while Article 5(3) outlines the division of competencies according to subsidiarity 'either at central level or at regional and local level'. Though national democracy is well represented in the Treaties, local

[44] F Palermo and K Kössler, *Comparative Federalism: Constitutional Arrangements and Case Law* (Hart Publishing 2017) 114 ff.

[45] NP Alessi, *A Global Law of Diversity. Evolving Models and Concepts* (Routledge 2024).

[46] Constant (n 39).

[47] Also referred to as 'the Constitutional Treaty', it was an unratified international treaty intended to create a consolidated constitution for the EU. Although having been signed on 29 October 2004 by both the existing Member States and the just entered Central and Eastern Europe Countries (CEECs), it never came into force as a consequence of the rejection of the document by French and Dutch voters in May and June 2005.

[48] See further, S Peers et al (eds), *The EU Charter of Fundamental Rights: A Commentary* (Bloomsbury Publishing 2021).

[49] U Allegretti, 'Democrazia Partecipativa' (2011) *Enciclopedia del Diritto* 295.

democracy is mentioned only implicitly in the TEU Preamble ('[The Member States are] resolved to continue the process of creating an ever closer union among the peoples of Europe, in which decisions are taken as closely as possible to the citizen in accordance with the principle of subsidiarity'), and Article 2 of the Protocol on Subsidiarity and Proportionality ('before proposing legislative acts, the Commission shall consult widely. Such consultations shall, where appropriate, take into account the regional and local dimension of the action envisaged'). Despite internal power allocation being a Member State prerogative[50] and, as a consequence, regional and local levels being overlooked in the Treaties,[51] all levels – supranational, national, regional and local – are recognised. In the light of that, democracy in the EU[52] can be better understood if we break it down into its fours levels (or tiers): the supranational level of EU democracy; democracy at the national level of the Member States; subnational democracy, as the third level of democracy which includes both the regional and the – much more important in our research – local level (our fourth level).[53] It is important, indeed, to understand democracy as a system of government according to its different levels, as the debates depending on the level are diverse.[54] The multi-level dimension of democracy therefore refers to the different levels where state–society relations are taking place: on one side, with regard to the (institutional organisation of the) democratic form of *representation* in the Union, while on the other with regard to the opportunities for experimenting with new forms of citizen *participation*.[55]

(d) The supranational EU level. The supranational level of democracy refers to democracy at the highest level within the EU legal order: the level of the EU

[50] Boggero is very clear on this point: 'Each member State is free to determine how its local government system should be arranged, and the Union cannot pass measures which directly impinge upon this power. However, one has to bear in mind that local and regional authorities, as they are subject to domestic law, are also subject to EU substantive law': G Boggero, *Constitutional Principles of Local Self-Government in Europe* (Brill 2018) 68 f. See also, J van Zeben, 'Local Governments as Subjects and Objects of EU Law: Legitimate Limits?' in S Bardutzky and E Fahey (eds), *Framing the Subjects and Objects of Contemporary EU Law* (Edward Elgar Publishing 2017): 'The picture of local government in the EU is one where local governments' legal positions are firmly based on Member States' constitutional arrangements. This is unlikely to change in the foreseeable future' (138).

[51] Also commentaries on EU Treaties do not consider relevant nor comment on the local level (and the regional one) when analysing Article 4 TEU: see, for example, M Kellerbauer, M Klamert and J Tomkin (eds), *The EU Treaties and the Charter of Fundamental Rights: A Commentary* (Oxford University Press 2019) 35 ff.

[52] This book always refers to 'democracy in the EU' and not to 'EU democracy' or 'European democracy'.

[53] C Panara and M Varney, *Local Government in Europe: The 'Fourth Level' in the EU Multilayered System of Governance* (Routledge 2013).

[54] This also raises the question as to whether a multi-level dimension is quintessential to democracy or not: for an introduction on this debate see further, Sommermann (n 19).

[55] ibid 11–12. See also F Palermo, 'Participation, Federalism, and Pluralism: Challenges to Decision Making and Responses by Constitutionalism' in C Fraenkel-Haeberle et al (eds), *Citizen Participation in Multi-Level Democracies* (Brill-Nijhoff 2015) 44 who states that the wider the subnational and local autonomy is, the wider space for participatory experiments exists. We will deal with new forms of participation, in particular, in Part III (chs 5 and 6) with the Italian model of civic participation through the commons, and in ch 7 for initiatives of participation through the commons in other EU cities.

institutions.[56] At the supranational EU level we have both representative and participatory democracy, and the concept of democracy has been developed in its own way, emancipating itself from its understanding in the context of nation states.[57] With concern to representative democracy – whose institutions are, pursuant to Article 10(2) TEU, the European Parliament,[58] the European Council and the Council – it can also exist without a European demos,[59] while conversely it is a fundamental element in nation states. When referring to the participatory form of democracy at the EU level, the reference goes to the supranational forms of participation that citizens can exercise for trying to influence the EU level decision-making process.[60]

(e) The national level. Democracy at the national level refers to the system of government at the national level. While all EU Member States are founded on representative democracies, the provisions on participatory forms of democracy, or even other forms like 'direct democracy', 'deliberative democracy' or other complementary forms of citizens' inclusion in the decision-making processes at the national level, are diverse. The provisions on forms of democracy at the national level can be found – if in existence – in national constitutions or national level legislation.[61]

(f) The subnational level: regional and local. The subnational level – regional and local – is the closest to citizens. While the EU treats them as a single third, subnational tier of government,[62] this book identifies the local level as a distinct, fourth level.[63] In the EU context, the third level refers to regions, the fourth, to local authorities. Representative democracy functions at both levels, but participatory democracy also thrives, especially at the local level, since proximity fosters innovation and experimentation that could eventually also influence and bring change to upper levels of democracy. As the first level of elected government, the local tier is the book's primary focus.[64]

[56] Using the term 'level' for the EU may imply a hierarchy, as noted in G Della Cananea, 'Is European Constitutionalism Really "Multilevel"?' (2010) 70 *Heidelberg Journal of International Law* 283. While 'tier' could be more accurate, this book adopts 'level' in a broad sense, referring to competences conferred by Member States.

[57] von Bogdandy and Bast (eds) *Principles* (n 8) 52.

[58] On the (lack of) representativeness of the European Parliament, see further, S Russack, 'EU Parliamentary Democracy: How Representative?' in S Blockmans and S Russack (eds), *Representative Democracy in the EU: Recovering Legitimacy* (Rowman & Littlefield Publishers 2019).

[59] von Bogdandy 'European Democracy' (n 16) 1.

[60] See further ch 2. For an introduction see A Alemanno and J Organ, 'The Case for Citizen Participation in the European Union: A Theoretical Perspective on EU Participatory Democracy' in J Organ and A Alemanno (eds), *Citizen Participation in Democratic Europe: What Next for the EU?* (ECPR Press/Rowman & Littlefield Publishers 2021).

[61] For some examples and comparative considerations on citizen participation in some federal and regional states (Austria, Italy, Switzerland, UK, Canada) see further, C Fraenkel-Haeberle et al (eds), *Citizen Participation in Multi-Level Democracies* (Brill-Nijhoff 2015) 207–308.

[62] As can be seen in the Treaties text, where 'regional and local' aspects go always together, and as the denomination of the 'Committee of the Regions' also shows, with the local level being absorbed in the wider spectrum of local and regional authorities across the EU.

[63] Panara and Varney (n 53).

[64] It is indeed local democracy the 'front line' level where innovation occurs as a consequence of intense interactions between public authorities and citizens: see further, F Hendriks et al, 'European

In sum, democracy in the EU can be classified according to both forms and levels. This book specifically addresses one of those forms –the participatory – and one of these levels –the local:[65] the representative form of democracy and the other EU/national/regional levels are not covered by this book. The following table aims to clarify our conceptualisation of democracy in the EU by outlining its various forms and levels as derived from the text of the Treaties and serves as a foundation for the analytical perspective adopted in this book.

Table 1 Multi-form and multi-level dimensions of democracy in the EU: the 'democracy' cell in dark grey marks the book's analytical focus (author's elaboration)

DEMOCRACY IN THE EU				
LEVELS / FORMS	**EU**	**NATIONAL**	**SUBNATIONAL**	
			REGIONAL	**LOCAL**
REPRESENTATIVE	Democracy	Democracy	Democracy	Democracy
PARTICIPATORY	Democracy	Democracy	Democracy	**Democracy**

III. Problem (Re)Definition: Is Democracy in Crisis?

It is very common today to talk about 'the crisis of democracy',[66] a trend affecting many regions worldwide.[67] In the EU, this crisis reflects a deeper erosion of core values,[68] with some Member States actively undermining democracy and the rule of law.[69] While crises have shaped the EU since its founding, this one strikes at its

Subnational Democracy: Comparative Reflections and Conclusions' in J Loughlin, F Hendriks and A Lidström (eds), *The Oxford Handbook of Local and Regional Democracy in Europe* (Oxford University Press 2012) 739 ff.

[65] On participation and the participatory form of democracy, ch 2 will contribute through an investigation of the principle of civic participation. On the local level of democracy, ch 3 will assist through the study of the principles of subsidiarity and local self-government, highlighting the rising role of 'cities' as a specific unit among other local authorities.

[66] The concept is used in different disciplinary contexts for looking from different angles at the same phenomenon. For some starting points, see: Fraenkel-Haeberle et al (n 61) 5; Palermo and Kössler (n 44) 114 ff; H Kriesi, 'Is There a Crisis of Democracy in Europe?' (2020) 61 *Polit Vierteljahresschr* 237; Kochenov, 'Europe's Crisis of Values' (n 34); Nicolaïdis, 'European Demoicracy' (n 25).

[67] F Fukuyama, 'Against Identity Politics: The New Tribalism and the Crisis of Democracy' (2018) 97(5) *Foreign Affairs* 90, 91: 'in recent years, the number of democracies has fallen, and democracy has retreated in virtually all regions of the world'.

[68] Kochenov, 'Europe's Crisis of Values' (n 34). In addition to this important debate, another phenomenon is usually linked to the crisis of democracy in the EU, namely the so-called 'democratic deficit': ie, the lack of public engagement at the EU level and the absence of a common public sphere and common demos, as it is for national democracies. For an introduction, see A Follesdal and S Hix, 'Why There is a Democratic Deficit in the EU: A Response to Majone and Moravcsik' (2006) 44 *Journal of Common Market Studies* 533. *cf* RD Kelemen, 'Europe's Other Democratic Deficit: National Authoritarianism in Europe's Democratic Union' (2017) 52(SI2) *Government and Opposition* 211, and von Bogdandy 'European Democracy' (n 16) 17.

[69] In particular, the reference goes to Hungary and Poland, on which there is a vast literature. For a summary of the latest development towards a model of illiberal democracy see Halmai (n 23) 184 f. For a summary of the initiatives that the EU has taken against their backsliding see Pech (n 3). The

foundation, posing a systemic threat to integration. Yet, as noted,[70] crisis is intrinsic to democracy – a project and process[71] in constant flux. Looking at democracy in the EU through its different forms and levels, not all dimensions of democracy should be considered to be in crisis.[72]

When it comes to forms of democracy, we can say more precisely that what we are witnessing is a crisis of representation,[73] which is occurring at all levels. The relation of trust[74] between the people and their delegates has been constantly diminishing, within a model of democracy that is built around politicians and the party system, elections and representative assemblies. If we look at representation at the EU level, we can see that the main actor devoted to representation – the European Parliament – has witnessed a decline in total election turnout from 61.99 per cent in the first elections in 1979 to 50.74 per cent in the latest election in 2024, even though the election turnout in 2024 was the highest since 1994 (56.67 per cent).[75] If we go one level lower to the national level, then – according to data – the voter turnout of parliamentary elections in EU Member States is declining almost everywhere.[76] The same declining trend

model of 'illiberal State' is the one defined by Prime Minister Viktor Orbán's Speech at the 25th Bálványos Summer Free University and Student Camp, 26 July 2014, Tusnádfürdő (Băile Tuşnad), Romania, where he outlined the ideal of a new type of democracy: 'the most popular topic in thinking today is trying to understand how systems that are not Western, not liberal, not liberal democracies and perhaps not even democracies, can nevertheless make their nations successful. The stars of the international analysts today are Singapore, China, India, Russia and Turkey … the new state that we are constructing in Hungary is an illiberal state, a non-liberal state'. On the interconnectedness of the rule of law and democracy, see A Jakab, 'What Can Constitutional Law Do Against the Erosion of Democracy and the Rule of Law?' 2019-15 MPIL Research Paper Series.

[70] SA Ercan and J-P Gagnon, 'The Crisis of Democracy Which Crisis? Which Democracy?' (2014) 1(2) *Democratic Theory* 1, 6. A more optimistic view is the one shared by Kriesi who thinks that despite the fact that dissatisfaction with (representative) democracy is widespread in the EU, there is no reason to over-dramatise, as the principle of democracy is still widely supported and shared among European citizens (see Kriesi (n 66) 256 f).

[71] BR Barber, 'Three Challenges to Reinventing Democracy' in PQ Hirst and S Khilnani (eds), *Reinventing Democracy* (Blackwell Publishers 1996).

[72] For some critical reflections on the concept of 'crisis' as a barely defined concept, see W Merkel and S Kneip, *Democracy and Crisis: Challenges in Turbulent Times* (Springer 2018) 12 ff.

[73] Manin (n 40) 193 ff.

[74] I Pernice, 'Multilevel Constitutionalism and the Crisis of Democracy in Europe' (2015) 11 *European Constitutional Law Review* 541. On the growing gap between elites and peoples see Y Mény, 'Conclusion: A Voyage to the Unknown' (2012) 50(S1) *Journal of Common Market Studies* 154.

[75] Data at: results.elections.europa.eu/en/turnout/.

[76] Data provided by the International Institute for Democracy and Electoral Assistance: www.idea.int (more precisely at: www.idea.int/data-tools/regional-entity-view/EU/40?st=par#rep). Austria: from 94.31% in 1945 to 75.59% in 2019; Belgium: from 90.30% in 1946 to 88.38% in 2019 (compulsory voting); Bulgaria: from 83.87% in 1991 to 49.11% in 2021 (compulsory voting from 2017); Croatia: from 84.54% in 1990 to 46.90% in 2020; Cyprus: from 75.85% in 1970 to 65.72% in 2021 (compulsory voting was abolished in 2017); Czech Republic: from 96.33% in 1990 to 65.39% in 2021; Denmark: from 86.29% in 1945 to 84.60% in 2019; Estonia: from 78.20% in 1990 to 63.67% in 2019; Finland: from 74.87% in 1945 to 68.73% in 2019; France: from 79.83% in 1945 to 48.70% in 2017; Germany: from 78.49% in 1949 to 76.58% in 2021; Greece: from 77.20% in 1951 to 57.78% in 2019 (compulsory voting); Hungary: from 65.10% in 1990 to 69.59% in 2022; Ireland: from 74.25% in 1948 to 62.77% in 2020; Italy: from 89.08% in 1946 to 72.93% in 2018 (compulsory voting abolished in 1993); Latvia: from 81.20% in 1990 to 54.58% in 2018; Lithuania: from 71.72% in 1990 to 47.80% in 2020;

in citizens' participation through representative schemes is also reflected at the subnational dimension. Looking at data, despite the fact that representation has never been fully covering the totality of represented people, it can be clearly observed that elections and other representative channels have, throughout the decades, lost their appeal and reliability, and capacity to respond to people's needs and expectations. This has led in recent times to consistent percentages of citizens not feeling represented by those running to being elected in the representative arenas, and as a consequence of that to possibly feeling indifferent to public life,[77] or looking for alternative channels for taking part in their communities. The reasons for the crisis of representation are many: in addition to the decline in voter turnout, it is possible to refer to the decline of parties as vehicle of mass participation, the general polarisation of the political landscape, and the rise of extremism and populism.[78] The low voter turnout, additionally, questions the legitimacy of (democratically elected) governments, that sometimes happen to be elected by a minority of the totality of voters.

When coming to the participatory form of democracy, at all levels, the discourse is different. While representation, despite its crisis, still constitutes the fundamental structure of democracy and as such is not questioned,[79] participation is gaining momentum as a tool to advance democratisation and counteract the shortcomings of the representation crisis. Participation is also aimed at overcoming failings coming from representative democracy as the 'rule of the majority'. The majoritarian principle, while a cornerstone of representative democracy,[80] often marginalises minority interests.[81] Thus, today's democratic crisis is primarily one of representation – not participation. Participation varies by level: the higher the level, the more difficult and unlikely participation usually is.[82] Though there is

Luxembourg: from 91.90% in 1948 to 89.66% in 2018 (compulsory voting); Malta: from 75.74% in 1947 to 85.63% in 2022; Netherlands: from 93.12% in 1946 to 78.71% in 2021; Poland: from 95.03% in 1952 to 61.74% in 2019; Portugal: from 91.73% in 1975 to 57.96% in 2022; Romania: from 79.69% in 1990 to 31.84% in 2020; Slovakia: from 96.33% in 1990 to 65.81% in 2020; Slovenia: from 85.90% in 1992 to 52.64% in 2018; Spain: from 76.96% in 1977 to 71.76% in 2019; Sweden: from 82.74% in 1948 to 87.18% in 2018.

[77] This refers to what has been defined as 'post-democracy' for talking about the growing alienation of citizens towards representative democracy: see C Crouch, *Post-Democracy After the Crises* (Polity 2020).

[78] H Landemore, *Open Democracy: Reinventing Popular Rule for the Twenty-First Century* (Princeton University Press 2020) 26 ff.

[79] Fraenkel-Haeberle et al (n 61) 6 f.

[80] Mény, 'Conclusion: A Voyage to the Unknown' (n 74) 162.

[81] On the negative effects of majority rule over minorities, see further, Palermo and Kössler (n 44) 117.

[82] With regard to the EU level, for a critical appraisal of the under-valorisation of participatory initiatives and for the need to institutionalise more stable channels for supranational citizen participation, see A Alemanno, 'Europe's Democracy Challenge: Citizen Participation in and Beyond Elections' (2020) 21 *German Law Journal* 35. Despite criticism, it has been suggested that the Conference on the Future of Europe goes in the direction of promoting participatory democracy at the EU level (A Alemanno, 'Unboxing the Conference on the Future of Europe' (2021) HEC Paris Research Series). With regard to the national level, some experiences of 'participatory constitutionalism' have been tried out for example in Iceland and Ireland: see further on that, F Palermo, 'Partecipazione come fonte di

usually no talk of a crisis of participatory democracy at the EU level, the EU level initiatives have often proved ineffective in engaging citizens.[83] National practices vary according to relevant legislation (if any), but most participatory activity – including deliberation[84] – happens at the subnational, especially local, level.

All in all, while representative democracy faces crisis at all levels, the same cannot be said about participatory democracy – especially locally – where instead experiments and innovations are taking place. This book focuses on the challenges and opportunities of democracy in its participatory form and at the local level.

IV. From Democratic Government to Democratic Governance

Until now, democracy has essentially been discussed in its institutional aspect as a system of *government* – a vertical structure separating rulers from the ruled. But to understand the participatory form of democracy at the local level, we must also view democracy as a system of *governance*. The concept of governance emphasises horizontal collaboration between state and non-state actors. Participation, indeed, involves actors outside formal institutions who still shape democracy. The dimension of governance is a horizontal one, in contrast to the vertical dimension of government, and it allows for widening the arena of non-governmental actors involved in the act of governing. This also affects how we view public authority and sources of law – where even non-binding acts (the so called 'soft law' in the EU) become relevant normative sources in democratic systems.

First developed in political science, the concept of 'governance' spread into legal studies,[85] despite often being criticised as vague and contested.[86] Since the 1980s,

legittimazione? Nuovi processi decisionali e sfide per il sistema delle fonti' in S Catalano et al (eds), *Processi decisionali e fonti del diritto* (Edizioni Scientifiche Italiane 2022) 60 ff.

[83] We are referring here to European Citizens' Initiatives (ECI), consultations, and other attempts to involve civil society organisations (which tend to be the preferred target of EU institutions rather than citizens). They will be further investigated in ch 2.

[84] As an introduction, see JS Dryzek et al, 'The Crisis of Democracy and the Science of Deliberation' (2019) 363 *Science* 1144 and C Chwalisz, 'The Pandemic Has Pushed Citizen Panels Online' *Nature* (12 January 2021), for the importance of social media in deliberation. Deliberative practices will be further included in ch 2.

[85] For some introductory reflections on the challenge presented by governance to traditional categories of constitutional law and on its revolutionary potential with regard to the system of sources of law, see M Dani and F Palermo, 'Della Governance e Di Altri Demoni (Un Dialogo)' (2003) 4 *Quaderni Costituzionali* 785. See also, S Cassese, 'Identità e Funzioni Delle Riviste Pubblicistiche' (2021) 4 *Forum Di Quaderni Costituzionali* 26: he criticises Italian constitutional scholarship for overlooking governance and urges scholars to engage with issues beyond court rulings to advance legal science.

[86] A great critique and deconstruction of the concept has been elaborated by one of its major critics, Roberto Bin, who considers (European) governance as non-existent in the light of a pure theory of sources of law. See R Bin, 'Contro La Governance: La Partecipazione Tra Fatto e Diritto' in G Arena and F Cortese (eds), *Per Governare Insieme: Il Federalismo Come Metodo* (Cedam 2011). Opposing, for the claim of governance as a form of law, see P Westerman, 'From Houses to Ships: Governance as a Form of Law' (2018) 14(4) *Le Libellio* 5.

scholars have defined it as broader than 'government', including civil society and focusing on managing networks, especially in service delivery.[87] Unlike the vertical structure of 'government' used for referring to the mere institution – the instrument of public power – 'governance' instead granted a new perspective on the public arena,[88] implying the necessary interaction between multiple institutions and actors in the decision-making process.[89] Decision-making processes and the interplay of diverse actors lie at the centre of governance. Governance consists of 'the production of authoritative decisions which are not produced by a single hierarchical structure, such as a democratically elected legislative assembly and government, but instead arise from the interaction of a plethora of "public and private, collective and individual actors"'.[90] This networked exercise of power is particularly visible in the European legal space, and more in general in the above-mentioned transnational law.

The EU is not only the regional context object of this book, but it also exemplifies the shift from government to governance, with dense networks operating below supranational institutions.[91] It disrupts national systems' hierarchy of

[87] For an introductory overview, see AM Kjaer, *Governance* (Wiley 2004) 1 ff. The disciplinary perspective on the term excluded from the very beginning the economic perspective, which on its side refers to the concept of 'corporate governance'. The broad and essential definition given by the author is that 'governance refers to something broader than government, and it is about steering and the rules of the game' (7), and that it has to do with 'how the centre interacts with society and asks whether there is more self-steering in networks' (11). See further, E-H Klijn, 'Trust in Governance Networks: Looking for Conditions for Innovative Solutions and Outcomes' in SP Osborne (ed), *The New Public Governance? Emerging Perspectives on the Theory and Practice of Public Governance* (Routledge 2010); SP Osborne, *The New Public Governance? Emerging Perspectives on the Theory and Practice of Public Governance* (Routledge 2010) 6 f. As explained by Osborne, the concept of governance in the public arena (the 'public governance') refers to 'public policy implementation and public services delivery', which is the object of study of the different theories and regimes of Public Administration (PA), New Public Mangament (NPM), and New Public Governance (NPG) studies. On the theory of NPG as the paradigm for capturing the latest developments in the evolution of the provisions of public services, see SP Osborne, 'The New Public Governance?' (2006) 8 *Public Management Review* 377. See also, B Kohler-Koch and B Rittberger, 'Review Article: The "Governance Turn" in EU Studies' (2006) 44 *Journal of Common Market Studies Annual Review* 27.

[88] The term 'arena' is used here as encompassing both the vertical and horizontal dimension (in contrast to the term 'level'), in line with the meaning given by Adrienne Hèritier, 'Introduction' in A Hèritier (ed), *Common Goods: Reinventing European and International Governance* (Rowman & Littlefield Publishers 2002).

[89] On the concept of 'interaction' and the recognition within a governance perspective of the necessary interdependence among actors, see J Kooiman (ed), *Modern Governance: New Government–Society Interactions* (Sage 1993) 4: 'No single actor, public or private, has all knowledge and information required to solve complex, dynamic and diversified problems'. The contribution of Kooiman represents a reference point for the debate on the shift from government to governance. In particular, he uses the term 'social-political governance' for referring to governance as the interaction between government and society. In addition to the concept of interaction, governance is strongly linked to the concepts of 'system': 'Governance is system specific. Interactions are in fact the definition of a system' (ibid 259).

[90] T Christiansen and S Piattoni (eds), *Informal Governance in the European Union* (Edward Elgar Publishing 2003) 6.

[91] Ladeur defines Europe as 'a network of (overlapping) networks where a new space is being created beyond the Westphalian duo of national law and international public law: a new space that is defined "transnational law"'. He points to the growing emergence of transnational networks which evolve within Europe, therefore contributing to creating an unexplored space. See K-H Ladeur, 'European Law as Transnational Law – Europe Has to Be Conceived as an Heterarchical Network and Not as a

sources of law and accelerates decision-making beyond the limits of the traditional tool of legislation considered too slow in a fast-moving economy.[92] This link with economic priorities has drawn sharp criticism: some describe EU governance as a 'form of neoliberal governmentality' that erodes[93] democracy by inviting private interests into public decision-making and blurring public–private boundaries. In addition to that, the increasing 'scientification of politics, particularly the use of experts' put the idea of governance in a questionable light, given its weakening of parliaments as representatives of the people, reinforcing a 'technocratic model of steering and managing … and advance a new form of elitism'.[94]

The governance turn in the EU took a precise term, that eventually became a buzz word among both scholars and EU civil servants and politicians: 'multilevel governance' (MLG).[95] The term comes from a prominent feature of governance in the EU context, which is its multi-level nature, that points to the interdependence of different actors (state and non-state actors, public and private) operating from diverse territorial levels (supranational, national, regional, local) in a non-hierarchical system of governance.[96] The decision-making power is therefore not monopolised by the governments of the Member States, but is diffused at different levels, among them the local level:[97] in this way, MLG has been described as contributing positively to democracy in the EU thanks to 'the involvement of democratic representative territorial authorities in the EU decision-making process'[98]

Superstate!' (2009) 10) *German Law Journal* 1357. He concludes by saying that: 'The nation-state is the product of a specific evolution in European history … It is time dependent. This is why the form of the state is in deep crisis at its traditional level. It is linked to the dominance of unity and homogeneity over plurality and fragmentation … The EU must be distinctive and it can only follow the new global rationality of difference, plurality, and acentric networks' (1365).

[92] One side supported new governance tools (eg, the Commission), while the other favoured traditional legislation (eg, national governments). See further Hèritier (n 88) 201.

[93] C Shore, '"European Governance" or Governmentality? The European Commission and the Future of Democratic Government' (2011) 17 *European Law Journal* 287. As the author underlines, it is not a coincidence that the development of the concept of governance in the EU occurred in parallel to the development of the concept of 'good governance' in the IMF and World Bank, as a dominant theme underlying policies towards aid in developing countries where these organisations were active (288).

[94] ibid 297 and 302. Additionally, for a critique of the technocratic governance of the EU institutions see M Castells, *Rupture: The Crisis of Liberal Democracy* (Polity Press 2018) 58.

[95] Among others, see P Stephenson, 'Twenty Years of Multi-Level Governance: "Where Does It Come From? What Is It? Where Is It Going?"' (2013) 20 *Journal of European Public Policy* 817; C Panara, *The Sub-National Dimension of the EU: A Legal Study of Multilevel Governance* (Springer 2015); S Piattoni, *The Theory of Multi-Level Governance* (Oxford University Press 2010).

[96] Kohler-Koch and Rittberger (n 87) 42.

[97] See P Popelier, 'Subnational Multilevel Constitutionalism' (2014) 6(2) *Perspectives on Federalism* 1: 'The European integration process resulted in a network of complex and interdependent relationships between national states, decentralized entities, supranational authorities, and non-state actors, generally described as a system of "multilevel governance"' (9).

[98] Panara (n 95) 174. The author also recognises some unresolved issues on the relationship between democracy and MLG (at 170–73). The contribution of Panara is key to understanding MLG not only as a political concept, but also with its legal side: he considers it to be a 'procedural principle' of the EU constitutional construction (73), that requires the involvement of subnational authorities in EU policy-making and law-making.

(alongside, however, with corporations and other private, non-democratically legitimated entities). Launched within a study of renewed European structural policy in the 1990s,[99] the concept of MLG became predominant in the governance debate among European integration scholars[100] who were looking for new concepts an as alternative to traditional state-centric forms of government. The term was also included in the work of the EU Commission and the Committee of the Regions (CoR) that issued two documents[101] that constitute the reference point on the concept within the EU legal order. The CoR, specifically, warned that MLG 'cannot be understood solely through the lenses of the division of powers',[102] and that it has to be considered as inextricably linked to the principle of subsidiarity (with subsidiarity in its vertical dimension referring to the responsibility of different tiers of government, and MLG to their interaction).

The shift from government to governance has triggered a proliferation of actors in the public arena and a parallel multiplication of normative sources, resulting in profound confusion known as the 'crisis of the sources of law'.[103] The 'equilibrium' created by MLG in the EU lacks constitutional legitimacy, making the division of competences often unclear.[104] This blurring of institutional powers has produced a regulatory landscape filled with non-legislative acts coming from

[99] G Marks, 'Structural Policy in the European Community' in AM Sbragia (ed), *Europolitics: Institutions and Policymaking in the 'New' European Community* (The Brookings Institution 1992).

[100] See G Marks et al, 'European Integration from the 1980s: State Centric v. Multilevel Governance' (1996) 34 *Journal of Common Market Studies* 341; L Hooghe and G Marks, 'Types of Multi-Level Governance' (2001) 5-11 European Integration Online Papers.

[101] Commission, 'European Governance. A White Paper' COM(2001)428, 25 July 2001; and Committee of the Regions. *The Committee of the Regions' White Paper on Multilevel Governance* (2009). While the Committee of the Regions (CoR) talks of MLG, the Commission refers in particular to the concept of 'good governance', and to the principle of participation as underpinning good governance: 'The White Paper proposes opening up the policy-making process to get more people and organisations involved in shaping and delivering EU policy. It promotes greater openness, accountability and responsibility for all those involved … A better use of powers should connect the EU more closely to its citizens and lead to more effective policies'. The CoR, on its side, refers to 'the need for local and regional authorities to be closely involved in shaping and implementing Community strategies', and sees MLG as reinforcing the democratic dimension of the EU for its contribution on stimulating participatory democracy.

[102] CoR, ibid 7. For further readings on this link between regions and subsidiarity see R Toniatti et al (eds), *An Ever More Complex Union: The Regional Variable as the Missing Link in the EU Constitution?* (Nomos 2004).

[103] The EU legal order does not fit within the Westphalian order founded on, on one side, nation states based on strictly defined internal systems of sources of law and, on the other, the separation of powers (legislative, executive and judiciary). Instead, it represents a new legal space for transnational law: see J Hage, 'Sources of Law' in J Hage et al (eds), *Introduction to Law* (Springer International Publishing 2017). On the progressive dismantling and crisis of the internal system of hierarchy of sources, see R Bin, 'Cose e Idee. Per Un Consolidamento Della Teoria Delle Fonti' (2019) 1 *Diritto Costituzionale* 11. Following Bin, for sources of law we refer to acts produced by bodies endowed with political legitimacy and produced through guaranteed procedures ('le fonti sono atti prodotti da organi dotati di una legittimazione politica e prodotti attraverso procedimenti garantiti', 24). The author concludes by saying that the crisis of the system of the sources of law is a consequence, at its core, of the crisis of politics.

[104] Marks et al (n 100) 372.

new centres of authority.[105] Many of these take the form of 'soft law': a variety of non-binding instruments with no legal sanctioning mechanisms against non-compliance,[106] yet they constitute rules of conduct that produce legal[107] and practical effects.[108] Though grounded in the instruments of recommendations and opinions in Article 288(5) TFEU, the actual range of soft-law tools is broad – also including frameworks, communications, guidelines, letters, codes, notices and others.[109] Such tools are issued by EU institutions, sometimes in partnership with non-institutional stakeholders,[110] and have spread rapidly in European governance despite their widely acknowledged legitimacy deficit.[111]

Participation at the local level has not been the object of legally binding regulations and relies heavily on informal and soft-law tools. It exemplifies the shift away from traditional representative procedures towards alternative forms of democratic legitimation.[112] While this mix of soft law and non-state law can blur legal sources, it may also be the case that soft law represents the ideal framework for participatory instruments in the EU, which operate beyond representative logic. Governance reframes democracy by integrating non-state actors – including individuals[113] – into decision-making at the local level, where new normative

[105] F Modugno, 'E' Possibile Parlare Ancora Di Un Sistema Delle Fonti?' (2008) *Associazione italiana dei costituzionalisti* 2.

[106] Kohler-Koch and Rittberger (n 87).

[107] On the legal effects that soft law could eventually produce, see O Stefan et al, 'EU Soft Law in the EU Legal Order: A Literature Review' (2019) King's College London Law School Research Paper (forthcoming). According to the author, soft law could 'provide a normative framework for future negotiations and for potential arguments or conflicts; binding the enacting institution and also the institutions' parties to an interinstitutional agreement; concretizing the duty of institutional cooperation; creating the expectation that the enacting institution will comply with the rules it laid down in a soft law instrument; producing a stand-still effect on the non-conforming conduct of a state or institutions; and influencing the legal rights and obligations of third parties. Soft law can impact on national and European legislation by expressing general principles of EU law, being part of the acquis communautaire, interpreting hard law provisions, and serving as a legal basis for the enactment of national legislation. In a court of law, the effects of soft law include, inter alia: providing the basis for judicial review; being the object of an action for annulment; being used in litigation by the parties to a trial; and serving as an aid in the interpretation of hard law provisions' (24–25).

[108] See F Snyder, 'The Effectiveness of European Community Law: Institutions, Processes, Tools and Techniques' (1993) 56 *Modern Law Review* 19, 32. On mainstays and downsides of soft law, see D Chalmers and A Tomkins (eds), 'Soft Law' in D Chalmers and A Tomkins, *European Union Public Law* (Cambridge University Press 2007).

[109] M Eliantonio et al (eds), *EU Soft Law in the Member States: Theoretical Findings and Empirical Evidence* (Bloomsbury Publishing 2021) 1.

[110] Stefan et al (n 107) 17.

[111] On this drawback of soft law, see ibid 34. Also the European Parliament took a negative stance on soft law with the Resolution of 4 September 2007 on institutional and legal implications of the use of soft-law instruments (2007/2028(INI)), saying that 'the use of soft law is liable to circumvent the properly *competent* legislative bodies, may flout the principles of democracy and the rule of law under Article 6 of the EU Treaty, and also those of subsidiarity and proportionality'.

[112] D Ferri, 'L'Unione Europea Sulla Strada Della Democrazia Partecipativa?' (2011) 2 *Istituzioni del Federalismo* 298. As she points out, Article 11 (TEU) would constitute the ideal legal basis on which an EU regulation could have been adopted on the topic of participation, but this has never been done (334).

[113] van Zeben (n 50) 123.

sources are tried.[114] This justifies speaking of local governance rather than local government, with participation at its core.[115]

All in all, democracy in the EU must be seen as a system of both government and governance, combining representative and participatory channels that reflect social pluralism. Local authorities, recognising the governance opportunities of EU policies and funding, also actively become subjects of a process of Europeanisation.[116] A governance approach is essential, as participation goes beyond state actors, their traditional representative legitimation and their system of sources of law: participation enters the domain of non-state actors and paves the way for new alternative sources of law.[117]

V. Participation in Local Democracy as the Forefront of Democracy in the EU

Democracy in the EU is not in crisis but in transformation. Defining the European legal space reveals democracy as a European constitutional principle with different forms and different levels. This multi-level understanding of democracy highlights the growing role of participatory democracy at the local level[118] conceived as a 'universe of practices, procedures and processes'.[119] Moreover, understanding democracy as a system of both government and governance underscores how non-state actors, through participatory legitimation, can complement legitimacy coming from traditional representative democracy channels.

This is already happening around Italian cities and other local authorities studied in Part III (chapters five and six), where mandatory institutional support for citizen initiatives is expanding the meaning of democracy beyond representative legitimation and towards participatory legitimation. In this sense, the commons – as we will see – are offering an interesting laboratory for new types of civic participation not only in Italian, but also in other EU local authorities, revealing opportunities for citizen involvement as well as deep societal challenges. Local democracy, due to its proximity to citizens, is best placed to foster innovative types

[114] Like collaboration pacts in ch 6.

[115] On this shift see further, P John, *Local Governance in Western Europe* (SAGE Publications Ltd 2001); N Kersting et al, *Local Governance Reform in Global Perspective* (VS Verlag für Sozialwissenschaften 2009).

[116] John, ibid 8.

[117] Palermo, 'Partecipazione Come Fonte Di Legittimazione? (n 82).

[118] 'When it comes to assessing concrete and practical models of participation, it is noteworthy that the local level, supported by the regional level, is configurated as a "laboratory" for participation. This occurs not because of the creativity, variety and richness of the practices, but mostly because it promotes a change in the way society interacts with institutions': M Nicolini, 'Theoretical Framework and Constitutional Implications: Participatory Democracy as Decision-Making in Multilayered Italy' in F Palermo and E Alber (eds), *Federalism as Decision-Making* (Brill-Nijhoff 2015) 447.

[119] Allegretti (n 49): 'la democrazia partecipativa costituisce una categoria generale comprensiva di un universo di pratiche e dispositivi (processi, procedure) … un complesso di fenomeni' 259.

of participation – especially what this book defines as civic participation through the commons (CPC).

All in all, civic participation through the commons can act as a 'niche innovation' that in the long term may eventually make a real impact on democracy in the EU by means of local democracy and later bring larger-scale societal change. Borrowed from transition literature,[120] this concept captures how local experiments can shift from one dynamic equilibrium to another through systemic change. Transitions are like innovations[121] in local democracy and participation, actively redefining these core concepts of the European legal space, showing that transnational democracy is broad enough to include the pluralism of innovative experiences coming from the local level. That is why the local level of democracy and its participatory form constitute the core dimensions of democracy explored in this book.

[120] D Loorbach et al, 'Sustainability Transitions Research: Transforming Science and Practice for Societal Change' (2017) 42 *Annual Review of Environment and Resources* 599. 'Transitions in their literal sense refer to the process of change from one state to another. In transitions research, the term refers to the process of change from one system state to another via a period of nonlinear disruptive change' (605); and transitions 'are considered to be societal processes of fundamental change including emergent and coordinated characteristics … a transition can be coordinated by creating shared future orientations and guiding values and at the same time creating space for experimentation and diversity in the short term (ed: niche innovations), allowing for new solutions and ways of organizing to emerge' (608).

[121] See ch 2.

2

The Principle of Participation

I. The Principle of Participation: An Introduction

This chapter analyses the principle of participation[1] within the European legal space, both constitutionally and through its diverse practices and instruments. Despite the absence[2] of a unified theoretical framework and shared definition of participation and its related concept of 'participatory democracy',[3] participation in Europe remains a melting pot of interpretations. Crucially, its broad scope has fostered innovative bottom-up practices across local to supranational levels.

Participation refers to a phenomenon of great complexity, rooted in and strictly related to the concept of democracy and its legitimation[4] through means that go beyond the mere representative instruments. First and foremost participation must be understood in contrast to representation: considered as the two legs[5] of democracy, as we saw in chapter one, the first referring to the direct form of democracy while the second to the indirect one, as it is based on delegation. At its core, participation defines how society engages with the State in decision-making.[6] Originating in ancient Greek city-states as 'political participation' where citizens could influence public powers through deliberative assemblies, it evolved

[1] The literature on the principle of (political) participation is extensive. As an introduction see J Morison and A Harkens, 'Principle of Participation' (June 2017) *Max Planck Encyclopedia of Comparative Constitutional Law* (*MPECCoL*). For an introduction on participatory democracy, see U Allegretti, 'Democrazia Partecipativa' (2011) *Enciclopedia del Diritto* 295.

[2] On the persistent lack of a constitutional theory on participatory democracy, see F Palermo, 'Participation, Federalism, and Pluralism: Challenges to Decision Making and Responses by Constitutionalism' in C Fraenkel-Haeberle et al (eds), *Citizen Participation in Multi-Level Democracies* (Brill 2015) 35, 44.

[3] A recent contribution conducted a study on the framing of participatory democracy within constitutional law by using a comparative approach (Austria, Italy, Spain, US, Canada): see M Trettel, *La democrazia partecipativa negli ordinamenti composti: Studio di diritto comparato sull'incidenza della tradizione giuridica nelle democratic innovations* (Edizioni Scientifiche Italiane 2020) 17. Trettel also recognised the fundamental contribution of administrative law for its precise tools and procedures to implement the constitutional principle of participation. For a contribution from a political science perspective see, for example, H Heinelt, *Handbook on Participatory Governance* (Edward Elgar Publishing 2018) 1–16.

[4] F Palermo, 'Partecipazione come fonte di legittimazione? Nuovi processi decisionali e sfide per il sistema delle fonti' in S Catalano et al (eds), *Processi decisionali e fonti del diritto* (Edizioni Scientifiche Italiane 2022).

[5] D Borgonovo Re, *Le quattro stelle della Costituzione. Per una cittadinanza responsabile* (Il Margine 2013) 105.

[6] M Nigro, 'Il nodo della partecipazione' [1980] *Rivista Trimestrale di Diritto e Procedura Civile* 225.

with nation states via representative channels. Today, the internationalisation of democracy challenges traditional institutions to seek legitimation beyond representation and delegation.[7]

Political participation today spans diverse contexts and refers to people's diverse contributions depending on their social capital[8] and competences.[9] Popularised in the 1960s through student demands for more participation on matters affecting them,[10] participatory democracy emerged as a response to the classical theory of democracy at that time, with a narrow focus on voting and elite involvement.[11] The demand for more participation went beyond politics into workplaces and local communities,[12] serving multiple democratic functions: influencing decision-making, fostering inclusion, building civic skills, supporting public deliberation, and strengthening the legitimacy of decisions.[13]

Generally speaking, because of the difficulties in defining precisely what participation is, 'political participation' could be used as a concept for referring to all those voluntary activities of citizens directed at the government, the state, politics, or more generally at solving community problems (this is sometimes defined, more specifically, as 'civic participation')[14] through citizens' involvement,

[7] For these three historical transformations of democracy see RA Dahl, 'A Democratic Dilemma: System Effectiveness versus Citizen Participation' (1994) 109 *Political Science Quarterly* 23.

[8] Social capital refers to individuals coming together in associations to contribute to their community. Robert Putnam, in his influential work R Putnam, *Making Democracy Work* (Princeton University Press 1993), argued that democracy's quality relies on the level of social capital. He emphasised values like mutual trust, social cooperation and civic consciousness, advocating for reform at the local rather than national level. See additionally, F Fukuyama, 'Social Capital, Civil Society and Development' (2001) 22 *Third World Quarterly* 7.

[9] The issue of competences belongs to the long-standing problem of civic competences in democracies, addressed in RA Dahl, 'The Problem of Civic Competence' (1992) 3(4) *Journal of Democracy* 45. He called it an issue for all democracies, old and new, worsened by the scale of public life, the complexity of political issues, and the impact of ICT, which impose 'ever stronger demands on the capacities of citizens' (51).

[10] The landmark contribution bringing the argument for a participatory theory of democracy, and the first one talking of 'participatory democracy' is C Pateman, *Participation and Democratic Theory* (Cambridge University Press 1970). Pateman identified John Stuart Mill and Jean-Jacques Rousseau as foundational to participatory democracy: Rousseau for his emphasis on the individual participation of each citizen in political decision-making, while Mill for his concern on individuals being prepared to participate at the local level and, eventually, also at the national level.

[11] The predominant theory of democracy in those years was the one of Schumpeter: JA Schumpeter, *Capitalism, Socialism and Democracy* (Geo Allen & Unwin 1943).

[12] See Pateman, *Participation and Democratic Theory* (n 10) and BR Barber, *Strong Democracy* (University of California Press 1984). In particular, Barber defined the concept of 'strong democracy' in relation to participation 'defined as politics in the participatory mode where conflict is resolved in the absence of an independent ground through a participatory process of ongoing, proximate self-legislation and the creation of a political community capable of transforming dependent, private individuals into free citizens and partial and private interests into public goods' (132).

[13] A Michels, 'Innovations in Democratic Governance: How Does Citizen Participation Contribute to a Better Democracy?' (2011) 77 *International Review of Administrative Sciences* 275, 277.

[14] P Đurman, 'Participation in Public Administration Revisited: Delimiting, Categorizing and Evaluating Administrative Participation' (2020) 20 *Croatian and Comparative Public Administration* 79. The author distinguishes between political, civic and administrative participation. The literature, however, is confusing on the distinction between political and civic participation, often using the 'political' meaning for also including the 'civic' one.

empowerment, engagement, inclusion.[15] Because of its implicit reference to citizens, participation has also been referred to as 'citizen participation', which in a nutshell consists in citizen power, remarkably conceived through a ladder of citizen participation – each rung corresponding to a different gradation of participation.[16]

Participation varies by actors, modes and instruments of involvement. Alongside 'political participation' – that is citizens' engagement in the wider public arena – 'administrative participation' emerged,[17] involving citizens directly in administrative decision-making procedures. Here, private individuals act as external contributors in regulatory processes.[18] Both are referred to participation in the decision-making process for which the state is responsible, even through different means.

A great boost to participation came more recently with information communication technology (ICT), which has dramatically expanded political participation by multiplying channels and opportunities for citizen engagement. Known as *e-participation*,[19] it includes diverse digital forms worldwide[20] that make public decision-making and opinion forming more accessible. Formats include e-information, e-petitions, e-initiatives, e-campaigning, e-deliberation, e-consultation, e-budgeting and e-voting,[21] serving functions like monitoring, agenda-setting and input to decision-making.[22] E-participation enhances e-democracy (electronic democracy),[23] which is 'the support and enhancement of traditional democracy by means of ICTs'.[24] While its impact on the quality of

[15] JW van Deth, 'A Conceptual Map of Political Participation' (2014) 49 *Acta Politica* 349, 353.

[16] Arnstein defined citizen participation as citizen power arranged in a ladder pattern, where each rung corresponded to 'the extent of citizens' power in determining the plan and/or program': see SR Arnstein, 'A Ladder of Citizen Participation' (1969) 35 *Journal of the American Planning Association* 216. There were eight rungs on Arnstein's ladder of citizen participation: from the lower to the highest degree of citizens' participation we have: (1) manipulation, (2) therapy, (3) informing, (4) consultation, (5) placation, (6) partnership, (7) delegated power and (8) citizen control. For the recent proposal of adding a further rung to the ladder of citizen participation see D Ciaffi, 'Sharing the Commons as a "New Top" of Arnstein's Ladder of Participation' (2019) 45 *Built Environment* 162, where the author suggests the need to recognise a new frontier of participation in the collaborative attitude emerging in many urban (but also rural) contexts where active citizens contribute to the general interest of their community through autonomous initiatives of care for the commons (or 'common goods') on an equal level with public authorities.

[17] For an introduction on participation in administrative procedures in continental Europe, see R Caranta, 'Participation into Administrative Procedures: Achievements and Problems' (2010) 2 *Italian Journal of Public Law* 311.

[18] See Đurman (n 14).

[19] L Hennen et al, *European E-Democracy in Practice* (Springer Open 2020).

[20] 'Advances in e-participation today are driven more by civic activism of people seeking to have more control over their lives, rather than by the availability of financial resources or expensive technologies' (5): see United Nations E-government Survey 2016, publicadministration.un.org.

[21] For an analysis of all these forms see G Aichholzer and G Rose, 'Experience with Digital Tools in Different Types of E-Participation' in L Hennen et al (eds), *European E-Democracy in Practice* (Springer Open 2020).

[22] ibid.

[23] For an introduction, see L Pratchett and R Krimmer, 'The Coming of E-Democracy' (2005) 1(3) *International Journal of Electronic Government Research* 1.

[24] See the European Parliament resolution of 16 March 2017 on e-democracy in the European Union: potential and challenges (2016/2008(INI)) at: www.europarl.europa.eu/doceo/document/TA-8-2017-0095_EN.html.

democracy is still debated,[25] concerns remain about risks[26] as well as democratic legitimacy if such digital tools operated outside institutional frameworks.[27]

All in all, existing findings confirm that citizen participation strengthens democracy.[28] Participation's positive impact is undeniable, even though only a small portion of the population engages and some groups remain excluded and underrepresented. This chapter examines participation and participatory democracy (section II), the contribution of the EU and Council of Europe (CoE) legal orders (sections III–IV), and diverse participatory practices and instruments, especially at the local level (section V). The conclusion addresses current limits and challenges in the current understanding of participation within the European legal context (section VI).

II. Participatory Democracy as Distinct from Deliberative and Direct Democracy

Within the general principle of participation we can find the roots of what has been defined as 'participatory democracy'. Participation and participatory democracy are not the same thing. Participation refers to a general concept not precisely defined and often ambiguous, whose essence regards the relationship between society and public authorities, and that has links with many other topics like local autonomy, federalism as a method of government and governance,[29] and the role of civil society organisations.[30] Participatory democracy refers to a complex of specific and clearly characterised processes.[31] The two concepts of

[25] P Nijkamp and G Cohen-Blankshtain, 'Opportunities and Pitfalls of Local E-Democracy' in U Allegretti (ed), *Democrazia partecipativa: esperienze e prospettive in Italia e in Europa* (Firenze University Press 2010) 213.

[26] See Morison and Harkens (n 1).

[27] For the relationship between democratic legitimacy and sovereignty in the age of digital tools, see S Rodotà, *Iperdemocrazia: Come Cambia La Sovranità Democratica Con il Web* (Laterza 2013) 20 ff. The author claims that we are witnessing a turning point in our democratic societies because new technologies are self-legitimating themselves, outside the sovereignty granted by representative channels. The essential question concerns, therefore, the very notion of sovereignty and the possible extent of the democratic process.

[28] We refer to the study in Michels (n 13), which draws on empirical evidence from 120 cases across Western countries.

[29] On the link between participatory democracy and federalism, see F Palermo and K Kössler, *Comparative Federalism: Constitutional Arrangements and Case Law* (Hart Publishing 2017). As they observe, 'there is a link between federalism and participatory democracy and … it lies in their 'common innate connection with pluralism … Both are expressions of pluralism: institutional and societal, respectively' (114).

[30] U Allegretti, 'Basi Giuridiche Della Democrazia Partecipativa in Italia: Alcuni Orientamenti' (2006) 3 *Democrazia e Diritto* 151.

[31] On this distinction Allegretti is very clear: see U Allegretti, 'Democrazia Partecipativa: Un Contributo Alla Democratizzazione Della Democrazia' in U Allegretti (ed), *Democrazia partecipativa: esperienze e prospettive in Italia e in Europa* (Firenze University Press 2010) 12; Allegretti, 'Basi Giuridiche' (n 30).

participation and democracy are, however, strictly intertwined to the extent that both the terms 'democratic participation'[32] and 'participatory democracy' are commonly used.

The term 'participatory democracy' first appeared in 1960, emphasising its role in personal growth as 'an important role in enabling a person to develop his constructive and creative powers and achieve greater happiness'.[33] It inspired 1960s US student movements pushing for broader participation in decision-making processes, and gained widespread importance through the influential 'Port Huron document' by the Students for a Democratic Society.[34] This document became a key reference for demands for more participation beyond universities, challenging conservative authority. Simultaneously, peace, civil, women and workers' rights movements also demanded greater participation in decision-making processes.[35] The Port Huron document constitutes a fundamental reference[36] in discourses on participatory democracy because it also established some essential theoretical 'root principles' of this concept: trust in human self-governance, independence grounded in fraternity and the capacity to contribute to the common good, and the call for maximal participation in decision-making at all societal levels.[37] Since then, scholars of democracy theory have linked participatory democracy to both socialist ideals and radical liberalism.[38] In a nutshell, scholars advocating for a participatory turn of democracy were rejecting the solely representative dimension of democracy,[39] where individuals' political capacities, responsibilities, autonomy, self-government and self-determination, bottom-up social protagonism and virtues of active citizenship were not contemplated.

A second stage within the debate on participatory democracy occurred in the 1980s, when democracy scholars[40] began advancing 'beyond participatory

[32] This book, however, uses the term 'participatory democracy' rather than 'democratic participation'.

[33] AS Kaufman, 'Human Nature and Participatory Democracy' (1960) 3 *NOMOS: American Society for Political and Legal Philosophy* 266, 273. The deliberative aspect was already recognised as a fundamental dimension of participation.

[34] The inspiration on the concept of participation came from the work of Kaufman himself (ibid), who was one of the advisers to the students for drafting the document (reported by F Cunningham, *Theories of Democracy: A Critical Introduction* (Routledge 2002) 123).

[35] Pateman, *Participation and Democratic Theory* (n 10).

[36] By JJ Mansbridge, *Beyond Adversary Democracy* (University of Chicago Press 1983) 376 as reported in A Floridia, 'Participatory Democracy versus Deliberative Democracy: Elements for a Possible Theoretical Genealogy. Two Histories, Some Intersections' 7th ECPR General Conference Sciences Po (Bordeaux, 4–7 September 2013) 3.

[37] Floridia, 'Participatory Democracy' (n 36) 3 f.

[38] Notably the two contributions of Carole Pateman and CB MacPherson are those that have allowed great circulation to the concept of participatory democracy: Pateman's participatory democracy was the strand more in line with the ideas of the American new left, in accordance with the socialist ideal; MacPherson participatory democracy, on the opposite, was a model of democracy perceived perfectly in line with liberal theory, pursuing the idea of a free and autonomous citizen. See further Pateman, *Participation and Democratic Theory* (n 10) and CB Macpherson, *The Life and Times of Liberal Democracy* (Oxford University Press 1977).

[39] On this point, see Floridia, 'Participatory Democracy' (n 36) 5.

[40] The reference goes to B. Barber and J. Mansbridge, that are considered two important precursors to the deliberative theory of democracy. See further Barber (n 12), Mansbridge (n 36).

democracy' and paving the way for the new theoretical paradigm of 'deliberative democracy' (even though still not mentioned in this transition phase).[41] They introduced a plural and empirical perspective, analysing varied participatory initiatives that emphasised equal participation and consensus-based decision-making.[42] Another key development was the concept of 'strong democracy',[43] which deepened the participatory model by highlighting civic virtues. In this vision, citizens actively pursue the common good through participatory institutions, sustaining civic autonomy and resisting power delegation.

A later third wave of participatory democracy emerged in 1988 with Porto Alegre's pioneering 'participatory budget', empowering citizens to directly decide how public funds are allocated.[44] Participatory budgeting became a global model, alongside other participatory tools that started circulating and became institutionalised[45] across diverse regions.[46] This momentum culminated in the 1998 Aarhus Convention, adopted by the United Nations Economic Commission for Europe (UNECE),[47] which established civic participation in

[41] Floridia considers this period as a 'transition phase' towards deliberative democracy theory: see Floridia, 'Participatory Democracy' (n 36) 10.

[42] Mansbridge (n 36): the author used the term 'participatory democracies' for referring to diverse local communities' initiatives. In particular, the author conducted an empirical study of 'a Town Meeting Government' in a little village in Vermont, and of a 'participatory workplace'.

[43] It was Barber who theorised the idea of strong democracy 'which can be formally defined as politics in the participatory mode where conflict is resolved in the absence of an independent ground through a participatory process of ongoing, proximate self-legislation and the creation of a political community capable of transforming dependent, private individuals into free citizens and partial and private interests into public goods' (Barber (n 12) 132.

[44] For an introduction on participatory budget, see G Allegretti, 'Giustizia Sociale, Inclusività e Altre Sfide Aperte per Il Futuro Dei Processi Partecipativi Europei' in U Allegretti (ed), *Democrazia partecipativa: esperienze e prospettive in Italia e in Europa* (Firenze University Press 2010).

[45] 'Institutionalisation' refers to 'the process by which organizations and procedures acquire value and stability', as observed in SP Huntington, *Political Order in Changing Societies* (Yale University Press 1968) 21. The concept also has an important significance in the legal discourse, as it refers to the recognition by legal means of certain values and practices that already exist within society transforming them into formal rules. For the two forefathers of institutionalism – namely Maurice Hauriou and Santi Romano – see further, A Salvatore (ed), *Maurice Hauriou. La Teoria Dell'istituzione e Della Fondazione* (Quodlibet 2019), and R Cavallo Perin et al (eds), *Attualità e Necessità Del Pensiero Di Santi Romano* (Editoriale Scientifica 2019).

[46] See C Pateman, 'Participatory Democracy Revisited' (2012) 10 *Perspectives on Politics* 7. See also U Allegretti (ed), *Democrazia partecipativa: esperienze e prospettive in Italia e in Europa* (Firenze University Press 2010) and its overview of participatory processes around Europe. Worth mentioning is the Regional law of Toscana 69/2007 that is among the first laws on participatory democracy in the world that included civic participation in regional and local decision-making processes (see l.r.n.69/2007 on '*Norme sulla promozione della partecipazione alla* elaborazione delle politiche regionali e locali'). See on that M Brunazzo, 'Istituzionalizzare La Partecipazione? Le Leggi Sulla Partecipazione in Italia' (2017) 3 *Istituzioni Del Federalismo* 837. See further, R Lewanski, 'Institutionalizing Deliberative Democracy: The "Tuscany Laboratory"' (2013) 9 *Journal of Public Deliberation* Article 10, which talks of 'deliberative participation', claiming that deliberative theories were included in civic participation procedures.

[47] United Nations Economic Commission for Europe (UNECE), Convention on Access to Information, Public Participation in Decision-Making and Access to Justice in Environmental Matters, Aarhus, 25 June 1998, available at: unece.org/fileadmin/DAM/env/pp/documents/cep43e.pdf. The EU and its 27 Member States are all Parties to the Aarhus Convention, which entered into

public decision-making on environmental matters. Accordingly, authorities are now required to involve affected citizens and NGOs, consider their input, and explain final decisions.

In parallel to participatory democracy, however, the principle of participation in its broadest meaning also constitutes the conceptual reference for a wide variety of phenomena which may also occur at different levels of government. More in general, the principle refers to all those forms of democracy that are not based on the traditional representative channels. Specifically, deliberative democracy and direct democracy implement some kind of citizen participation – yet with differences from participatory democracy.

'Direct democracy' has been defined as 'a form of democracy in which the demos expresses its political will without any intermediate elected body'.[48] Unlike representative democracy, it allows citizens to intervene directly in specific decisions through tools like referenda, citizens' initiatives and the right to petition. Compared with participatory democracy, which seeks continuous engagement, direct democracy is occasional and limited in scope – focused on expressing support or opposition to particular issues. Its reliance on voting underscores a weaker, less sustained form of participation. Although most constitutions favour representative democracy and rarely mention 'direct democracy' explicitly, referenda are widely embedded in constitutions worldwide.[49]

For 'deliberative democracy'[50] the discourse becomes more complex. While absent from constitutional texts,[51] it originated in American constitutional thought in debates on the interpretation of the US Constitution.[52] First introduced in an

force on 30 October 2001 and was approved on behalf of the European Community by Council Decision 2005/370/EC of 17 February 2005. Today, it is considered as the leading international agreement on environmental democracy.

[48] Definition provided in A Gamper, 'Direct Democracy' in *Max Planck Encyclopedia of Comparative Constitutional Law* (MPECCoL, 2019). See this contribution for an introduction on direct democracy and further references. The author understands both participatory and deliberative forms of democracy as variants of direct democracy. There are many diverse categorisations of the forms of democracy, so this one should only be considered as one among many.

[49] An empirical survey was conducted by Gamper ibid (see paras 10–15).

[50] It should be noted that this form of democracy is currently mainly referred to by scholars of political sciences: it entered the legal debate only recently, where it is usually referred to within the broadest field of participatory democracy, even though there is no shared theory yet.

[51] For comparative research in world constitutions, this book used the platform 'Constitute', available at: constituteproject.org/?lang=en. Inaccuracies are possible, primarily due to the language barrier, since the research was conducted using the database with translations in English. By searching the term 'deliberative democracy' on its research platform it shows it has no explicit references in currently established constitutions. On the contrary, the term 'participatory democracy' entered many constitutions (Algeria, Angola, Gambia, Honduras, Maldives, Morocco, Portugal, South Africa, Suriname, Tunisia, Uganda). It is true, however, that the constitutional charters in the majority of cases do not explicitly mention the participatory aspect of democracy (nor the deliberative) usually because of the historical phases where they were adopted, when the concept of participation was not widespread (see on this point U Allegretti, 'La democrazia partecipativa in Italia e in Europa' (2011) 1 *Rivista dell'Associazione Italiana dei Costituzionalisti* 4, 7). The term 'direct democracy', for its part, could be explicitly found in five constitutions: Ecuador, Georgia, Nicaragua, Ukraine and Vietnam.

[52] Floridia, 'Participatory Democracy' (n 36) 27.

important essay in 1980,[53] the concept emphasised the role of elected representatives who should be able to understand the 'deliberative sense of the community', that is the expression of the 'public voice' emerging from citizens and their public debates.[54] Deliberative democracy prioritises procedures and inclusive dialogue over immediate outcomes, contrasting with the more result-driven participatory democracy. Despite diverse interpretations,[55] and a wide variety of deliberative procedures,[56] more generally, we could talk of a deliberative approach, that puts at the core of democracy procedural rules and the method of argument-based discussion (which is the meaning of 'deliberation') over and above the results, and where all the diverse and contrasting interests and points of view are included. This is in contrast to participatory democracy, whose more pragmatic perspective is aimed at reaching a concrete output and impact on the decision-making process. What the two have in common is their aim of countering the shortcomings of representative democracy and its elitist vision prevailing in that historical context, based on majority rule.[57] That is also the reason why often the difference between the two is blurred, and there is no consensus in the literature on the relation between them. In fact, some authors have claimed that they are two different theories of democracy but have contrasting views on their precise origins (in particular on participatory democracy).[58] Some scholars wrote that deliberative democracy is a specific type of participatory democracy with more circumscribed and defined contours;[59] some others believe the opposite is true;[60] some have suggested that they are actually two ways of approaching democracy that are destined to intersect and thus mutually benefit;[61] some have worked on the concept of 'participatory

[53] JM Bessette, 'Deliberative Democracy: The Majority Principle in American Government' in RA Goldwin and WA Schambra (eds), *How Democratic is the Constitution?* (AEI Press 1980). He claims that 'the Constitution was designed to make the deliberative majority the effective ruling power in the United States', in sharp contrast to 'aristocratic' or 'elitist' interpretations of the Constitution (112 ff).

[54] ibid.

[55] Among others, there are philosophical, legal-constitutionalist, social theory, and political science approaches. For a summary of those perspectives and their further references, see A Floridia, 'The Origins of the Deliberative Turn' in A Bächtiger et al (eds), *The Oxford Handbook of Deliberative Democracy* (Oxford University Press 2018).

[56] OECD, *Innovative Citizen Participation and New Democratic Institutions Report: Catching the Deliberative Wave* (2020). This report studied 282 cases of 'representative deliberative practices' in OECD countries, labelling them as 'innovative citizen participation'. It views participation broadly, including deliberative democracy. Notably, 52% of these practices occur at the local level (16).

[57] With reference to participatory democracy and deliberative democracy, 'both aim to attenuate the most negative effects of majority rule, most notably, the marginalisation of minority interests through polarised and polarising yes-or-no decisions': see Palermo and Kössler (n 29) 117.

[58] Floridia, 'Participatory Democracy' (n 36) 7 traces the origins of both participatory and deliberative democracy to the US, noting later intersections and overlaps. Another view links participatory democracy to Porto Alegre's participatory budgeting in Latin America, and deliberative democracy in the Anglo-Saxon context: see on that, U Allegretti, 'La democrazia partecipativa in Italia e in Europa' (n 51) and L Bobbio, 'Dilemmi Della Democrazia Partecipativa' (2006) 4 *Democrazia a Diritto* 11, 14.

[59] Bobbio, ibid, 14.

[60] R Bifulco, 'Democrazia deliberativa, partecipativa e rappresentativa: tre diverse forme di democrazia' in U Allegretti (ed), *Democrazia partecipativa: esperienze e prospettive in Italia e in Europa* (Firenze University Press 2010).

[61] Allegretti, 'La democrazia partecipativa in Italia e in Europa' (n 51) 4.

deliberative democracy' as one unique conception of democracy mixing participation and deliberation aspects.[62]

All in all, the scholarly debate on participatory democracy remains complex due to overlapping definitions with direct and deliberative democracy and its varied applications across time, place and levels of institutionalisation. This book adopts a clear focus: participatory democracy as a form of democracy viewed through a public and constitutional law lens within the European legal space. We also acknowledge federalism's role in shaping participation in multi-level systems[63] (see chapter four), and we address its legal positioning at the intersection of constitutional and administrative law. We treat 'participation' as a broad, constitutionally grounded term, examining how the EU and CoE enshrine it among their founding principles.

III. The Constitutional Contribution of the EU Legal Order

The concept of participation[64] (and participatory democracy) has been adopted by both EU Member States and the Union, that made it a pillar of its constitutional construction. Seen as a way of building a political community without a common *demos*,[65] the EU developed this principle by including civil society in decision-making, in this way emphasising governance over government. The process began in 1957 with the Treaty of Rome[66] that established the European Economic and Social Committee (EESC), a consultative body (still in existence) composed of the representatives of various social and economic activities:[67] its advisory role aimed at ensuring that organised civil society contributes directly to EU decision-making through formal advisory opinions, amplifying the voices of interested parties. The Treaty of Amsterdam (Article 138) reaffirmed the Commission's recognition of the consultative role of the social parts in the social policy field. Later for the first time

[62] D della Porta, *Can Democracy Be Saved? Participation, Deliberation and Social Movements* (Polity 2013) 8. See further, J Bohman and W Rehg (eds), *Deliberative Democracy: Essays on Reason and Politics* (MIT Press 1997); J Elster (ed), *Deliberative Democracy* (Cambridge University Press 1998); A Bächtiger et al (eds), *The Oxford Handbook of Deliberative Democracy* (Oxford University Press 2018): in particular, see the chapter of E Stephen. 'Deliberative and Participatory Democracy'.

[63] This is particularly true in so far as federalism is based on a culture of shared powers and autonomy. Federalist studies, indeed, include a research strand on participation and participatory democracy: Palermo and Kössler (n 29) 111–22. For the further contribution of federalism, in particular, to the local democracy and to the identification of the 'city' as an independent subject, see ch 4.

[64] When referring to 'participation' we are implicitly always referring to political/civic participation, as already explained above (n 14).

[65] We already referred to this debate in ch 1 (see n 26 and further references).

[66] We are referring to the Treaty establishing the European Economic Community (TEEC), signed in 1957 in Rome.

[67] The EESC is defined as a 'transnational participatory forum' in D Ferri, 'European Citizens … Mind the Gap! Some Reflections on Participatory Democracy in the EU' (2013) 5(3) *Perspectives on Federalism* 56, 62.

the concept of participation entered EU constitutional discourse explicitly in the (draft) Treaty establishing a Constitution for Europe (TECE) – at Article I-47 titled 'the principle of participatory democracy' – recognising participatory democracy alongside representative democracy as a distinct form of democratic legitimation. In contrast to almost[68] all the Member States whose democratic legitimation is founded – also because of historical reasons – on the principle of representation, the EU constitutes a landmark recognition of a democratic legitimation founded on both representative democracy and elements of participatory democracy, therefore paving the way for a new relationship between the state (or more correctly, the public side) and society.[69] The content of Article I-47 comprised four parts: (1) the need for public institutions to grant citizens and representative associations the public exchange of their opinion on matters relating to the EU's field of action; (2) the need for institutions to 'maintain an open, transparent and regular dialogue with representative associations and civil society'; (3) the provision of consultations to be carried out by the Commission with parties concerned with its actions; (4) the opportunity to initiate a European citizens' initiative (ECI) addressed to the Commission for proposing a legislative action on a certain matter. Despite the draft Treaty's failure, the substance of Article I-47 remained in EU law, later appearing in Article 11 TEU, though without the term 'participatory democracy'.

Looking at the constitutional ground of the EU legal order, explicit references to the principle of participation can currently be found in different Articles of the Treaties, together with some implicit ones also referring to the concept of participatory democracy.[70] It goes without saying that the core of the constitutional provisions on participation are contained in Title II of the TEU labelled

[68] Within the EU, only Portugal's Constitution (Article 2) explicitly includes participatory democracy alongside representative democracy.

[69] In fact, 'EU democracy is not founded on the principle of popular sovereignty that has been proclaimed in the national constitutions inspired by social contract tradition' (128) and 'the establishment of participatory democracy as one of the EU's normative bedrocks is a potentially important step because it makes clear that representation, that pillar of liberal democracy, cannot be the sole means to a legitimate regime in the EU' (130, quoted from A Warleigh): see V Cuesta Lopez, 'The Lisbon Treaty's Provisions on Democratic Principles: A Legal Framework for Participatory Democracy' (2010) 16 *European Public Law* 123.

[70] In addition to the provisions at Articles 9–12, further (implicit and explicit) references at the EU constitutional level could be found in other Articles contained in the Treaties and in the Charter of Fundamental Rights of the European Union (CFR) (proclaimed in Nice on 7 December 2000, and that according to Article 6(1) TEU has the same legal value as the European Treaties), and precisely at: Article 1(2) TEU on the need for decisions to be taken at the level closest to citizens (principle later also referred to in Article 10(3) TEU); Article 24 TFEU on the European citizens' initiative, on the possibility for every citizen to the right to petition the European Parliament, to apply to the Ombudsman, and to write to any of the EU institutions or bodies; Article 15 TFEU on the participation of civil society and the promotion of good governance, and on the right of access to documents of the Union's institutions, bodies, offices and agencies; Article 42 CFR on the right of access to documents; Article 227 TFEU on the right to petition (also at Article 44 CFR); Article 228 TFEU on the right to write complaints to the European Ombudsman (also at Article 43 CFR). See further on this, Fabio Raspadori, 'La partecipazione dei cittadini all'Unione Europea e lo spettro della democrazia' (2022) *Federalismi.it*. According to all the Treaties and CFR provisions, he classifies civic participation through 3 different labels: (1) participation as control; (2) participation in public deliberations; and (3) participation as information, training and discussion.

'Democratic participation', showing clearly the correlation between participation and democracy.[71] This Title comprises four Articles, 9–12:[72] Article 9 contains the principle of democratic equality and defines EU citizenship; Article 10 founds the Union on representative democracy, adding to that a citizens' 'right to participate' to the democratic life of the Union, and defining the principle of transparency and the role of political parties; Article 11 refers to citizens' dialogues and consultations, and defines the ECI; and Article 12 outlines the role of national parliaments in the EU legislative process and other processes.

Articles 10(3) and 11 are the EU's strongest constitutional commitment to participatory democracy. They provide broad legal backing for participatory practices at all levels and serve as a shared reference. These Articles emphasise the role of EU citizens and civil society organisations in EU governance beyond traditional representative channels. The provision of citizens' right to participate laid down in Article 10(3) TEU complements the fundamental choice of representative democracy as the Union's democratic model, even though this right is not conceived there as an enforceable subjective right.[73] According to this Article, transparency and proximity constitute fundamental aspects of the decision-making processes of the Union so that decisions could be seen as more legitimate, demonstrating the link between participation and the other European constitutional principle of subsidiarity (Article 5(3) TEU).[74] In line with Article 10(3), Article 11 TEU goes further in defining what participatory democracy means within the EU legal order, through the definition of specific participatory tools. The first three paragraphs aim at granting effective participation through (1) the involvement of citizens and representative associations by means of better communication,[75] (2) a civil dialogue[76] between EU institutions and representative associations

[71] J Mendes, 'Participation and the Role of Law after Lisbon: A Legal View on Article 11 TEU' (2011) 48 *Common Market Law Review* 1849: 'For the first time at Treaty level participation in decision-making beyond political representation is explicitly linked to democracy. The democracy of the Union now rests, by force of Article 11 TEU, also on the links it establishes directly with its citizens' (1850). At the core of her contribution, the author argues that 'Article 11 TEU postulates a transition from the instrumental usages of participation typical of participatory governance to participation conceived as a basis of participatory democracy. Participation is therefore one of the foundations of democracy in the EU' (1850).

[72] See further, M Kellerbauer et al (eds), *The EU Treaties and the Charter of Fundamental Rights: A Commentary* (Oxford University Press 2019) 103 ff.

[73] Cuesta Lopez (n 69) 130.

[74] On this link among the two, see Kellerbauer et al (eds) (n 72) 111.

[75] Even though it is not clear what 'publicly exchange their views' means on a practical level, nor how the difference between this public exchange of views and civic dialogues and consultations is defined: see Mendes (n 71) 1858 f.

[76] 'The Commission has traditionally engaged in dialogue through external consultations which are expressly encouraged in Article 11(3) TEU. The European Parliament has channelled civil dialogue primarily through informal public hearings (Cuesta Lopez (n 69) 132). The practice of civil dialogue had been initiated by the Commission a long time before, with its introduction in 1996 by the DG responsible for social policy in order to grant interactions with civil society organisations in parallel to the interactions occurring with social partners already occurring through the 'social dialogue' (institutionalised already with the Maastricht Treaty, eventually included in Article 155 TFEU). See further on that, Ferri (n 67) 66.

and civil society, and (3) consultations carried out with parties concerned by the Commission. While paragraphs 1, 2 and 3 constitute a formal recognition of previous institutional practices, paragraph 4 introduces what has been defined[77] as the real major innovation among participatory democracy tools, namely the ECI. Despite the not unanimous account regarding its nature,[78] this book places it among the other tools of participatory democracy that the EU equips its citizens with under the principle of participation. Under the condition that a minimum of one million EU citizens launch an ECI on a certain matter legally relevant for the implementation of the Treaties, the Commission could submit a legislative proposal.[79] High expectations concerning the democratic potential of this tool should, however, be avoided since whatever initiative is subject to the political will of the institutions,[80] its scope of action cannot propose treaty change nor acts that are not legal.[81] All together, these participatory tools serve the scope of involving EU citizens and civil society organisations in the decision-making process, and therefore in the processes of governance as defined in chapter one. Article 24 TFEU outlines additional participation tools: the right to petition the European Parliament and to contact the European Ombudsman.[82] While participatory democracy tools target EU citizens, these rights extend to all natural or legal persons residing or with their office being registered in the EU.[83]

Alongside EU primary law – namely the Treaties (and by some Articles of the CFR)[84] – another key act referenced participation before the draft TECE and Lisbon Treaty: the 2001 White Paper on European Governance.[85] Issued by the EU Commission, it is a soft-law document which promoted good governance principles (openness, accountability, effectiveness, coherence and participation)[86] – later included in Article 11 TEU. It aimed to boost 'input legitimacy'[87] by enhancing

[77] Mendes (n 71) 1849.

[78] Authors like Kellerbauer define it as a tool of direct democracy (Kellerbauer et al (eds) (n 72) 115); others like Alemanno brings it back into the realm of participatory democracy: A Alemanno, 'Beyond Consultations. Reimagining European Participatory Democracy' (Carnegie Europe, HEC Paris Research Paper, 2018) 6.

[79] The procedural steps required to launch a ECI are: registration, successful submission, and a positive decision by the Commission. All of that is laid down in Regulation (EU) No 211/ 2011 of the European Parliament and of the Council of 16 February 2011 on the citizens' initiative [2011] OJ L65/1 (regulation which is based on Article 24(1) TFEU). For an exhaustive account on how the ECI works see Ferri, 'European Citizens' (n 67) 76 and 79.

[80] Position expressed by Cuesta Lopez (n 69) 136 f.

[81] These two are the main limitations underlined by Kellerbauer et al (eds) (n 72) 115.

[82] Further analysis of them could be found in Kellerbauer et al (eds) (n 72).

[83] Kellerbauer et al (eds) (n 72) 111.

[84] Within the EU Charter of Fundamental Rights (Nice Charter), two references are included on participation with regard to the rights of the elderly (Article 25) and the integration of persons with disabilities (Article 26). See also ch 1 (n 48).

[85] Commission, 'European Governance. A White Paper' COM(2001)428, 25 July 2001.

[86] As noted by Kellerbauer et al (eds) (n 72) 114. See also Cuesta Lopez (n 69) 134.

[87] Ferri, 'European Citizens (n 67). Input legitimacy is described as a 'discrepancy between the pervasive effects of the regulative power of the EU and the weak authorization of this power through the citizens of the Member States who are specifically affected by those regulations' (57).

citizen participation and EU governance legitimacy. The White Paper focused on reforming governance to be more participatory, while the Lisbon Treaty gave participation constitutional and legal status.[88] Another recent soft-law act is the Commission's recommendation of 2023, which encourages Member States to promote 'participation frameworks' to provide more opportunities for citizens and civil society organisations to effectively participate in public policy-making processes.[89]

In addition to soft law, secondary law also contributed somehow to providing legal ground to the principle of participation beyond its mere outlining as a principle: that is particularly evident in EU environmental law, where it emerges that European participation (especially in environmental matters) cannot simply be linked to participation in the way it is conceived at the national level, but needs to be understood in accordance with a supranational understanding closely related to the concept of European democracy.[90] Lastly, more recent initiatives show us the importance of the principle of participation and of the concept of participatory democracy. Among the others, we refer to the EU urban policy, with its latest New Leipzig Charter issued in 2020 defining the principle of participation (together with co-creation) as one of the key principles of 'good urban governance',[91] and to the Competence Centre on Participatory and Deliberative Democracy[92] of the European Commission, recently created within the Joint Research Centre directorate-general in order to support participatory and deliberative projects and policies at the EU level and to foster best practices in participatory and deliberative democracy across different levels of governance in the EU.

The list of EU contributions to participation and participatory democracy via binding and non-binding acts is longer and not exhaustive. We conclude

[88] This is the core of the contribution of Mendes (n 71) 1849.

[89] Commission Recommendation (EU) C(2023) 8627 of 12 December 2023 on promoting the engagement and effective participation of citizens and civil society organisations in public policy-making processes.

[90] For an introduction on participation in EU environmental law through both primary and secondary Union law, see B Peters, 'Towards the Europeanization of Participation? Reflecting on the Functions and Beneficiaries of Participation in EU Environmental Law' in C Fraenkel-Haeberle et al (eds), *Citizen Participation in Multi-Level Democracies* (Brill 2015) 311 ff. The author underlines that despite the great variety of legal sources, the Aarhus Convention 'remains the central point of reference for participation in environmental matters' (332). On the Aarhus Convention see above (n 47). See also, T Etty et al, 'Legal, Regulatory, and Governance Innovation in Transnational Environmental Law' (2022) 11 *Transnational Environmental Law* 223, where the authors claim that the emergence of a transnational environmental law is occurring through parallel legal, regulatory and governance innovation.

[91] *The New Leipzig Charter. The Transformative Power of Cities for the Common Good* (November 2020): it was adopted at the informal ministerial meeting on urban matters on 30 November 2020. The Charter (an instrument of soft law) defines its set of strategic principles of good urban governance providing a framework for EU Member States to coordinate their post-2020 urban policies. These principles are: (1) urban policy for the common good; (2) an integrated approach; (3) participation and co-creation; (4) multi-level governance; and (5) a place-based approach. Interestingly, despite the vagueness of the meaning of 'participation', the Charter refers to the need to design new forms of (public) participation able to help cities in urban development processes and to strengthen local democracy.

[92] See: knowledge4policy.ec.europa.eu/participatory-democracy_en.

with four brief points on participation in the EU, useful for the next steps: (1) on its limits and underuse; (2) on the relationship between participation and representation; (3) on the lack of a clear legal framework; and (4) on its level of application.

First, it is not a mystery that the different tools of participatory democracy at the EU level 'remain unknown, scattered, and underused by the average European citizen'[93] and have not 'evolved into a self-standing practice'.[94] In fact, despite the inclusion of participation within the Lisbon Treaty, the EU governance process still remains far removed from citizens,[95] and even worse it seems that the principle of political equality under which all the provisions on participatory democracy should be interpreted[96] is actually not properly applied, in so far as forms of elitism in European public policy-making at the Brussels level[97] continue to occur. Therefore, alongside its underuse, limits could also be observed with regard to the actual (limited) inclusiveness of participatory tools.[98]

Second, what emerges from the EU legal order is the fact that participation is not an autonomous source of legitimation of the Union, but it remains in a subordinate position to representative democracy.[99] The aim of participatory democracy consists therefore in a desire to bring European citizens closer to the institutions, whose legitimacy has already been guaranteed by the principle of representative democracy.

The third observation targets all those scholarly arguments on the need for the EU to institutionalise supranational participatory channels through a clear legal framework in order to improve citizen participation.[100] Despite the fact that Articles 10–11 TEU would have provided for an ideal constitutional ground for the enactment of secondary law,[101] so far a more informal approach based on soft law has been favoured.

[93] A Alemanno, 'Europe's Democracy Challenge: Citizen Participation in and Beyond Elections' (2020) 21 *German Law Journal* 35.

[94] A Alemanno, 'Levelling the EU Participatory Playing Field: A Legal and Policy Analysis of the Commission's Public Consultations in Light of the Principle of Political Equality' (2020) 26 *European Law Journal* 114, 118.

[95] Ferri, 'European Citizens' (n 67) 80, which defines the EU governance as '*muddy*' and technocratic.

[96] Cuesta Lopez (n 69) 131.

[97] A Kutay, 'Limits of Participatory Democracy in European Governance' (2015) 21 *European Law Journal* 803, 810 f. The author contests the narrow definition of European civil society, that he thinks it is structurally confined only to those associations that are willing and able to participate (812).

[98] On this point, Alemanno 'Levelling the EU Participatory Playing Field' (n 94): Commission's Public Consultations. In particular, he criticises the unconstrained discretion of the EU Commission on consultations (for example, how to frame them, and what to do with the outcome) (124), advocating for a redesign of consultations legal and policy framework (130).

[99] ibid, and Kutay (n 97) says that 'participation relies and depends on representation'.

[100] A Alemanno and J Organ, 'The Case for Citizen Participation in the European Union: A Theoretical Perspective on EU Participatory Democracy' in A Alemanno and J Organ (eds), *Citizen Participation in Democratic Europe: What Next for the EU?* (ECPR Press/Rowman & Littlefield Publishers 2021). Additionally, see Ferri, 'European Citizens' (n 67) 81.

[101] D Ferri, 'L'Unione Europea Sulla Strada Della Democrazia Partecipativa?' (2011) 2 *Istituzioni del Federalismo* 298, 334 f.

The last consideration regards the level of application of the EU constitutional provisions on participation and participatory democracy, which is clearly the supranational level. Indeed, the principle of participation and its related concept of participatory democracy within the EU legal order do not refer in any way to the national and subnational levels, but is limited to participation in EU level decision-making.[102]

All in all, according to the EU legal order, participation and participatory democracy complement representative democracy without replacing it. The EU's constitutional principle of participation adds a channel of legitimacy building on a wider supranational governance perspective beyond the mere nation states' governmental one based on representation. Although lacking a formal legal framework, this has not stopped a multitude of participatory practices and tools from developing across borders, especially locally, even without normative support.

IV. The Constitutional Contribution of the Council of Europe (CoE) Legal Order

The 27 EU Member States are subject not only to the EU legal order, but also to the legal order of the CoE, whose treaties belong to the sphere of international law and therefore constitute a constitutional commitment for each signatory and ratifying state. Interestingly, within the CoE, the contribution to citizen participation has occurred in relation to both democracy in the broad sense,[103] and to local democracy more specifically. In fact, while in the EU the relation is between participation

[102] This consideration builds on what has previosuly been briefly covered in ch 1, section II.

[103] Many and of diverse type are the CoE documents about participatory democracy and the principle of participation, the most relevant ones with an explicit mention of participation (legally binding or not) being the following. (1) Council of Europe Conventions: the European Charter of Local Self-Government. ETS No 122, 1985, with its Additional Protocol to the European Charter of Local Self-Government on the right to participate in the affairs of a local authority, CETS No 207, 2009; European Convention on the Participation of Foreigners in Public Life at Local *Level*, ETS No. 144, 1992. (2) Committee of Ministers, Recommendations: Recommendation CM/Rec(2009)1 of the Committee of Ministers to member states on electronic democracy (e-democracy), (which recognises that information and communication technology (ICT) facilitates wider democratic participation); Recommendation CM/Rec(2009)2 of the Committee of Ministers to member states on the evaluation, auditing and monitoring of participation and participation policies at local and regional level (which includes a self- assessment tool for citizen participation at the local level, the C.L.E.A.R. tool); Recommendation CM/Rec(2011)14 of the Committee of Ministers to member states on the participation of persons with disabilities in political and public life; Recommendation CM/Rec(2018)4 of the Committee of Ministers to member States on the participation of citizens in local public life. (3) Committee of Ministers' Guidelines: CM(2017)83-final 'Guidelines for civil participation in political decision making'. (4) Congress of Local and Regional Authorities: Revised European Charter on the Participation of Young People in Local and Regional Life, adopted by the Congress of Local and Regional Authorities of Europe (10th session – 21 May 2003 – Appendix to Recommendation 128). (5) Conference of INGOs of the CoE: Code Of Good Practice For Civil Participation In The Decision-Making Process Revised, 2019. (6) Centre of Expertise for Good Governance of the Council of Europe: the 'Civil Participation In Decision-Making Toolkit', 2020.

and democracy at the EU level, the CoE has focused since the very beginning on the relationship between participation and the local level of democracy, advocating for a true right to participate in the public affairs of local authorities.

At the treaty level, the highest status of the CoE legal instruments, we can find three main texts dealing with participation at the local level, and they constitute the object of our analysis: (1) the European Charter of local self-government (the Charter) (1985); (2) the Additional Protocol to the European Charter of local self-government on the right to participate in the affairs of a local authority (2009); and (3) the Convention on the participation of foreigners in public life at local level (1992). Among them, of paramount importance is without any doubt the Charter,[104] that thanks to its constitutional value can be said to have paved the way for establishing a European constitutional local government law.[105] Since 1985, the CoE Charter on local democracy sets international legal standards protecting local autonomy. Within this scope, its preamble first recognises the 'right of citizens to participate in the conduct of public affairs', rooted in all CoE member states' constitutional traditions. The origin of citizens' right to participate, however, can be traced back much earlier[106] to the Charter adopted by the General Assembly of the Council of European Municipalities[107] in 1953, namely the European Charter of Municipal Liberties. That Charter proclaimed municipal self-government 'as the bulwark of personal liberties' against the encroachments of the nation state, recognising that 'municipal rights are based on centuries-old traditions', among them being the right of citizens to work together for the development of municipalities that must 'strive to enable them to participate in the town's life'. The 1985 Charter commits[108] the Parties to recognising the principle of local self-government in domestic legislation and, if possible, in their constitution (Article 2). The Charter not only has a legal value, but also a political dimension: this emerges from the monitoring work of the CoE's internal body, the Congress of Local and Regional authorities of Europe (the Congress),[109] that regularly

[104] Its importance derives also from the status of its ratification: since its promulgation in 1985, it has been ratified by *all* the 46 CoE member states (table of ratifications available at: www.coe.int/en/web/conventions/full-list?module=signatures-by-treaty&treatynum=122). Unlike that, the Additional Protocol has been ratified by 23 Member States (data available at: www.coe.int/en/web/conventions/full-list?module=signatures-by-treaty&treatynum=207), while the 1992 Convention by 9 (data available at: www.coe.int/en/web/conventions/full-list?module=signatures-by-treaty&treatynum=144).

[105] G Boggero, *Constitutional Principles of Local Self-Government in Europe* (Brill 2018).

[106] CMG Himsworth, *The European Charter of Local Self-Government: A Treaty for Local Democracy* (Edinburgh University Press 2015) 16.

[107] Later it became the Council of European Municipalities and Regions.

[108] On the ambivalence of the Charter, see Himsworth (n 106) 68 ff. The author addresses the well-known critique to the effectiveness of the Charter: while on one side 'it was to be a fully binding treaty, imposing legal obligations', on the other 'there was a tendency to weaken the effectiveness of those obligations'. This gets clearer when looking at Article 12 of the Charter, that permits each State to consider itself bound by only a certain number of paragraphs, which are up to each State to choose.

[109] Originally established in 1957, the Congress of Local and Regional Authorities is an institution of the CoE, responsible for strengthening local and regional democracy in its 46 Member States. Its main aim is to safeguard the implementation of the European Charter of Local self-government, through the assessment of the situation of local and regional democracy in the CoE member states.

carries out monitoring missions in the 46 Member States and issues reports and recommendations addressed to states assessing their compliance with Charter implementation.[110] Constituted by the two elements[111] of political autonomy, and its democratic nature (Article 3), the principle of local self-government is a right and ability of local authorities, and is regarded as a vital contribution to democracy. At the same time, the Charter recognises that this right should not interfere with all those 'forms of direct citizen participation where it is permitted by statute' (among which, assemblies of citizens or referendums, as pointed out in Article 3(2)). The Charter itself only briefly addresses public participation in local government,[112] an aspect not expanded on.[113] Even the explanatory report simply notes local authorities' role due to their proximity to citizens, making them the right level of government for effective citizen participation in decisions affecting daily life.[114]

To build on this, the 2009 Additional Protocol on the right to participate in the affairs of a local authority was introduced. This legal instrument, equal in status to the main Treaty, focuses entirely on citizen participation, reaffirming the 'right to participate' stated in the Charter's preamble. The right to participate is here further described as 'the right to seek to determine or to influence the exercise of a local authority's power and responsibilities' (Article 1.2), in order to have 'better policies and services'[115] at the local level. In order to guarantee that, and since the provisions of the Protocol are not self-executing, it is stipulated that subsequent domestic law 'shall provide means of facilitating the exercise of this right' (Article 1.3). This obligation is better described in Article 2, where – despite criticism raised on the generality of these provisions[116] – it is outlined that this could occur through: (a) the empowerment of local authorities 'to enable, promote and facilitate' the exercise of this right; (b) the establishment of local level procedures for involving people, procedures for accessing documents, measures for the inclusion of people that are outside participatory channels, procedures for answering complaints and suggestions[117] of citizens

[110] On the political value of the Charter and the Congress' work on keeping 'local autonomy issues on domestic political agendas', see also Himsworth (n 106) 129 and 147. The monitoring reports and recommendation for each party State can be found at: www.coe.int/en/web/congress/congress-reports{%2254213415%22:[]}. For a comparative analysis between States and compliance with the Charter Articles, see: www.congress-monitoring.eu/en/.

[111] C Panara and M Varney, *Local Government in Europe: The 'Fourth Level' in the EU Multilayered System of Governance* (Routledge 2013) 372.

[112] Himsworth (n 106) 40.

[113] An implicit reference to citizen participation lies in Article 5 of the Charter, where the need for consultations of the local community concerned, possibly by referenda, in case of any change in the boundaries of a local authority, is reported.

[114] Council of Europe, *Explanatory Report to the Additional Protocol to the European Charter of Local Self-Government on the Right to Participate in the Affairs of a Local Authority* (2009).

[115] ibid 3.

[116] Himsworth (n 106) 83.

[117] Article 2(2), ii, d) outlines that measures for granting the right to participate in the affairs of a local authority shall secure the establishment of 'mechanisms and procedures for dealing with and responding to complaints and suggestions regarding the functioning of local authorities and local

concerning the work of local authorities; and (c) the encouragement for the use of ICTs to foster participation. The Protocol[118] requires local authorities to support citizens' participation, foreseeing more obligations on them towards their citizens and their rights. It establishes an individual right to participate in local affairs alongside the Charter's local self-government right of local authorities.[119] Participatory rights apply broadly, covering not only 'citizens' *in strictu senso* (Article 3.2 Charter), but also 'nationals' (Article 1.4.1 Protocol), matching CoE terminology[120] from the 1992 Convention on the participation of foreigners in public life at local level.

In addition to the international legal guarantee concerning the right to participate provided by the 1985 Charter and the 2009 Protocol, the 1992 Convention also contributed to the principle of participation. The Convention specificially addresses all those 'foreign residents' who are not nationals of the state, but reside lawfully on its territory (Article 2), granting them participatory rights in the decision-making process: the right of voting and standing for elections in local authorities after five years of residency in the host country; the right to freedom of expression, to freedom of peaceful assembly and to freedom of associations; and, the provision for the creation of consultative bodies for the representation of foreign residents in relation to local public life.[121] Through this legal framework there has been an extension of participation rights beyond the mere boundaries of the legal concept of 'citizen'.[122]

All in all, the CoE's main contribution to participation is its inclusion in treaty documents and the link to local democracy. The 1985 Charter, its 2009 Protocol and the 1992 Convention form the key constitutional basis for participation, despite some national courts' reluctance to recognise the Charter's constitutional value.[123] Although these Treaties do not explicitly mention participatory

public services': by using the word 'suggestions' the Protocol in this way seems to welcome any kind of contribution that could come from the citizens' side as a spontaneous initiative towards the local community.

[118] Himsworth (n 106) 83.

[119] In accordance with a recent critique, it would actually be better to talk of 'territorial authorities' instead of 'local authorities' if we observe that Article 13 of the Charter also considers within 'all the categories of local authorities' the regional authorities, therefore creating confusion about the precise target of the Charter. Despite this confusion, however, the Charter was originally 'intended to apply first and foremost to public territorial authorities with a truly local dimension and not to those higher-level authorities from which local authorities are delegated powers and/or are being supervised' (91). See on this point, Boggero, *Constitutional Principles* (n 105) 87 ff.

[120] CoE, *Explanatory Report* (n 114). See also Boggero, *Constitutional Principles* (n 105) 133.

[121] 'Local public life' shall mean all matters, services and decisions and in particular the management and administration of the affairs relating to or concerning a local community (CM/Rec(2018)4).

[122] L Kirchmair, 'International Law and Public Administration: The European Charter of Local Self-Government' (2015) 3 *Pro Publico Bono* 124, 133.

[123] For a further in-depth reading on the jurisprudence of Member States on the status of the Charter, see G Boggero, 'La Carta Europea Dell'autonomia Locale Nella Giurisprudenza Degli Stati Europei' (2015) 43 (5–6) *Le Regioni* 1077. In particular, for the experience of the Italian Constitutional Court – which qualifies the Charter provisions as mere generic policy rules – see 1099–1107. In a similar way, the Charter provisions are seen as being only of programmatic value and 'not sufficiently precise for

democracy, the CoE frequently uses the term, notably in its Secretariat General's Division of Elections and Participatory Democracy.[124] Together, these treaties form the CoE's constitutional roots[125] for citizen participation at the local level.

V. From the Constitutional Roots to Practical Instruments: The Contribution of Democratic Innovations

The majority of the experiences of participatory democracy in the world are occurring at the local level, within municipalities or even smaller districts, and the vast majority of them often begin with an informal character[126] before eventually starting to circulate as more structured and institutionalised models considered as best practice. Over the last decades a wide variety of participatory practices have been tried out in Europe, as well as in other parts of the world, at all levels of government, even though the local level seems to be favoured because of its proximity with citizens: from this perspective, indeed, the wider the local autonomy, the more this level of government can invent and experiment innovative forms of citizen participation.[127] Because of that, in this section we will do a run-through of some common examples of participatory democracy practices, instruments or processes that are occurring at the local level, in order to give us an idea of the participatory European scene. This is not exhaustive, as a full study would require separate research and a complex systematisation of diverse ground-level participatory experiences, which also need varied research methods beyond traditional legal ones. In fact, there is currently no shared overall understanding nor theoretical framework over participatory democracy practices occurring specifically at the local level and within the EU legal space, whether they have been institutionalised or not. Rather than typologies and systematisations of participatory practices, it is indeed more common to find just lists of examples.[128] One already

local governments to directly rely on them in courts'; also in Germany and Austria: see K Kössler and A Kress, 'European Cities Between Self-Government and Subordination: Their Role as Policy-Takers and Policy-Makers' in E Hirsch Ballin et al (eds), *European Yearbook of Constitutional Law 2020: The City in Constitutional Law* (Springer 2020) 279.

[124] It can be found at: www.coe.int/en/web/participatory-democracy.

[125] We define the contribution of these CoE Treaties as constitutional in line with that phenomenon defined as the 'constitutionalisation of international law' and 'internationalisation of constitutional law' elaborated in F Palermo, 'Internazionalizzazione Del Diritto Costituzionale e Costituzionalizzazione Del Diritto Internazionale Delle Differenze' (2009) European Diversity and Autonomy Papers no 2.

[126] H Addink, *Good Governance: Concept and Context* (Oxford University Press 2019) 140.

[127] Palermo, 'Participation, Federalism, and Pluralism' (n 2) 47: 'To be effective, participation needs to be carried out with some passion, to be moving and even exciting for people, motivating them to engage. Participation is therefore more likely to occur on issues at the heart of people's interests. These issues are normally either very local, or very foundational, such as constitutional questions'.

[128] See, eg, G Sgueo, *The Practice of Democracy: A Selection of Civic Engagement Initiatives* (Study, European Parliament 2020).

existing category defined by political scientists is 'democratic innovations' (DIs) – a field and umbrella term aimed at rethinking the relationship between the state and society by increasing opportunities for civic participation. This category is key for studying participation as it covers the main participatory experiences.

On the border between participatory and deliberative traditions, this category has been elaborated by democracy scholars trying to systematise within one theoretical framework citizens' forms of participation around the world, obviously too many to analyse in detail.[129] New participation types occur locally, aided by the governance shift described in chapter one; though governance and DIs stem from political science, many other sciences discuss ways to innovate democracy. While this term generally suffers from a lack of clarity and eludes general characterisation because of the wide diversity among innovations, one recent definition seems to better describe and frame the phenomenon as the most recent and (almost) all-encompassing. Accordingly, democratic innovations could be described as 'processes or institutions that are new to a policy issue, policy role, or level of governance, and developed to reimagine and deepen the role of citizens in governance processes by increasing opportunities for participation, deliberation and influence'.[130] Citizens are seen not just as voters or policy recipients, but are re-imagined as co-producers and problem-solvers who contribute individually beyond organised civil society groups.[131] What emerges is a clear link between the method of participation (alongside deliberation and influence) and the concept of governance as a relationship between the state and all those non-state actors contributing to democracy in some ways beyond representation. Given the many diverse practices of DIs, a recent classification into four families is helpful:[132] (1) mini-publics; (2) participatory budgeting; (3) referenda and citizens' initiatives; (4) collaborative governance. In addition to these, digital participation (also referred to as e-participation) constitutes a common trend that can be observed in each family.[133] The first family referred to as mini-publics, comprises all those consultative bodies made of citizens who deliberate on specific issues in order to

[129] For a worldwide perspective on participatory practices on the ground, the online crowdsourcing platform *Participedia* provides for a useful tool; see: participedia.net/.

[130] S Elstub and O Escobar, 'Defining and Typologising Democratic Innovations' in S Elstub and O Escobar (eds), *Handbook of Democratic Innovation and Governance* (Edward Elgar Publishing 2019) 11. Before this definition, worth mentioning is the definition of DIs by Smith as 'institutions that have been specifically designed to increase and deepen citizen participation in the political decision-making process' (see G Smith, *Democratic Innovations: Designing Institutions for Citizen Participation* (Cambridge University Press 2009) 1).

[131] Elstub and Escobar 'Defining and Typologising' (n 130) 15. On co-production, see further, SP Osborne et al, 'Co-Production and the Co-Creation of Value in Public Services: A Suitable Case for Treatment?' (2016) 18(5) *Public Management Review* 639.

[132] See Elstub–Escobar's definition.

[133] The advent of new information and communication technologies (ICTs), in fact, revitalised the debate over participatory theories in reference to the contribution that digital tools could bring to citizen participation: as an introduction, see V Lember et al, 'Engaging Citizens in Policy Making: The Potential and Challenges of e-Participation' in T Randma-Liiv and V Lember (eds), *Engaging Citizens in Policy Making: E-Participation Practices in Europe* (Edward Elgar Publishing 2022).

support the work of political representatives' bodies, providing them with recommendations to be considered in public decision-making. This family is, in turn, diversified, and all those practices of 'citizens' assemblies', 'citizens' juries', 'consensus conferences', 'deliberative polling' and 'planning cells' are considered to be all types of mini-publics. Mini-publics seems to represent the favoured method for the institutionalisation of deliberative democracy,[134] since at their core they have deliberation as a method for reaching a shared position on a specific issue: their deliberation, however, remains connected to representative decision-making.[135] The second family – participatory budgeting – refers to processes where ordinary citizens can participate through their direct say in deciding how public budget ought to be allocated. Porto Alegre[136] in 1989 was the first city in the world to elaborate and implement this instrument for engaging citizens in decisions relating to public finances: a novelty at that time, it rapidly circulated in a great number of local authorities around the world, becoming a best practice everywhere recognised as such (and institutionalised) for citizen participation.[137] With regard to the referenda and citizens' initiatives – the third family – the reference goes to multiple cases of direct democracy that have been often institutionalised in EU countries through the contribution of laws or included in constitutional texts.[138] The initiative could come from both parts –governmental as well the citizens'– and its result could be legally binding as well as not.[139] Proceeding with the last family, it has been referred to as the most internally diverse.[140] In fact, under the term

[134] C Harris, 'Mini-Publics: Design Choices and Legitimacy' in S Elstub and O Escobar (eds), *Handbook of Democratic Innovation and Governance* (Edward Elgar Publishing 2019) 48.

[135] For an introductory overview on mini-publics, see further, O Escobar and S Elstub, 'Forms of Mini-Publics: An Introduction to Deliberative Innovations in Democratic Practice' (New Democracy, Research and Development Note 4, 2017), available at: www.newdemocracy.com.au/2017/05/08/forms-of-mini-publics/.

[136] For the experience of Porto Alegre, see G Allegretti (n 44).

[137] For further readings, see E Ganuza and G Baiocchi, 'The Long Journey of Participatory Budgeting' in S Elstub and O Escobar (eds), *Handbook of Democratic Innovation and Governance* (Edward Elgar Publishing 2019).

[138] With concern to referenda, the majority of EU Member States have a constitutional provision on them (two exceptions are Cyprus and the Netherlands, which have no mention of them in their Constitutions): see the Constitute project online platform for comparing Constitutions (www.constituteproject.org/?lang=en).

[139] See M Jäske and M Setälä, 'Referendums and Citizens' Initiatives' in S Elstub and O Escobar (eds), *Handbook of Democratic Innovation and Governance* (Edward Elgar Publishing 2019) for an introductory systematisation of referenda and citizens' initiative within the field of DIs.

[140] Elstub and Escobar, 'Defining and Typologising' (n 130) 27. With reference to the field of collaborative governance, four different strands of research were suggested: collaborative management; co-creation; collaborative public innovation; and participatory and deliberative governance (see E Sørensen et al, 'Political Boundary Spanning: Politicians at the Interface between Collaborative Governance and Representative Democracy' (2020) 39 *Policy and Society* 530, 532). See also the definition of collaborative governance provided in C Ansell and A Gash, 'Collaborative Governance in Theory and Practice' (2008) 18 *Journal of Public Administration Research and Theory* 543 which still constitutes a reference point: 'A governing arrangement where one or more public agencies directly engage non-state stakeholders in a collective decision-making process that is formal, consensus-oriented, and deliberative and that aims to make or implement public policy or manage public programs or assets' (544).

'collaborative governance' we could find a great variety of practices, mostly occurring at the local level, that in a nutshell seek to allow for a collaboration between state actors and citizens often through the mediation of other stakeholders like NGOs or community groups in order to produce specific policy outcomes.[141] Because of its focus on citizens as active contributors to the production and delivery of public policies and services,[142] the concept of collaborative governance intercepts not only the stream of democratic theory, but also the one of public administration scholarship.[143] This systematisation of democratic innovations is helpful, though at times it may not be immediately evident how certain forms of participation – like urban planning,[144] community gardens, neighbourhood theatres,[145] or large public debates of a consultative nature like the French débat public[146] – fit within the four main categories.

In comparison to the contribution of political sciences, law has been much more limited. From this perspective, the analysis builds on on the core concept of legal pluralism, recognising that law is not exclusively state-derived, but also develops through societal practices.[147] The institutionalisation of participatory practices via legal means usually comes only at a second phase, after ground-level experiences have already been put in practice and consolidated. In addition to the variety of practices that we have only briefly listed, it is useful to note that certain participatory experiences have also been institutionalised at different levels of government, even though the majority remain in operation without the

[141] S Bussu, 'Collaborative Governance: Between Invited and Invented Spaces' in S Elstub and O Escobar (eds), *Handbook of Democratic Innovation and Governance* (Edward Elgar Publishing 2019) 62.

[142] ibid 60.

[143] L Blomgren Amsler, 'Collaborative Governance: Integrating Management, Politics, and Law' (2016) 76 *Public Administration Review* 700.

[144] We may refer here to further readings: see, for example, D Laws and J Forester, *Conflict, Improvisation, Governance: Street Level Practices for Urban Democracy* (Routledge 2015) for the concept of '*doing democracy*' for referring to street level democratic processes and governance in (participatory) urban planning.

[145] These participatory practices could be found on *Participedia* (n 129).

[146] See further, A Nicotina, 'A Procedural Idea of Environmental Democracy: The "Débat Public" Paradigm within the EU Framework' (2021) 14(2) *Review of European Administrative Law* 85.

[147] On this point see as a starting point, E Ehrlich, *Fundamental Principles of the Sociology of Law* (Harvard University Press 1936), where he challenged the state-centred conception of law by introducing the concept of 'living law' – the law practised by society, as opposed to that enforced by the State. He thus proposed a pluralism of legal orders existing in parallel to state law, arguing that not all legal phenomena originate from the State. This concept later laid the foundation for the modern theory of legal pluralism, which reconceptualises the relationship between law and society by adopting a post-modern view that recognises multiple sources of legitimacy beyond state law. Legal pluralism is therefore framed as an alternative to the Westphalian paradigm, encompassing both state and non-state law: for an overview, see BZ Tamanaha, 'Understanding Legal Pluralism: Past to Present, Local to Global' (2008) 30(3) *Sydney Law Review* 375. For a position in support of legal pluralism as the breeding ground for transnational law, see A Bostan, 'Transnational Law – A New System of Law?' (2021) 11 *Juridical Tribune* 332. Additionally, see M Avbelj, 'The Theory of Principled Legal Pluralism' in M Avbelj (ed), *The European Union under Transnational Law* (Hart Publishing 2018), where the author argues that new legal pluralism includes collectively binding norms not posited by the state (defined as 'anti-state legal pluralism', 26).

need for regulatory frameworks and even though the majority of such experiences are one-off. Among others, some examples of institutionalised experiences come from the Italian region of Tuscany, the Austrian Land of Vorarlberg, the Autonomous Community of Aragon, or the French national law on public debate.[148] Interestingly, for all those participatory practices occurring at the local level the lack of an explicit anchorage in the constitution or in a law does not prevent their realisation. Moreover, sometimes it could even seem that a legal framework is not actually needed as these practices could easily keep on circulating without that. Notwithstanding that, developing a legal framework could facilitate participatory practices, providing them with broader legitimacy and institutional recognition; a general trend toward institutionalisation, indeed, has been growing in recent years.

In sum, beyond constitutional texts many participatory practices at different levels of government creatively engage citizens beyond mere representation. Such innovative practices often blend doctrinal distinctions, constituting participatory practices founded on deliberative methods that can be grouped under the term 'democratic innovations' as they aim at renewing representative democracy. Democratic innovations fit within the broader field of 'participation',[149] and their constitutional significance – also that of local level grass-roots participatory practices – lies in their capacity to implement the European constitutional principle of participation.[150]

VI. Limits and Challenges

All in all, this gap between constitutional principles and on the ground implementation is what guarantees local governments the freedom to innovate with democratic innovations, turning constitutional vagueness into an advantage. Considering this, some limits and challenges could be pointed out.

[148] M Trettel, 'Rethinking Participatory Democracy through Federalism: Citizen Participation, Power-Sharing and Decision-Making Processes' in NP Alessi and M Trettel (eds), *Federalism and the Law of Diversity* (Brill Nijhoff 2025) 141–45. For other experiences of institutionalised participation see further, M Trettel, 'Democratic Innovations in (Subnational) Constitution-Making: The Institutionalized Case(s) of the Italian Provinces of Trento and Bolzano'. *Innovation: The European Journal of Social Science Research*, 2021; E Alber and A Valdesalici, 'Framing Subnational "Institutional Innovation" and "Participatory Democracy" in Italy: Some Findings on Current Structures, Procedures and Dynamics' in F Palermo and E Alber (eds), *Federalism as Decision-Making* (Brill Nijhoff 2015).

[149] Evidence coming from other scholars also points to participation and participatory democracy as the broad field where democratic innovations are rooted, recognising the undeniable influence of participation on DIs beyond the mere deliberation: see on this point Elstub and Escobar, 'Defining and Typologising Democratic Innovations' (n 130) 16 (and their further references), and H Asenbaum, 'Rethinking Democratic Innovations: A Look through the Kaleidoscope of Democratic Theory' (2021) 20 *Political Studies Review* 680.

[150] We use 'participation' instead of 'deliberation' because national constitutions as well as EU and CoE constitutional treaties refer to participation, not deliberation, which is more common in political science. See above (n 50).

Debates on democracy have long focused on moving beyond representation towards greater legitimacy through participation. Thanks to this awareness, participatory practices are growing inside and outside the EU, with and without government support. However, full legitimisation of participation remains limited, and challenges persist. A first considerable limitation could be seen at the EU level, where EU democracy has been accused of 'keeping citizens in a box':[151] accordingly, looking at citizen participation in contributing to the EU agenda, criticism has been raised towards the Union's machinery as it seems to keep on perceiving citizen participation as undesirable, and therefore dealing with it from a position of resistance. When it comes to citizens' involvement, indeed, the EU often keeps on being understood by its citizens as a fundamentally elitist and bureaucratic construction within the Brussels bubble that, despite declarations of principles and legal contributions, still struggles to ensure appropriate channels of citizen involvement and to guarantee meaningful forms of participation beyond representation. A second limitation consists in a centralised view of democracy, which overlooks the diverse local experiences in the EU. This is probably the consequence of the difficulty of the subnational level across the EU to define clear frameworks of participatory democracy – absent in the EU – capable of systematising the countless number of practices circulating and being tried out at regional and local levels. Thus, limitations exist at all levels. While democratic innovations highlight the need for interdisciplinary input, this does not finalise systematisation. A third key limitation is that most participatory practices remain top-down, allowing citizens' input in decision-making processes, but leaving final decisions with public authorities.[152]

This very limitation is useful as it points to the direction of the next challenges in the broad field of participation, and one primarily: that is the challenge of recognising forms of participation not only in decision-making processes, but also in concrete actions, where citizens are legitimised and empowered for taking practical initiatives in their communities. The frontier of this principle is, therefore, an action-oriented version of participation (a *participation in doing*)[153] which allows citizens not only to contribute to a public decision, but also to a concrete action of 'doing' something tangible relating to the public sphere through pragmatic activism.[154] The two forms of participation aimed at a practical doing consist of:[155]

[151] P Leino, 'Disruptive Democracy: Keeping EU Citizens in a Box' in I Govaere et al (eds), *Critical Reflections on Constitutional Democracy in the European Union* (Hart Publishing 2019).

[152] On this point, see L Bherer et al, 'The Participatory Democracy Turn: An Introduction' (2016) 12 *Journal of Civil Society* 225.

[153] For the distinction between the two types of *participation in deciding* and *participation in doing*, see further ch 5.

[154] On the idea of a '*do-it-ourselves democracy*' based on pragmatic activism and close to an action-oriented version of participatory democracy, see further F Hendriks, 'Democratic Innovation beyond Deliberative Reflection: The Plebiscitary Rebound and the Advent of Action-Oriented Democracy' (2019) 26 *Democratization* 444. The author advocates extending citizen participation through the recognition of practical collective actions beyond the formulation of decisions.

[155] Allegretti, 'Democrazia Partecipativa' (n 1) 305 is the scholar who qualifies these two forms of participation ('sussidiarietà' and 'autogestione') as having as their object a specific 'doing'. This is carried

(1) participation as self-governance; and (2) participation as enhanced by the principle of subsidiarity.

Participation as self-governance[156] refers to the ability of individuals to be autonomous in determining the rules underlying their relations with others, rather than relying on the state and governmental authorities.[157] The individual, indeed, is considered by a relevant strand of research[158] as the basic unit in democracy in which the importance of their self-governance through horizontal relationship complements vertical governmental relationships. Any collective unit of self-governance (for example, associations) comes only as a secondary concern, as created by individuals and their capacity to self-govern.[159] Self-governance has also been defined as the distinctive characteristic of polycentric systems – which are those systems based on polycentricity as a theory of governance.[160] Polycentricity, for its part, is the concept used to express societal capacity to self-govern through the active participation of citizens that, in time, will eventually bring about 'a complex system of governance institutions'[161] with many centres of authority, and where rules are not exclusively imposed by the State at all its levels. Self-governance constitutes, therefore, the capacity of individuals to participate by practical means in the societal groups they belong to,[162] thanks to the exercise of their individual autonomy.

out within a relationship with public institutions (subsidiarity) or autonomously (self-governance). The author also distinguishes them from other forms of participation within decision-making procedures implemented by institutions.

[156] Sometimes also referred to as 'self-organisation', see J van Zeben, 'Polycentricity as a Theory of Governance' in J van Zeben and A Bobić (eds), *Polycentricity in the European Union* (Cambridge University Press 2019) 14.

[157] Definition taken and adjusted from J van Zeben and A Bobić, 'The Potential of a Polycentric European Union' in J van Zeben and A Bobić (eds), *Polycentricity in the European Union* (Cambridge University Press 2019). However, as it has been critically argued, 'pure self-governance … in reality seldom exists': F van Laerhoven and C Barnes, 'Facilitated Self-Governance of the Commons' in B Hudson et al (eds), *Routledge Handbook of the Study of the Commons* (Routledge 2019).

[158] See further the studies on self-governance as linked to polycentrism by V Ostrom: 'The character of a democratic society is revealed by the willingness of people to cope with problematical situations instead of presuming that someone else has the responsibility for them … Most people have the opportunity to be active citizens in their local communities in addition to being spectators watching the games of politics being played out in distant places. As de Tocqueville recognized, municipal institutions are the basic sources of vitality in a free society. Citizens cannot achieve self-organizing and self-governing capabilities without the experience of actively associating with their fellow citizens to accomplish tasks that require their joint efforts. Citizens are essential coproducers of the patterns of life constitutive of human communities': see V Ostrom, *The Meaning of American Federalism: Constituting a Self-Governing Society* (Institute for Contemporary Studies 1991) 256.

[159] Van Zeben (n 156) 18.

[160] We will go further into this topic in ch 4, section I.

[161] Van Zeben (n 156) 16.

[162] The concept of self-governance is taken up in subsequent studies of Elinor Ostrom on community-based management of common pool resources, where it means that 'the resource users are the ones who define the rules by which the resource is managed' (van Zeben (n 156) 19). The landmark work is E Ostrom, *Governing the Commons: The Evolution of Institutions for Collective Action* (Cambridge University Press 1990).

This type of participation as self-governance, however, can be better exercised if it receives institutional support: in doing so, subsidiarity plays a key role. Subsidiarity in fact provides great potential for supporting an action-oriented form of participation and for strengthening the principle of participation itself, in so far as public authorities could be allies of individuals contributing to society at diverse levels, providing them with incentives and support for their initiatives. This is, specifically, what emerges from the innovative form of civic participation through the commons (CPC) – a totally new form of action-oriented participation that goes beyond the mere decision-making process – that is being supported and promoted by local public authorities in Italy in accordance with the constitutional principle of subsidiarity.[163] Recently considered as democratic innovations,[164] the commons indeed constitute a new field of experiences, practices and institutions for a new form of action-oriented participation (and democracy), where subsidiarity could play a fundamental role.[165]

In conclusion, the principle of participation in the European legal space is a complex, evolving phenomenon, like a jigsaw puzzle still difficult to fully grasp and systematise. The 'puzzle of participation' in the EU legal space is composed of both the constitutional entrenchment of this principle in the two legal orders of the EUnion and of the Council of Europe, as well as a myriad of practices invented, tested and circulating in institutionalised or non-institutionalised forms at all levels of government, with a greater presence at the local level. Participation, at the same time, is shifting towards new action-oriented forms beyond mere decision-making input. Though lacking direct and clear supranational legitimation, these local practices are a local phenomenon *within* the wider European constitutional space, and as such are part of a broader European democratic transformation.

[163] See Part III.

[164] In Asenbaum 'Rethinking Democratic Innovations' (2021) 6f, where the author claims that 'commons do not only consist of the resource itself but propose an innovative institutional arrangement, including a set of participatory rules and a community of people'. Previously, on the mentioning of 'urban commons as a democratic innovation' see Sheila R Foster and Christian Iaione, 'The City as a Commons' (2016) 34 *Yale Law & Policy Review* 326.

[165] See Parts III–IV.

PART II

Democracy at the Local Level

3

The Principles of Subsidiarity and Local Self-Government

I. The Local Level in the European Legal Space: An Introduction

Building on what emerges from the participation puzzle (chapter two), and our understanding of democracy according to forms and levels (chapter one), focusing on the local level of democracy within the European legal space becomes a crucial next step. Since most participatory practices – often called 'democratic innovations' – occur at this level,[1] it is essential to examine how local governments support these practices and the constitutional space that enables them.

The 'local level' of democracy in this book refers to the level of government which is the closest to citizens, and that is the first governmental level constituted through representative schemes. Many and diverse are the terms used for referring to what could be considered as 'the local level'. The most common are: 'local governments'; 'local self-government'; 'local autonomy'; 'local authorities'; 'local entities'; 'local governance'; 'local self-determination'; 'municipal government'; 'municipalities'; and 'cities'. These are used in addition to 'territorial autonomies'; 'subnational authorities'; 'subnational entities'; and 'regional and local authorities'; which refer indistinctly to the two regional and local dimensions together, or to the regional dimension without real importance and recognition given to the local one which is considered as included in it. The choice of terms depends on a multitude of aspects, spanning from the disciplinary lenses used, historical reasons, national perspective usage, the diverse definitions of different branches

[1] As claimed by U Allegretti, 'Participatory Democracy in Multi-Level States' in C Fraenkel-Haeberle et al (eds), *Citizen Participation in Multi-Level Democracies* (Brill 2015) 207. See also F Hendriks et al, 'European Subnational Democracy: Comparative Reflections and Conclusions' in J Loughlin, F Hendriks and A Lidström (eds), *The Oxford Handbook of Local and Regional Democracy in Europe* (Oxford University Press 2012) 741: 'Democratic innovation often centres on the local level … Local democracy serves as a field of democratic experimentation that also influences supralocal institutions of democracy. Quite often, democratic innovations travel 'upwards' in the system of home administration … Local government is also in the frontline'. Also Trettel demonstrates that citizens' participation is more frequent at the subnational level as a consequence of the fact that decentralised systems of government allow for a wider space for democratic experimentations: see M Trettel, *La democrazia partecipativa negli ordinamenti composti: Studio di diritto comparato sull'incidenza della tradizione giuridica nelle democratic innovations* (Edizioni Scientifiche Italiane 2020).

within the same discipline: these could be the reasons, for example, why scholars with a wider social science approach seem to prefer using 'local governments' while legal scholars prefer 'local authorities/entities'; why 'local governance' is more recent than 'local government' (as a consequence of the governance turn in the EU in the 1990s);[2] why each national legal tradition has its own terminological preference;[3] or why constitutional and administrative scholars have different terminological preferences. This book uses the term 'local democracy' to refer to the local level in the European legal space.

For legal scholars the local level has usually been object of study as a topic of administrative law, while for political scientists as an issue of local governance or local politics: until recently there was almost no interest in deepening that from a (European) constitutional law perspective.[4] Historically, the local level has been governed by national constitutions and state laws, often positioning local authorities as extensions of central government,[5] in line with the Westphalian model of state sovereignty.[6] Yet, the local level *predates* modern states in the form of what we are used to calling a 'city'. While states emerged in the seventeenth century through the Peace of Westphalia, cities as forms of societal organisational have existed for millennia as independent centres of civilisation, continuously evolving from Neolithic towns to today's diverse urban forms.[7] This highlights a key terminological point: unlike state-derived terms like 'local', the 'city' stands as an autonomous spatial and cultural concept.

Concerning the city as such (and not, more generally, the local level), it is interesting to note that the term is spanning disciplinary differences, as tremendous interest in cities spread long ago throughout human and social sciences,

[2] However, it is very common for the two terms of 'local government' and 'local governance' to be used interchangeably with no distinction between them: as an example, see the usage of them in E Vodyanitskaya, 'Local Government' (2016) *Max Planck Encyclopedia of Comparative Constitutional Law (MPECCoL)*.

[3] The two official versions of the CoE European Charter on local self-government – in English and in French – recognise the diversity of legal traditions in Europe. The concept of local autonomy is referred to as 'local self-government' and 'local authorities' as well as '*autonomie locale*' and '*collectivités locales*'. For more on terminology, see G Boggero, *Constitutional Principles of Local Self-Government in Europe* (Brill 2018) 12–17.

[4] As observed by C Panara and M Varney, *Local Government in Europe. The 'Fourth Level' in the EU Multilayered System of Governance* (Routledge 2013) 369.

[5] Well known is the definition of city provided by Frug as a 'powerless creature of the State': see GE Frug, 'The City as a Legal Concept' (1980) 93 *Harvard Law Review* 1057, 1063, 1120. Frug also reflects on this connection between cities and participatory democracy: 'But surely a more likely source of participatory democracy has always been the cities, in part because of the tradition of local participatory democracy from the colonial era to as recently as de Tocqueville's time. Why are cities today governed as bureaucracies, rather than as experiments in participatory democracy? … Thus, state control has prevented cities from becoming experiments in participatory democracy' (1073).

[6] On that, see J Hoeksma, 'Replacing the Westphalian System' (The Federal Trust, 2020) available at: fedtrust.co.uk/wp-content/uploads/2020/10/Replacing-the-Westphalian-system.pdf, and his observations on the EU as the system that is actually replacing the Westphalian system.

[7] L Mumford, *The City in History* (Harcourt Brace Jovanovich Inc 1961) 30.

from philosophy,[8] to political theory,[9] geography,[10] history,[11] economics,[12] urban studies,[13] sociology[14] and digital innovation[15] (but the list could be much longer) in a way that our times have been defined as 'city century'.[16] On the other hand, an absolute silence has prevailed until recently in general public law,[17] as we will

[8] H Lefebvre, *Il diritto alla città* (Ombre Corte 2013) (Italian translation of the 1967 book *Le Droit à la ville*), and D Weinstock, 'Cities and Federalism' in JE Fleming and JT Levy (eds), *Federalism and Subsidiarity* (New York University Press 2014).

[9] eg, see W Magnusson, *Politics of Urbanism: Seeing Like a City* (Routledge 2011): 'When we see like a state, we assume that the state is the necessary solution to the problem of sovereignty … To see like a city is to accept a certain disorderliness, unpredictability, and multiplicity as inevitable, and to pose the problem of politics in relation to that complexity, rather than in relation to the simplicity that sovereignty seeks' (120). See further also, BR Barber, *If Mayors Ruled the World: Dysfunctional Nations, Rising Cities* (Yale University Press 2013), where the author argues that cities and their mayors are at the forefront in solving problems, and are dealing with them more effectively than states.

[10] D Harvey, 'The Right to the City' (2003) 27 *International Journal of Urban and Regional Research* 939.

[11] For a historical account on the European city as a political entity whose importance has been neglected since the birth of nation states, and on its roots in the distinction between *urbs* and *civitas*, see F Hörcher, *The Political Philosophy of the European City: From Polis, through City-State, to Megalopolis?* (Lexington Books 2021) 1 ff.

[12] On economic challenges occurring in cities, see R Florida, *The New Urban Crisis* (Basic Books 2017).

[13] J Jacobs, *The Death and Life of Great American Cities* (Vintage Books 1961), and R Sennett on the concept of 'open city' (R Sennett, 'The Open City' (Urban Age, LSE Cities, 2006), available at: urbanage.lsecities.net/essays/the-open-city). For the idea of 'creative city' on the use of creativity in cities for solving urban problems by harnessing people's imagination and talent (also through a 'creative bureaucracy') see C Landry, *The Creative City: A Toolkit for Urban Innovators* (Earthscan 2008).

[14] eg, see S Sassen, 'The Global City: Introducing a Concepts' (2005) 11(2) *Brown Journal of World Affairs* 27.

[15] When referring to the field of digital innovation the reference goes to the contribution of digital means and networks to the transformation and development of cities, which is a phenomenon that usually goes under the name of 'smart city'. See on that, C Ratti and M Claudel, *La città di domani: Come le reti stanno cambiando il futuro urbano* (Einaudi 2017) – Italian translation of *The City of Tomorrow: Sensors, Networks, Hackers, and the Future of Urban Life* (Yale University Press 2016); and E Morozov and F Bria, *Rethinking the Smart City: Democratizing Urban Technologies* (Rosa Luxemburg Stiftung 2018). These authors, in particular, advocate for a bottom-up approach to the smart city paradigm where citizen participation through digital means could shape cities therefore preventing a purely top-down setting. Additionally, see C Moreno et al, 'Introducing the "15-Minute City": Sustainability, Resilience and Place Identity in Future Post-Pandemic Cities' (2021) 4 *Smart Cities* 93 for the introduction of the increasingly popular concept of the '*15 minute-city*', which has been inspired by the idea of the smart city itself, with regard to a model of city based on the four dimensions of proximity, density, diversity, digitalisation. Lastly, digital innovation in cities includes the idea of platform urbanism, an evolution of the smart city that examines how digital platforms reshape ties between corporations, cities and citizens (F Caprotti et al, 'Beyond the Smart City: A Typology of Platform Urbanism' (2022) 4 *Urban Transformations* 1).

[16] See M Bloomberg, 'City Century. Why Municipalities Are the Key to Fighting Climate Change' (October 2015) *Foreign Affairs* 116, that refers to a new urban age where the predominant institutional actor would be the city.

[17] Within public law, the two landmark contributions that broke the silence are: R Hirschl, *City, State: Constitutionalism and the Megacity* (Oxford University Press 2020) in constitutional law theory, and J-B Auby, 'Droit de La Ville. An Introduction' (2013) 5(2) *Italian Journal of Public Law* 302 in administrative law. Additionally, public international law is a key protagonist in a re-awakening of this field of research with respect to the urban age: HP Aust and JE Nijman (eds), *Research Handbook on International Law and Cities* (Edward Elgar Publishing 2021). For an introduction on this research turn, see G Nesi, 'The Shifting Status of Cities in International Law? A Review, Several Questions and a Straight Answer' (2021) 30 *Italian Yearbook of International Law Online* 15, where the author – despite

further investigate later in chapter four (sections I and III). Worth mentioning is also the recent acknowledgement of the role played by cities beyond nation states within the European integration process itself, that since the very beginning has been the prerogative of nation states.[18] Since in European public and constitutional law, the terms 'local government' (and 'local authority') are commonly used, it will therefore be the preferred terminology in this book. Key constitutional law concepts tied to local government include decentralisation, subsidiarity,[19] federalism[20] and urban citizenship.[21] However, looking at the local level through the prism of the European legal space, one should examine the legal orders of the EU and the Council of Europe, which means focusing on the core principles of 'subsidiarity' and 'local self-government' found in both legal frameworks.

II. Subsidiarity and Local Self-Government in the EU Legal Order

Subsidiarity and local self-government, both key concepts in the EU Treaties, reflect different perspectives: subsidiarity aligns with the state and the EU's view on power distribution, while local self-government reflects local authorities' aim to retain autonomy from higher levels of government. Despite a general overlook at the local level in the Treaties mostly as a consequence of the fact that it

a very clear position on the primacy of states in international law as the sole actors – recognises the emerging role of cities and other local authorities in implementing international treaties on the ground especially through 'transnational city networks'. For the first works within local government law scholarship on cities in international law, see Y Blank, 'The City and the World' (2006) 44 *Columbia Journal of Transnational Law* 875, and GE Frug and DJ Barron, 'International Local Government Law' (2006) 38 *The Urban Lawyer* 1, and more recently CF Swiney, 'The Urbanization of International Law and International Relations: The Rising Soft Power of Cities in Global Governance' (2020) 41 *Michigan Journal of International Law* 227. For the recent link between human rights (as a specific sub-field of international law) and cities see B Oomen and M Baumgärtel, 'Frontier Cities: The Rise of Local Authorities as an Opportunity for International Human Rights Law' (2018) 29 *European Journal of International Law* 607, who recognise the importance of local authorities in the protection and enhancement of human rights in the negligence of nation states. See also the position of the international law scholar Papisca on the topic: he was much in favour of a more important role for cities in international law and human rights protection, because cities are much closer to citizens, and constitute the roots of democracy. See A Papisca, 'Relevance of Human Rights in the Glocal Space of Politics: How to Enlarge Democratic Practice beyond State Boundaries and Build up a Peaceful World Order' in K de Feyter et al (eds), *The Local Relevance of Human Rights* (Cambridge University Press 2011).

[18] On this observation, see J Zielonka, 'The Remaking of the EU's Borders and the Images of European Architecture' (2017) 39 *Journal of European Integration* 641.

[19] As an introduction, on the distinction between subsidiarity and decentralisation, see J Drew and B Grant, 'Subsidiarity: More than a Principle of Decentralization – A View from Local Government' (2017) 47 *Publius: Journal of Federalism* 522.

[20] On the awakening of the federalist theory moving from a two-tier systematisation to a three-tier one see, above all, F Palermo and K Kössler, *Comparative Federalism: Constitutional Arrangements and Case Law* (Hart Publishing 2017) 281 ff. See further ch 4.

[21] As an introduction, see the 'Urban citizenship' debate on *Verfassungsblog* in 2020 at: verfassungsblog.de/category/debates/urban-citizenship-debates/.

belongs to the exclusive competence of each Member State,[22] the explicit recognition of these two concepts as founding principles of EU law can be found most importantly in two points, Articles 4(2) and 5(3) of the Treaty on European Union (TEU). While Article 4(2) TEU recognises the national identities of each Member States 'inclusive of regional and local self-government' and, as a consequence, it also recognises domestic democracy at the level of all territorial autonomies, Article 5(3) matters for the vertical division of competences between the EU and the Member States, 'either at central level or at regional and local level' (which is the so-called 'subsidiarity principle'). To frame subsidiarity in the EU legal order, we first outline its origins and its current (vertical) interpretation (section II.A), then examine the concept of local self-government and the neglected role of local authorities (section II.B), ending with the forgotten horizontal dimension of subsidiarity towards civil society (section II.C).

A. Subsidiarity

The roots of subsidiarity can be traced a long way back before the creation of the European Economic Community, in the constant tension between individuals' liberty and autonomy in contrast with the role exercised by a higher authority,[23] and in the constant search for a balance between human dignity and the common good.[24] In a nutshell, the principle looks at how the relationship between the state and society should be structured. Subsidiarity centres on competences, grounded in the idea that individuals should be free to shape their lives and contribute to the community, countering centralised authority. It therefore contributes to providing

[22] On the exclusive competence of each Member State on its local level, see J van Zeben, 'Local Governments as Subjects and Objects of EU Law: Legitimate Limits?' in S Bardutzky and E Fahey (eds), *Framing the Subjects and Objects of Contemporary EU Law* (Edward Elgar Publishing 2017), and Boggero, *Constitutional Principles* (n 3) 69. Additionally, see M Finck, 'Challenging the Subnational Dimension of Subsidiarity in EU Law' (2015) 8 *European Journal of Legal Studies* 5, where the author claims that subnational authorities (SNAs) 'doubtlessly exist; yet the European Treaties largely ignore their existence' (8). An obvious consequence of the EU's lack of competence on the local level is the absence of recognition of cities and local governments as political communities by the European judiciary, rendering them effectively invisible (see F Nicola, 'Invisible Cities in Europe' (2012) 35 *Fordham International Law Journal* 1282).

[23] For an introductory perspective on the political philosophy behind the concept of subsidiarity and the importance of considering it as a constitutional principle, see C Millon-Delson, *Il principio di sussidiarietà* (Giuffrè Editore 2003).

[24] J Drew, *Reforming Local Government* (Springer 2020): 'The Principle of Subsidiarity seeks to balance the needs of persons and persons in association, on the one hand, with the need to cultivate the common good, on the other. It is a principle that cautions against concentrations of power and competence and celebrates the plurality of associations critical for human flourishing' (123). The author points to Johannes Messner as 'the greatest interpreter of the Principle of Subsidiarity' (106) whose lucid outlook on subsidiarity was the consequence of his first-hand experience as an adviser to the Chancellor of Austria Dollfuss before the advent of Nazism, through which he understood the importance of this (back then totally neglected) principle, lamenting 'the "parental" conception that citizens had increasingly transferred onto government' (107).

a solution to the problem of scale raised by the fundamental question about the appropriate level of where to allocate competencies. The principle is usually said to come from the Latin word *subsidium* with reference to the military reinforcements meant to provide support during a battle (the so called *subsidiariae cohortes*).[25] Although the Catholic social doctrine, notably Pope Pius XI's *Quadragesimo Anno* (1931),[26] for the first time explicitly recognised subsidiarity as central to societal organisation, its origins go further back. Observing the complexity of society, and the growing power of states in regulating individuals' lives (also at the expense of the Church itself), Pope Pius XI's call to subsidiarity was essentially aimed at protecting the individual and their freedom against the growing power of the state and the hegemonic ambitions of fascism:[27] according to him, individuals should be considered as competent and responsible participants in society, also within the autonomy of intermediate bodies, and supported while not suppressed by the state in achieving their freedom in accordance with the common good. The Christian social doctrine, however, did not invent subsidiarity, but rather took it from the previous centuries-old tradition of social philosophy – in doing so constituting only the modern reference to this principle.[28] In fact, early roots appear first in Mosaic law, advising Moses to decentralise authority.[29] Aristotle also endorsed higher authority stepping in only to aid individuals in achieving autonomy through the *polis*, understanding politics as the government of autonomies. The idea evolved through Medieval Scholasticism into an idea of a subsidiary society articulated in a multitude of autonomous groups and units cooperating with a view of a common destiny. Later, it featured in federalist thought (for example, Althusius),[30] state theorists like de Tocqueville and Hegel, liberal advocates of limited state interference towards lower levels of government (for example, Locke), and eventually

[25] TE Frosini, 'Sussidiarietà (Principio Di) (Dir.Cost.)' (2008) *Enciclopedia del Diritto* 1134.

[26] Pope Pius XI, *Littera Encyclica Quadragesimo Anno*, 1931, at point 80 on the role of the state and the restoration of the social order: 'The supreme authority of the State ought, therefore, to let subordinate groups handle matters and concerns of lesser importance, which would otherwise dissipate its efforts greatly. Thereby the State will more freely, powerfully, and effectively do all those things that belong to it alone because it alone can do them: directing, watching, urging, restraining, as occasion requires and necessity demands. Therefore, those in power should be sure that the more perfectly a graduated order is kept among the various associations, in observance of the principle of "subsidiary function", the stronger social authority and effectiveness will be the happier and more prosperous the condition of the State'.

[27] L Antonini, *Sussidiarietà fiscale. La frontiera della democrazia* (Guerini 2005) 67.

[28] J Luther, 'La sussidiarietà come principio sussidiario del diritto pubblico comune europeo' in D Ciaffi and FM Giordano (eds), *Storia, percorsi e politiche della sussidiarietà. Le nuove prospettive in Italia e in Europa* (Il Mulino 2020).

[29] By B Gussen, *Axial Shift City Subsidiarity and the World System in the 21st Century* (Palgrave Macmillan 2019) 200, where he refers to Exodus 18: 13–27. Also FM Giordano, 'Subsidiarity, a Transformative Principle for the Future of European Democracy' (2021) 4 *De Europa* 99, 101 refers to Exodus as the possible original source of subsidiarity.

[30] See, eg, E Arban, 'An Intellectual History of Federalism: The City and the "Unit" Question' in E Arban (ed), *Cities in Federal Constitutional Theory* (Oxford University Press 2022); A Føllesdal, 'Survey Article: Subsidiarity' (1998) 6 *Journal of Political Philosophy* 190; G Macdonald, *Sussidiarietà Orizzontale: Cittadini Attivi Nella Cura Dei Beni Comuni* (Aracne editrice 2018).

nineteenth-century Catholic social thought,[31] which opposed excessive state intrusion into individual life.

The re-emergence of subsidiarity in the European context has been explained[32] to be mainly as a result of three reasons: the gradual construction of the EU as a political organisation; the crisis of Western European states' providentialism as a consequence of the depletion of the public sector; and the fall of totalitarianism in Eastern European states. The period of time we are referring to is the 1990s. These events have posed the need for European states to balance the demands of autonomy and those of authority within a wider supranational organisation, for which the constitutionalisation of the principle of subsidiarity has offered a solution. The Treaty of Rome of 1957 already contained the first implicit traces of the principle in some of its provisions on the division of competences between the Community and the Member States.[33] The principle first appeared in the Single European Act (1987),[34] and was fully established in Article 3b EC of the Maastricht Treaty,[35] becoming a general principle for all areas falling outside the exclusive competence of the Community, reinforced by its inclusion in the preamble and Article A, which emphasised decisions being taken 'as closely as possible to the citizen'. The Maastricht Treaty later became the basis for the further elaboration of the principle in the (failed) Treaty establishing a constitution for Europe,[36] and eventually in the Lisbon Treaty in Article 5(3) TEU as we know it today.

The principle of subsidiarity entered the EU legal order amid debates in the 1990s over competence allocation between the EU and its Member States. Scholars identify three main roots of the EU's interpretation of subsidiarity:[37] (1) Catholic social philosophy; (2) German federalism; and (3) British conservative ideology. Catholic social philosophy sees the state as overreaching by usurping the functions of smaller societal groups such as families, associations and local communities. This view stands out from the others because it emphasises private individuals' contributions

[31] The reconstruction of these steps is made on the basis of the contribution of Millon-Delson (n 23) 7 ff.

[32] By Millon-Delson (n 23) 2.

[33] Articles 100 and 235 EEC: for this historical development of subsidiarity in the EU, see K Granat, 'The Subsidiarity Principle in the EU Treaties' in K Granat, *The Principle of Subsidiarity and its Enforcement in the EU Legal Order: The Role of National Parliaments in the Early Warning System* (Hart Publishing 2018).

[34] Article 130r(4) EEC on Community action in the area of environmental policy.

[35] As inserted by Article G(5) TEU. Also known as the 'Treaty on European Union', it was concluded in 1992 and became effective on 1 November 1993.

[36] For a study on subsidiarity in the draft Constitution, see further NW Barber, 'Subsidiarity in the Draft Constitution' (2005) 11 *European Public Law* 197, and I Massa Pinto, 'Il principio di sussidiarietà nel progetto di trattato che istituisce una Costituzione per l'Europa' (2003) II *Diritto Pubblico Comparato ed Europeo* 1220.

[37] On these three roots see, above all, J Peterson, 'Subsidiarity: A Definition to Suit Any Vision?' (1994) 47 *Parliamentary Affairs* 116, 117 ff; M Wilke and H Wallace, 'Subsidiarity Approaches to Power Sharing in the European Community' (1990) RIIA Discussion Paper No 27, 1. Additionally, see Granat (n 33).

to the common good, believing that 'small social groups should be autonomous and sovereign in a pluralist society'.[38] Such groups are seen as better suited to carry out many societal tasks and support individual talents.[39] German federalism viewed subsidiarity as requiring a clear, constitutionalised static division of powers across government levels, aiming for an EU federal structure like Germany.[40] The third view, British conservative ideology, saw subsidiarity as a safeguard against the European Community's overreach, ensuring national primacy over the Community in decision-making processes and rejecting any federal model. These differing views delayed consensus, but subsidiarity was included in the Maastricht Treaty as a safeguard tool 'to placate those member states … who feared that too much power was shifting from the national to the European level'.[41] The British view, favoring national primacy, became dominant,[42] reflecting a bicentric perspective of the European Community,[43] focused on the two national and European levels.

Today, subsidiarity in the EU consists in a legal-political[44] principle guiding the allocation of powers among levels of government, based on the idea that public functions should be carried out as close to citizens as possible. It has a dual nature: a negative aspect limiting central intervention when local levels are sufficient, and a positive one allowing central action when objectives are better achieved at higher levels.[45] Since the Lisbon Treaty, the EU has moved beyond a purely bicentric model by explicitly also recognising local and regional levels.

[38] On the principle of subsidiarity as conceived by Catholic social thought, see Peterson (n 37) 117 f; NW Barber, 'The Limited Modesty of Subsidiarity' (2005) 11 *European Law Journal* 308, 310–14; Wilke and Wallace (n 37) 12 f; Drew and Grant (n 19) 524 ff. The quotation can be found in particular in Peterson (n 37) 118. Additionally, see FH Mueller, 'The Principle of Subsidiarity in the Christian Tradition' (1943) 4(3) *American Catholic Sociological Review* 144, and Føllesdal 'Survey Article: Subsidiarity' (n 30) 207 ff.

[39] A well-known representative of this approach to subsidiarity was Jacques Delors, who also became 'the leading exponent of the principle of subsidiarity': see Wilke and Wallace (n 37) 30. On Delors' contribution to European subsidiarity, see also Giordano (n 29) 99 ff and further references.

[40] Peterson (n 37) 119.

[41] NW Barber 'The Limited Modesty' (n 38) 314.

[42] See Peterson (n 37) 119. *cf* Granat (n 33) argues that the main inspiration for European subsidiarity came from German federalism.

[43] It was the Maastricht Treaty in 1993 that replaced the 'European Community' with 'European Union'.

[44] S Pazos-Vidal, *Subsidiarity and EU Multilevel Governance: Actors, Networks and Agendas* (Routledge 2019) 1; C Panara, 'The Enforceability of Subsidiarity in the EU and the Ethos of Cooperative Federalism' (2016) 22 *European Public Law* 305, 306; P Craig, 'Subsidiarity: A Political and Legal Analysis' (2012) 50(S1) *Journal of Common Market Studies* 72. As Panara interestingly writes: 'With specific reference to subsidiarity, Nettesheim has recently proposed the oxymoronic notion of "politisches Recht" (political law), indicating those legal provisions which are only or principally enforceable through forms of political coordination (politische Koordination) … Subsidiarity is a constitutional principle of the EU whose observance is achieved by cumulating judicial review and political cooperation in the lawmaking process' (24 and 27).

[45] See G Martinico, 'Federalism, Regionalism and the Principle of Subsidiarity' in E Arban et al (eds), *Federalism and Constitutional Law: The Italian Contribution to Comparative Regionalism* (Routledge 2021); Drew and Grant (n 19) 526.

However, the Treaties fail[46] in embracing a truly polycentric approach,[47] as subsidiarity remains framed mainly between the EU and the Member States. Competences remain mainly divided between the EU and nation states – exclusive, shared, or supporting[48] – with subnational levels viewed as part of Member States' domain. Where the EU lacks exclusive competence, subsidiarity protects Member States' authority. This 'vertical subsidiarity'[49] focuses on governments and has enabled the EU's multi-level integration. The principle has a practical impact on legislative procedures: in particular the role of national parliaments[50] has, indeed, been strengthened with the Lisbon Treaty, as well as that of the Court of Justice[51] in monitoring compliance with the principle, and that of the Committee of the Regions (CoR).[52] Despite the fact that subsidiarity as a legal principle of European constitutional law is strictly related to the concept of democracy as its introduction was expected to reduce the EU democratic deficit[53] through the favour for proximity,[54] the critiques and limits to this principle as such are diverse, the main three being: (1) its difficult justiciability; (2) its centralising effect; and (3) the total overlook of its subnational dimension. Concerning the first critique, since its introduction in the Maastricht Treaty in 1992, the EU principle of subsidiarity has raised questions concerning its justiciability before the Court of Justice of the European Union (CJEU),[55]

[46] Finck 'Challenging' (n 22). As the author argues, 'it must thus be concluded that while subsidiarity seemed to bear the promise of recognising local and regional authorities as regulators of EU law, under its current formulation and implementation, Article 5(3) TEU limits this promise to pure rhetoric rather than actual substantive change' (17). See also, M Finck, 'Fragmentation as an Agent of Integration: Subnational Authorities in EU Law' (2017) 15 *ICON* 1119.

[47] K Nicolaïdis and J van Zeben, 'Polycentric Subsidiarity' in J van Zeben and A Bobić (eds), *Polycentricity in the European Union* (Cambridge University Press 2019). See further ch 4, section I.

[48] Articles 2, 3, 4 and 6 TFEU on the division of competences within the EU.

[49] E Arban, 'Re-Centralizing Subsidiarity: Interpretations by the Italian Constitutional Court' (2015) 25 *Regional & Federal Studies* 129; additionally, see F Giglioni, 'Subsidiary Cooperation: A New Type of Relationship between Public and Private Bodies Supported by the EU Law' (2010) 2 *Rivista Italiana di Diritto Pubblico Comunitario* 485, 491.

[50] See Article 5(3) TEU (second sub-paragraph), Article 12 (b) TEU, and Protocol (No 2) on the application of the principles of subsidiarity and proportionality. National parliaments can have a say in the EU legislative process through the issuing of a reasoned opinion where they state why they believe that the principle of subsidiarity has been violated by an EU draft legislative Act: this is what has been defined as the 'early warning system' (EWS). Regional parliaments with legislative powers may also be involved in the EWS by national parliaments. On the EWS as a tool for safeguarding the respect of subsidiarity see Finck, 'Challenging' (n 22) 5ff.

[51] Article 8 of the Protocol (2).

[52] Article 8 of the Protocol (2). On the role of the CoR in the implementation of subsidiarity see C Panara, *The Sub-National Dimension of the EU: A Legal Study of Multilevel Governance* (Springer 2015) 120–21.

[53] M Bartl, 'The Way We Do Europe: Subsidiarity and the *Substantive* Democratic Deficit' (2015) 21 *European Law Journal* 23.

[54] On the relationship between subsidiarity and proximity, see M Cahill, 'Subsidiarity as the Preference for Proximity' (2021) 66 *American Journal of Jurisprudence* 129.

[55] For an analysis of the case law on the principle of subsidiarity before the CJEU, see C Panara, 'Subsidiarity v Autonomy in the EU' (2022) 28 *European Public Law* 269. The author counts 44 cases

about which many had doubts. Despite being relatively scarce, case law of the CJEU on the EU principle of subsidiarity does exist, and the justiciability experience of certain EU Member States proves that to be possible:[56] however, the difficulty in doing that goes unquestioned, also as a consequence of subsidiarity itself being seen by some as a threat to EU integration.[57] Secondly, EU subsidiarity tends to centralise power by promoting a subsidiarity-as-efficiency model, concentrating competences at the EU level due to its perceived efficiency, often at the expense of lower authorities.[58] Thus, while subsidiarity should protect Member States' and subnational autonomy in theory, in practice efficiency is prioritised over autonomy.[59] The third critique, linked to the second, points to a total overview of the regional and local dimensions of subsidiarity.[60] While subsidiarity is usually seen as recognising autonomies in the EU, its role in control by local and regional authorities is often overestimated.[61] The Lisbon Treaty's inclusion of these levels seems more rhetorical than substantive, despite their potential to strengthen subsidiarity and democracy in the EU's multi-level governance system.[62]

B. Local Self-Government

The second principle recognising the local level from a constitutional perspective within the EU legal order is local self-government under Article 4(2) TEU. Generally, treaties treat subnational levels as passive recipients of EU law, but Article 4(2) acknowledges their function of self-government. Self-government is used for referring to all those subnational authorities that enjoy some degree of autonomy towards central government, and that are expression of their local community in so far as they have elected representatives.[63] Constitutional law has until very recently[64] rarely dealt with the principle of local self-government

since 1993, and through his study demonstrates that the interpretation of subsidiarity by the CJEU is not a safeguard clause for autonomy of MSs and their subnational entities, but instead a tool for reinforcing EU governance aim of efficiency. See additionally, Nicolaïdis and van Zeben (n 47) 86 ff.

[56] Panara, 'Subsidiarity v Autonomy in the EU' (n 55). The two cases that the author, in particular, analyses are Germany and Italy.

[57] As argued by Estella and reported in Panara, 'The Enforceability of Subsidiarity' (n 44) 306.

[58] Among the others, Millon-Delson (n 23) 67; Nicolaïdis and van Zeben (n 47) 86 ff; M Cahill and G O'Sullivan, 'Subsidiarity and the City: The Case for Mutual Strengthening'. In E Arban (ed), *Cities in Federal Constitutional Theory* (Oxford University Press 2022). Nicolaïdis and van Zeben argue that 'the EU's interpretation of the principle of subsidiarity meant to restrain the expansion of EU competences has not been able to stop the expansion of EU competence – and has arguably facilitated it, despite pre-legislative and post-legislative control' (ibid 8).

[59] This is the central thesis argued in Panara, 'Subsidiarity v Autonomy' (n 55) (2022). See also on that, Finck, 'Challenging' (n 22).

[60] See Finck, Challenging' (n 22); van Zeben, 'Local Governments as Subjects' (n 22).

[61] As reporetd in van Zeben (n 22) 133, 'the only direct representation of local interests is through the Committee of the Regions (CoR), whose mandate is exclusively advisory'.

[62] Panara and Varney (n 4) 413.

[63] ibid 20.

[64] As pointed out in Panara and Varney, ibid, 369.

(or local autonomy)[65] from a wider EU perspective, that is also reflected in the fact that the reference to local (and regional) authorities was introduced only with the Lisbon Treaty. Local self-government includes two key elements: political autonomy and local democracy.[66] Political autonomy 'implies that a local community is entitled to make their own decisions on issues falling within their remit',[67] allowing for a certain degree of autonomy in those areas allowed by law or constitutional provisions, so that the local level of government would not be a mere executor of decisions taken at higher levels of authority. Local democracy 'implies that local communities are entitled to elect the governing bodies of local authorities (local council, mayor)':[68] this refers, in a nutshell, to the representative dimension of the local level as the first level of democracy. The recognition of the importance of this principle in the EU legal order comes from its constitutionalisation by the CoE in the European Charter of local self-government (Article 2), that since 1985 has drawn attention to this level of government beyond nation states. However, many nation-state constitutions mentioned this as early as in the eighteenth century.[69] Democracy, for its part, constitutes a fundamental aspect of local self-government, in so far as local governments are recognised to have not only representative channels, but also participatory instruments for citizens' contribution to democracy, so that they could be involved at the level of government which is closer to them. The recognition of local self-government in the EU Treaties is, therefore, fundamental for providing an EU constitutional basis for the local level of government as an actor and not only receiver of the wider EU governance system: this explicit mention, however, 'is not an European guarantee for the existence of such structures'.[70] Scholarship[71] and the CJEU[72] generally interpret Article 4(2) TEU as protecting

[65] Acknowledging the identification between these two terms, this book predominantly uses the term 'local self-government' in accordance with the EU and CoE jargon. Sometimes it also uses the term 'local autonomy' in accordance with the literature found. In this work they should be considered as interchangeable, and this is in line with the Congress of Local and Regional authorities: *A Contemporary Commentary by the Congress on the Explanatory Report to the European Charter of Local Self-Government*. 12February2020,availableat:rm.coe.int/a-contemporary-commentary-by-the-congress-on-the-explanatory-report-to/16809cbf8c.

[66] Panara and Varney (n 4) 372. To define local self-government, the authors use the European Charter of local self-government of the CoE.

[67] ibid.

[68] ibid.

[69] The concept of local self-government found its place in the French Constitution of 1795 for the first time: for a list of historical mentions of this principle among European constitutions, see Panara and Varney (n 4) 374 f.

[70] A Schnettger, 'Article 4(2) TEU as a Vehicle for National Constitutional Identity in the Shared European Legal System' in C Calliess and G van der Schyff (eds), *Constitutional Identity in a Europe of Multilevel Constitutionalism* (Cambridge University Press 2019) 25.

[71] Paradigmatic is one recent commentary on the EU Treaties: M Kellerbauer et al (eds), *The EU Treaties and the Charter of Fundamental Rights: A Commentary* (Oxford University Press 2019), where the concept of local self-government included at Article 4(2) TEU is not specifically mentioned or explained (see 35–60).

[72] On the dominant interpretation of Article 4(2) TEU see, among the others, G Martinico, 'Taming National Identity: A Systematic Understanding of Article 4.2 TEU' (2021) 27 *European Public Law* 447; and B de Witte, 'Article 4(2) TEU as a Protection of the Institutional Diversity of the Member States'

the 'national identity' and constitutional structure of Member States, reflecting the EU's bicentric focus on the EU and national levels. This interpretation overlooks subnational authorities, concentrating instead on nation states. The EU seems, in conclusion, not to have fully incorporated the value of autonomy, and of local autonomy in particular: its constitutional recognition is still too broad to wholly acknowledge the decisive contribution of the local level of government and of local democracy itself to the wider EU governance. Despite that, 'local governments are routinely affected by, and affect, EU law in their roles as public service providers and conduits for political participation':[73] they are subject not only to domestic law – since they are the exclusive competence of nation states – but also indirectly to EU substantive law.[74] Local authorities are not just passive receivers of EU and national laws; they can also 'influence EU law through their norm-generating capacity'.[75] In fact, EU law often incorporates norms upon inspiration by subnational governments, in practice making these local and regional levels key players in the EU integration process alongside national and supranational levels.[76] So, the bicentric Union model turns out to be outdated given the growing role of local governments – and of cities in particular – as important public law actors beyond nation-state borders within the wider European legal space.

(2021) 27 *European Public Law* 559. De Witte advocates (also through the analysis of some case law) for a strict interpretation of the principle as a mere guarantee for the internal constitutional structure of each Member State, against a broader meaning that would open doors 'to abusive and superficial uses of identity as a justification for non-compliance with EU obligations from the side of the member States' (560). Martinico, on his side, warns in particular about the nationalist-sovereigntist interpretation of the principle by some national courts (as the Hungarian case shows) that have carried out an abusive interpretation of the principle, which has gone far beyond mere respect for the institutional autonomy outlined by the text of the Article.

[73] van Zeben (n 22) 124.

[74] Boggero, *Constitutional Principles* (n 3) 68–69.

[75] Finck, 'Fragmentation' (n 46) 1122. The example brought by the author is the *Omega* case, which established that a local authority may limit the freedom to provide services – a fundamental element of market integration – when aiming to safeguard public policy and human dignity. The author explains that Bonn banned laser games based on its own specific and localised understanding of human dignity – an interpretation not commonly held across Germany or in other EU Member States. Despite this, Bonn chose to enforce a stricter standard of protection than was required under national constitutional law. The court not only allowed this interpretation but also endorsed the idea that human dignity is a general principle of EU law. By doing so, it effectively incorporated Bonn's localised interpretation of dignity into the broader framework of EU law (see 1122–23). On this norm-generating capacity of local governments the author continues, saying that 'cities like Bonn have no formal competence to influence EU law, yet through the interactions of their own norms with those of the Union they can influence supranational law's substantive core. What is striking about Omega and the other rulings subject to analysis here is that the Court treats subnational measures in the same manner as those of the Member States. This technique allows municipal norms to have identical generative effects in EU law that Member State norms are known to have' (1123).

[76] This is the central thesis argued in Finck, 'Fragmentation' (n 46) 1119. The author claims that despite the schematic picture drawn by EU primary law which fundamentally envisages a bicentric structure, the fragmentation of subnational authorities (regional and local) does actually constitute an agent of EU integration in so far as their policies often influences and inspire higher levels of government. Subnational authorities should therefore be regarded not only as receivers but also as exporters of norms.

C. A Forgotten Meaning of Subsidiarity Grounded in Local Self-Government

Within the EU constitutional construction, the principle of subsidiarity puts at its core the relationship between public authorities and citizens not only through a vertical distribution of powers among different levels of government, but also through a horizontal sharing of competences not tied to the territorial level between public and private actors. Although the current and dominant interpretation of the principle within the EU legal order as we have explained so far (section II.A) consists in its vertical dimension, it goes unquestioned that in the original debate in the 1990s a key role was played by the current of thought of the Catholic social philosophy, with its focus on the role played by autonomous private individuals in contributing to the common good.

This book, in particular, argues that the horizontal dimension of subsidiarity, or 'horizontal subsidiarity',[77] is the forgotten meaning[78] of this principle, which empowers local self-government as the level closest to citizens and civil society. Indeed, despite the fact that there is no explicit recognition of that in the Treaties as 'the EU seems to overlook the horizontal dimension of subsidiarity operating at different scales',[79] 'this does not mean the EU law is extraneous to the implicit values of it',[80] and the EU indeed 'does not exclude this understanding, though the current institutional approach to subsidiarity still centres on the representative model, focussing on decisions made in national parliaments'.[81] The horizontal dimension of the principle used also to be the distinctive perspective of one of the greatest advocates for subsidiarity, Jacques Delors,[82] President of the European Commission in those years where the debate on subsidiarity was taking place (1985–1995). Delors' understanding of subsidiarity was based on the centrality of the autonomy of the citizen and its social components, which

[77] Arban, 'Re-Centralizing Subsidiarity' (n 49) 129; Føllesdal, 'Survey Article: Subsidiarity' (n 30) 196.

[78] This forgotten meaning of subsidiarity is clearer and stronger in Italian cities due to the constitutional introduction of horizontal subsidiarity. See Part III. See also a shorter version of this section at C Salati, 'The Forgotten Meaning of the EU Principle of Subsidiarity – Horizontal Subsidiarity in Italian Local Governments' (2023) Diversity Governance Papers.

[79] Nicolaïdis and van Zeben (n 47) 81.

[80] Giglioni, 'Subsidiary Cooperation' (n 49) 494. The author goes further by saying that 'if horizontal subsidiarity defines an innovative method of managing the general interest, where sharing and integrating responsibilities constitute a distinctive element, it is understandable how this system has significant potential to be welcome into the EU law, that has been testing new models for taking care of general interests since its coming to existence' (497). See also, F Giglioni, 'Alla Ricerca Della Sussidiarietà Orizzontale in Europa' in D Donati and A Paci (eds), *Sussidiarietà e Concorrenza* (Il Mulino 2010) 131 for the author's considerations on the implicit contribution of the principle of subsidiarity understood in its horizontal dimension to democracy in the EU.

[81] B Peters, 'Towards the Europeanization of Participation? Reflecting on the Functions and Beneficiaries of Participation in EU Environmental Law' in C Fraenkel-Haeberle et al (eds), *Citizen Participation in Multi-Level Democracies* (Brill 2015) 317.

[82] On Delors, see Giordano (n 29) 99 ff.

was actually much wider than the narrow treaty provision on that. Horizontal subsidiarity, in fact, strengthens a participatory form of democracy beyond mere representation in a governance perspective aimed at the inclusion of other actors: in a nutshell, the book argues that there may be room in the Treaties to disclose unexplored meanings from constitutional principles, and horizontal subsidiarity – in the light of its original debate in the 1990s – and there is great potential in that.

Understood in its horizontal dimension, subsidiarity essentially recalls many other classic constitutional concepts, among which are those of individuals' sovereignty, solidarity, participation. The link with individuals' sovereignty[83] invokes the concept of self-organisation of individuals whom, in the horizontal meaning of subsidiarity, are considered as proactive and free units of societal organisation able to reach certain aims without the need for any public authority intervention.[84] This is also for its part linked to the concept of solidarity: solidarity, indeed, 'operates horizontally'[85] between groups or organisational units that share a relation of proximity, and refers to a responsibility of the individual towards the community at large or, more broadly, towards 'the common good'.[86] In fact, 'there is increasing empirical evidence that solidarity is an expression of active citizenship in a grass-roots political sense',[87] constituting therefore a de facto solidarity and not only a statement of principle. New forms of solidarity can emerge across the European space and at all government levels, and horizontal subsidiarity could help these grow beyond nation states, as it aligns with participation principles, especially local participation. Subsidiarity thrives with local democracy, as 'participation is furthered in small communities, since individuals there see the impact of their actions',[88] fostering active participation ('doing') beyond just 'deciding' (chapter two).

In the light of these traces of subsidiarity in other constitutional principles, the horizontal dimension of subsidiarity offers a new perspective on local self-government, tied to the concept of polycentricity[89] and 'polycentric subsidiarity.' This theory views subsidiarity as a horizontal distribution of power and self-governance, recognising actors beyond states' and individuals' roles, while emphasising the importance of various government scales, especially at the

[83] Contra, the principle of subsidiarity is for obvious reasons seen as a threat to national sovereignty, as essentially more in line with a decentralisation rather than centralisation perspective.

[84] On horizontal subsidiarity and individuals' sovereignty as self-organisation, see Gussen (n 29) 227: 'subsidiarity is a principle that is anchored in the concept of sovereignty of the individual, where all other levels of social organisation are given a subsidiary role, taking up only those tasks and responsibilities that are beyond the capacity of the individual'.

[85] ibid 206.

[86] On solidarity as relating to the concept of common good, see M Ross, 'Transnational Solidarity: A Transformative Narrative for the EU and its Citizens?' (2020) 56 *Acta Politica* 220, 224. On the concept of 'common good' and its relationship with human dignity see Drew and Grant (n 19) 525 f.

[87] Ross (n 86) 221.

[88] Føllesdal, 'Survey Article: Subsidiarity' (n 30) 198.

[89] See further ch 4 and ch 2, section VI.

local level.[90] Self-governance,[91] a key feature of polycentric systems, links to subsidiarity in its horizontal meaning by emphasising local governments' role in supporting individual and collective action.[92] This self-governance should not be seen 'as hostile towards, or incompatible with, governmental action. In fact, public officials are considered potential allies and teachers in the process of self-governance by supporting communities to identify and solve common problems'.[93] Despite this, the Treaties omit this horizontal subsidiarity clearly backed by polycentric theory due to Member States' continued centrality and their disfavour towards horizontal distribution of power.[94] However, this meaning of subsidiarity enables public authorities to better include bottom-up inputs from non-state actors, reflecting the EU's polycentric system of governance.[95] It highlights the need to recognise a horizontal subsidiarity dimension, aligning with the EU's evolving democracy where both government and governance dimensions[96] have legitimation.[97] Polycentric theory thus supports horizontal subsidiarity over the dominant vertical view.

In the absence of any explicit recognition of this horizontal dimension of subsidiarity within the Treaties text, only two vague and implicit references could be traced: in the preamble ('Resolved to continue the process of creating an ever closer union among the peoples of Europe, in which decisions are taken as closely as possible to the citizen in accordance with the principle of subsidiarity'); and in Article 10(3) TEU ('Decisions shall be taken as openly and as closely as possible to the citizen'). Both statements, however, constitute more a declaration of intent than concrete substance. More interesting is the fact that beyond the Treaties text this forgotten meaning of subsidiarity has unconsciously and invisibly survived within the EU legal space through

[90] Nicolaïdis and van Zeben (n 47) 96.

[91] As 'the ability of individuals to be autonomous in determining the rules underlying their relations with others, rather than relying on the State and governmental authorities' (ch 2, section VI).

[92] A key reference for 'collective action' is Elinor Ostrom's work, based on Vincent Ostrom's polycentricity: E Ostrom, *Governing the Commons: The Evolution of Institutions for Collective Action* (Cambridge University Press 1990).

[93] J van Zeben, 'Polycentricity as a Theory of Governance' in J van Zeben and A Bobić (eds), *Polycentricity in the European Union* (Cambridge University Press 2019) 20.

[94] On this point, see J van Zeben and A Bobić, 'Conclusions – Pathways to Polycentricity' in J van Zeben and A Bobić (eds), *Polycentricity in the European Union* (Cambridge University Press 2019) 311 ff. Curiously, Vincent Ostrom in 1996 had already observed that 'Principles of subsidiarity need to be extended to family, neighbourhood, and community far beyond the realm of nation-states as contemplated by the Maastricht Accord' (V Ostrom, 'Faustian Bargains' (1996) 7 *Constitutional Political Economy* 303, 307).

[95] This is the central thesis argued by J van Zeben and A Bobić (eds), *Polycentricity in the European Union* (Cambridge University Press 2019).

[96] See also the concept of 'multi-centred governance' as strictly linked to horizontal subsidiarity, used for defining the many political communities that contribute to the system of governance: K Nicolaïdis, 'Conclusion: The Federal Vision Beyond the Federal State' in K Nicolaïdis and R Howse (eds), *The Federal Vision: Legitimacy and Levels of Governance in the United States and the European Union* (Oxford University Press 2001) 466 ff.

[97] See on this ch 1, section IV.

indirect means thanks to the work of other institutional actors: this is the case, for example, of the European Economic and Social Committee (EESC).[98] It goes without saying that the EESC contribution does not compensate for the lack of its clear entrenchment in EU primary law. The EESC is an advisory body of the EU representing employers' and workers' organisations and other interest groups contributing to the three aspects of economic and social conditions, participatory democracy and EU integration. Its work is worth mentioning here in relation to the concepts of 'active citizenship'[99] and 'functional subsidiarity' (also named horizontal subsidiarity).[100] With regard to active citizenship, the EESC fundamentally refers to all those units of organised civil society that contribute to their community through various forms of participatory democracy aimed at problem solving, which are able to go much beyond casting a vote every few years. Individuals' capacities are placed at the centre when talking about both active citizenship as well as subsidiarity, which is conceived by the EESC as 'the most important principle of good governance', considering it 'not merely a principle of administrative technique and distribution of powers but the expression of a certain conception of the individual, its freedom, its responsibilities and the society it lives in'.[101] In parallel to its vertical dimension (also named 'territorial subsidiarity'), subsidiarity is understood by the EESC in its horizontal (or functional) dimension for giving 'recognition to the public role of private players, for example, citizens and representative civil society organisations and to their participation in policy-shaping and decision-making processes, through their specific consultative role, as well as the autonomous legislative role of social partners in the context of European social dialogue. In fact, this concept of horizontal subsidiarity 'is already implicitly recognised by the Treaties under Articles 152, 154 and 155 of the Treaty on the Functioning of the European Union (TFEU)[102] on social dialogue and the role of social partners'.[103] The EESC's view of horizontal (functional) subsidiarity focuses mainly on private actors' input through consultations and dialogues. The broader meaning that, instead, this book refers to is that which supports individuals' self-governance and active participation. Still, the EESC deserves credit for recognising private actors' role in the general interest in a governance perspective, reflecting subsidiarity's original roots in Catholic social philosophy.

[98] See Giordano (n 29) 107, where the EESC's work on subsidiarity has been more deeply analysed.

[99] See Active citizenship. For a better European Society, 6, 2012, available at: op.europa.eu/it/publication-detail/-/publication/1822448a-1e8f-4f3b-bd06-d60eb7fc0b78.

[100] See Opinion of the Economic and Social Committee, Opinion on 'European Governance – a White Paper' (COM(2001) 428 final).

[101] ibid.

[102] These Articles refer to the role of social partners through consultations and the social dialogue.

[103] Opinion of the European Economic and Social Committee on 'Improving the functioning of the European Union building on the potential of the Lisbon Treaty' and on 'Possible evolutions and adjustments of the current institutional set-up of the European Union' (2016/C 013/27), available at: eur-lex.europa.eu/legal-content/EN/TXT/?uri=uriserv%3AOJ.C_.2016.013.01.0183.01.ENG&toc=OJ%3AC%3A2016%3A013%3AFULL.

In addition to implicit traces of the horizontal dimension of subsidiarity in the EU legal order, it is curious that some traces have also been found by scholars in some national constitutions.[104] In fact, in addition to the Italian case (see further Part III), this is the case, for example, of Poland, where traces have been found in its preamble;[105] of Spain, where traces have been found in Articles 9.2 and 23.1 of the Constitution;[106] of the Netherlands, where horizontal subsidiarity has been reported as a distinctive trait of the Dutch political culture;[107] of Switzerland, where traces were found in Article 6 of the Constitution;[108] of France, where implicit traces were noted across the French legal order.[109]

In conclusion, the horizontal meaning of subsidiarity – rooted in Catholic social philosophy emphasising individuals' free contribution to the common good – has become lost in the EU's wording. Despite its presence in 1990s debates[110] and in the constitutions of some EU Member States, the EU Treaties overlook local self-government and the horizontal dimension of subsidiarity. However, it is this forgotten horizontal subsidiarity that could strengthen local self-government, which in turn supports individuals' spontaneous initiatives by implementing horizontal subsidiarity locally. In practice, subsidiarity and local self-government mutually reinforce each other. Subsidiarity, at its core, is much more than a

[104] See further, C Salati and E Arban, 'Sussidiarietà, Pluralismo e Autonomie: Un Canale Aggiuntivo Alla Partecipazione' in C Salati and E Alber (eds), *Partecipazione e innovazioni democratiche in Italia. Una prospettiva multidisciplinare e multilivello* (forthcoming 2026).

[105] 'Hereby establish this Constitution of the Republic of Poland as the basic law for the State, based on respect for freedom and justice, cooperation between the public powers, social dialogue as well as on the principle of subsidiarity in the strengthening the powers of citizens and their communities' (English official translation of the text of the Constitution, available at: www.sejm.gov.pl/prawo/konst/angielski/kon1.htm). For an overview of the principle of subsidiarity in Poland, see E Poplawska, 'The Principle of Subsidiarity under the 1997 Constitution of Poland' [1997] *Saint Louis-Warsaw Transatlantic Law Journal* 107 (the author, in particular, laments the lack of definition of subsidiarity in the Constitution). Additionally, see also Arban, 'Re-Centralizing Subsidiarity' (n 49) 137 f (in reporting the Polish case, Arban underlines the 'elasticity of this fundamental principle of EU law' at 138).

[106] J-P López Pulido, *Perspectiva Cognitiva y Nudge Público La Actuación Conductual de Los Poderes Públicos* (Editorial Aranzadi 2023). See, for a short introduction, *Labsus*, 'Dalla Spagna Una Nuova Interpretazione Del Diritto Amministrativo' (2023) *Labsus*, available at: www.labsus.org/2023/07/dalla-spagna-una-nuova-interpretazione-del-dirittoamministrativo/?fbclid=IwAR32Gg6co c8AcfIWhSBknR8Jb9Y5tjSEUkigjIwTwASpIv16TM58TDi9rrg. Additionally, see V Aguado i Cudolà, 'Nuevas Formas de Participación Ciudadana. En Especial, La Gestión y Administración Compartida' [2023] *Anuario del Gobierno Local* 235.

[107] LFM Besselink, HSJ Albers and WT Eijsbouts, 'Subsidiarity in Non-Federal Contexts: The Netherlands and the European Union', Report Prepared for the XVI FIDE Conference in Rome (1994), available at: www.researchgate.net/profile/Lfm-Besselink/publication/238607110_Subsidiarity_in_non_federal_contexts_The_Netherlands_and_the_European_Union/links/59004cccaca2725bd71e8cff/Subsidiarity-in-non-federal-contexts-The-Netherlands-and-the-European-Union.pdf.

[108] Føllesdal, *Subsidiarity* (Cambridge University Press 2025) 14.

[109] N Perlo, 'Le Principe de Subsidiarité Horizontale: Un Renouvellement de La Relation Entre l'Administration et Les Citoyens. Étude Comparée Franco-Italienne' (2014) 66 *Revue internationale de droit comparé* 983.

[110] Not even more recent studies on the principle included any mention of its horizontal dimension, for example, see the 'Task force on subsidiarity, proportionality and doing less more efficiently', established on 14 November 2017 by European Commission President Jean-Claude Juncker.

principle of decentralisation;[111] it requires the closest government level to 'actively promote the formation of associations and provide support – whether financial or purely facilitative – in a manner consistent with the concept of subsidium'[112] to benefit individual dignity and the common good. All in all, there is no need to wait for explicit recognition of horizontal subsidiarity in the Treaties since this dimension is already implicit in the European constitutional tradition.[113] It is up to local governments to voluntarily apply it, seeing it not just as a legal principle but as a new governance culture. Thus, exploring local government autonomy is crucial. The CoE plays a key role in that, as the next section will show. In conclusion, the following table aims to illustrate how the two dimensions of subsidiarity relate to the two forms of democracy in the EU, as well as their government and governance perspectives.

Table 2 Two dimensions of subsidiarity and their potential understanding within the EU legal order (author's elaboration)

Principle of subsidiarity	
Vertical dimension	**Horizontal dimension**
Representative form of democracy	Participatory form of democracy
Government perspective	Governance perspective

III. Subsidiarity and Local Self-Government in the Council of Europe (CoE) Legal Order

When looking at the local level of government within the European legal space, the input of the CoE is much more decisive than that of the EU for its constitutional contribution towards the recognition of local authorities beyond nation-state borders. Not only with concern to the principle of participation, but also on the principle of local self-government the most important benchmark among the CoE acts is the European Charter of local self-government of 1985. While the CoE's main contribution to participation was linking it to local democracy constitutionally via the Charter, this also laid the foundation for a European constitutional

[111] Drew and Grant (n 19). The interpretation of subsidiarity as decentralisation, they argue, essentially comes from the federalism literature which provides for a government-centric interpretation of the principle 'in an apparent obsession with the geographical proximity and scale of various tiers of government', but instead fails in acknowledging the 'positive obligation' as a must 'to provide *subsidium* when lesser associations become unable to perform their function for the common good' also towards persons within associations.

[112] ibid 15.

[113] And, as we saw earlier in this section, inside other European constitutional principles like individuals' sovereignty, solidarity, participation.

local government law recognising subsidiarity and local self-government as core European principles.

Entering into force in 1988, the Charter is a source of international law which has been ratified by all 47 CoE member states, and has binding effects whether under international law alone, or through Member State incorporation of it into domestic law (through direct or indirect effect).[114] Its status is, however, disputed in each national legal order, as the common trend for national courts is 'to declare provisions as being non self-executing to shield national legal systems from radical changes'.[115] Unlike other CoE treaties like the European Convention on Human Rights and the European Social Charter – explicitly mentioned in EU law (Article 6(2) TEU and Article 151 TFEU) – the Charter is not referenced in EU Treaties nor recognised by the CJEU as general EU law principles,[116] although some have argued that 'the Charter is the only yardstick setting out the minimum common standards which could be deemed being general principles of EU law and which should as such be abided by EU bodies when passing new legislation'.[117]

The Charter contains the very first implicit recognition[118] of the principle of subsidiarity in an international treaty in Article 4(3): 'Public responsibilities shall generally be exercised, in preference, by those authorities which are closest to the citizen. Allocation of responsibility to another authority should weigh up the extent and nature of the task and requirements of efficiency and economy'. Clearly it is the vertical (and not horizontal) dimension of subsidiarity that the Charter is referring to,[119] perfectly in line with the EU follow-up contribution. However, credit is due to the Charter for recognising the role of local government in power allocation since 1985, while the EU acknowledged this only theoretically with the 2009 Lisbon Treaty.[120] Article 4(3) argues that unless a

[114] For a comprehensive understanding of the rank of the Charter under domestic law of the CoE member states, see Boggero, *Constitutional Principles* (n 3) 73–82.

[115] Boggero, *Constitutional Principles* (n 3) 74. Usual exceptions occur in Central and Eastern European countries where the Charter is considered to be directly applicable as it has the same status as international treaties on human rights: see G Boggero, 'La Carta Europea Dell'autonomia Locale Nella Giurisprudenza Degli Stati Europei' (2015) 43 (5–6) *Le Regioni* 1077. In particular, the author claims that national courts seem to be rarely conscious of being immersed in an European common legal space where local autonomies are constitutionally recognised beyond national constitutions: 'I giudici nazionali chiamati ad applicare la Carta sembrano dunque scarsamente consapevoli di essere immersi in uno spazio giuridico comune in cui il ricorso alla comparazione diventa essenziale non soltanto per una corretta interpretazione del diritto pattizio, ma anche per assicurare l'effetto protettivo più forte alle autonomie locali garantite dalla Costituzione' (1111). See additionally ch 2 (n 123).

[116] Only some opinions by the Committee of the Regions and of the Advocate General have explicitly referred to the Charter as a legally binding source for both the EU itself and the Member States: see Boggero, *Constitutional Principles* (n 3) 67 f.

[117] Boggero, *Constitutional Principles* (n 3) 71.

[118] CMG Himsworth, *The European Charter of Local Self-Government: A Treaty for Local Democracy* (Edinburgh University Press 2015) 45.

[119] As observed by K Kössler and A Kress, 'European Cities Between Self-Government and Subordination: Their Role as Policy-Takers and Policy-Makers' in E Hirsch Ballin et al (eds), *European Yearbook of Constitutional Law 2020: The City in Constitutional Law* (Springer 2020) 280.

[120] ibid.

task requires higher-level intervention for efficiency or economy (which may centralise power),[121] the most local government level should handle it, embedding subsidiarity at the subnational level.

So, while it is the EU that gave a fundamental contribution to the principle of subsidiarity – more than the CoE– it is the CoE and its Charter which that granted wider attention to be given to the principle of local self-government. Outlined in Article 3 of the Charter, the principle provides the first real reference to local authorities[122] and their 'right and ability … within the limits of the law, to regulate and manage a substantial share of public affairs under their own responsibility and in the interests of the local population' (Article 3(1) of the Charter). This 'right and ability' consists, according to the Charter, of the first aspect of the concept of local self-government that pertains to local authorities that could be explained as the political autonomy of local authorities.[123] The concept of 'self-government' matches essentially that of 'autonomy', as it can be understood from the official version of the Charter in French, which uses the term '*autonomie locale*'.[124] Through the recognition of the political autonomy of local authorities, the Charter is basically promoting a perspective of institutional pluralism[125] within the European legal space. The second aspect of local self-government is 'the democratic nature of local self-government'[126] (Article 3(2)), which refers to the right and ability exercised by local authorities formed on representative democracy schemes, making them the first elected government level. However, the Charter's reference to local authorities is ambiguous.[127] Article 13 lets each State specify which 'local or regional authorities' the Charter covers, allowing the choice to any State to clarify that 'when depositing its instrument of ratification'. Despite this vagueness, the Charter targets public authorities with a genuine local dimension and links to higher central or regional government levels.[128]

The issue that arises at this point concerns the essence of self-government (or autonomy): in fact, currently there is no consensus on how to define what is self-government, nor on how to measure that,[129] and comprehensive studies addressing the different components of local self-government within an all-encompassing framework are lacking.[130] Among them, the Local Autonomy Index)[131] identified

[121] Boggero, *Constitutional Principles* (n 3) 154 ff.

[122] It is interesting to observe the frequency of the use of some terms in the (English text of the) Charter: the term 'local authorities' occurs 36 times; 'local authority' twice; 'local government' once; 'local self-government' 15 times; 'local autonomy' 0 times.

[123] Panara and Varney (n 4) 372 look at this first aspect of local self-government with (local) political autonomy.

[124] See above (n 3).

[125] Boggero, *Constitutional Principles* (n 3) 13.

[126] Panara and Varney (n 4) 372.

[127] Boggero, *Constitutional Principles* (n 3) 87 ff.

[128] ibid 91.

[129] Kössler and Kress (n 119) 276.

[130] This is the general claim expressed in A Ladner et al (eds), *Patterns of Local Autonomy in Europe* (Palgrave Macmillan 2019) 333.

[131] ibid.

seven dimensions of local autonomy:[132] (1) legal autonomy (on whether the local level has received constitutional cover or not); (2) policy scope (concerning the number of tasks a local authority fulfils); (3) political discretion (on whether the local authority has discretion in fulfilling its tasks or not); (4) financial autonomy (on its financial resources); (5) organisational autonomy (the capacity to organise its own administration); (6) non-interference (on the relationship between the local level and upper levels of government); and (7) access (on its capacity to influence higher levels).

While benchmarks for local autonomy remain vague and the Charter lacks measurable definitions,[133] its key value lies in establishing a common European constitutional local government law constituting a 'reference framework offering normative and in particular constitutional guidance for setting up a new local government system from its very foundations at domestic level … as well as for complementing the constitutional frameworks of those legal orders in which a local government system already exists'.[134] Unlike the EU legal system, the Charter recognises local authorities as active players beyond nation states, affirming their right and ability of self-government within a shared European constitutional context. They also recognise a right to associate (Article 10) beyond national borders within international organisations.

All in all, local self-government, alongside vertical subsidiarity, is recognised and guaranteed in all EU Member States through the CoE 1985 Charter, which constitutes the foundation of a common European constitutional local government law. The CoE plays a more decisive role than the EU in local self-government, while the EU leads on subsidiarity. The Charter, on one side, grants political autonomy to local authorities via democratic election and, on the other, supports citizens' participation rights (see chapter two, section IV). In conclusion, despite a prevailing state-centric view and limited awareness of the Charter's constitutional value, the local government level in the EU already rests on the constitutional foundation provided by the combination of the CoE and EU respective legal orders.

[132] ibid 333 f. In addition to the Local Autonomy Index, two other indexes could be mentioned: M Ivanyna and A Shah, 'How Close Is Your Government to Its People? Worldwide Indicators on Localization and Decentralization' (2012) World Bank Policy Research Working Paper No 6138; and JM Sellers and A Lindström, 'Decentralization, Local Government, and the Welfare State' (2007) 20 *Governance* 609.

[133] Worth mentioning here is the recent Congress of Local and Regional authorities: *A Contemporary Commentary by the Congress on the Explanatory Report to the European Charter of Local Self-Government* (12 February 2020), available at: rm.coe.int/a-contemporary-commentary-by-the-congress-on-the-explanatory-report-to/16809cbf8c.

[134] Boggero, *Constitutional Principles* (n 3) 291.

4

From Local Governments to Cities

I. Theorising the Local Level: Federalism and Polycentricity

Understanding the growing importance of the local level of government in the EU requires moving beyond its constitutional foundations, already established in EU and Council of Europe (CoE) legal orders. Scholarship has been key in advancing this shift, particularly through two influential theories: federalism, which frames the local level as a tier of government; and polycentricity, which recognises it as a hub of governance.[1]

Generally, the literature on federalism has for a long time been blind to the local level. It is only recently that scholars have begun to question the traditional two-tier approach of considering federal systems as consisting simply of national and subnational levels.[2] Increasingly, power is shared not only between these two levels but also with the local level of government, which is consequently receiving growing attention from a constitutional and legal perspective,[3] even though local government long predates the creation of (federal) nation-states.[4] Indeed, scholars contend with three main issues when discussing the conjunction of local government and federalism.[5] The first is local government's degree of autonomy; the second is its relationship with other

[1] For the government-governance dualism, see ch 1, section IV.

[2] The terms 'level', 'tier', 'order' or 'spheres' of government could be used interchangeably: F Palermo and K Kössler, *Comparative Federalism: Constitutional Arrangements and Case Law* (Hart Publishing 2017) 9. See also, ch 1 (n 64).

[3] N Steytler (ed), *The Forum of Federations Handbook on Local Government in Federal Systems* (Palgrave Macmillan 2024); C Saunders and E Arban, 'Federalism and Local Governments' in E Arban (ed), *Cities in Federal Constitutional Theory* (Oxford University Press 2022). As a starting point, see Palermo and Kössler (n 2) 281 ff, a work which refers to the local level as a 'third order of government'. Earlier considerations of local government in the debate on federalism may be found in N Steytler, 'Comparative Conclusions' in N Steytler (ed), *Local Government and Metropolitan Regions in Federal Systems* (McGill-Queen's University Press 2009). Here, the author notes the progressive recognition of local governments: '[I]t was only after the Second World War that local government gradually received constitutional recognition, resulting from linking democracy to decentralization' (406). Steytler back then also pointed out that 'the importance of local governments as an order of government is likely to grow' (434).

[4] As already seen in ch 3, section I.

[5] Saunders and Arban (n 3).

levels of government;[6] and the third is its place in the constitutional framework. In a related vein, local-level government is believed to bring at least three main strengths to federalism.[7] The first is its contribution to the quality of democracy. This comes about thanks to the addition of a further layer of elected government – one allowing for closer contact between people and their representatives, for a more concrete possibility of influencing political outcomes, and for more opportunities for participation and inclusion. The second strength is local government's capacity to be more responsive than higher levels of government in terms of policy-making and service delivery given its better understanding of the community from which it is elected. The third strength is the capacity of the local tier of government to contribute to the dispersal of power, thus facilitating a decentralisation of authority in the face of the centralising pressures exerted by higher levels of government.

The overall input of federalism is of special importance in view of the bearing it has on the distribution of power (or 'competences', in the parlance of EU Treaties) in multi-level systems. As such, theories of federalism have contributed to the field of state theory not only from a legal (constitutional) perspective but by way of other disciplines such as political science or political philosophy.[8] Federalism, in a nutshell, and in the absence of a widely accepted definition,[9] may then be described – according to one of its most recent theorisations[10] – as a value-based concept that 'refers to maintaining the proper balance between different levels of territorial authority'.[11] Federalism, that is to say, contributes to the essential function of guaranteeing institutional pluralism,[12] and has the potential to do so within a common constitutional framework. Within the EU

[6] For a critical account of how central governments could actually support local authorities in weakening intermediate levels of government, see further, JT Dickovick, 'Municipalization as Central Government Strategy: Central-Regional–Local Politics in Peru, Brazil, and South Africa' (2009) 37 *Publius: The Journal of Federalism* 1.

[7] Saunders and Arban (n 3).

[8] For the relationship between federalism and cities from a political science perspective, see L King, 'Cities, Subsidiarity, and Federalism' in JE Fleming and JT Levy (eds), *Federalism and Subsidiarity* (New York University Press 2014), and D Weinstock, 'Cities and Federalism' in JE Fleming and JT Levy (eds), *Federalism and Subsidiarity* (New York University Press 2014).

[9] Federalism could be 'simultaneously understood as a concept, an ideal (and an ideology), a system of government and a set of institutions and instruments': Palermo and Kössler (n 2) 2. In addition, Elazar's definition – based on 'self-rule plus shared rule' – entails that 'federalism has to do with the need of people and polities to unite for common purposes yet remain separate to preserve their respective integrities' (DJ Elazar, *Exploring Federalism* (University of Alabama Press 1987) 12, 33). In federalism, 'at least two entities … [are] part of a larger union while at the same time enjoying autonomy' (Palermo and Kössler (n 2) 18).

[10] P Popelier, *Dynamic Federalism: A New Theory for Cohesion and Regional Autonomy* (Routledge 2021). Popelier draws a clear terminological distinction between federalism (considered as a value), federalist systems (political organisations), and federations (forms of state) (at 46). She advances a new theory of federalism – dynamic federalism – in which it is redefined in terms of autonomy and cohesion (instead of the traditional pairing of self-rule and shared rule) and thereby able to encompass all forms of multi-tier systems.

[11] ibid 46.

[12] On the link between federalism and pluralism, see Palermo and Kössler (n 2) 6.

legal order, however, subsidiarity[13] – rather than federalism – was the guiding principle that allowed for the recognition of multiple levels of government in addition to the national and subnational ones (the latter generally referring to the regional level). Namely, they were the supranational EU level, and the local level – where the latter could be regarded as the fourth tier of government within the EU legal order.[14]

Scholarship on federalism has the merit of having introduced a notable term into academic debate, one that relates to a specific phenomenon within the local level of government: the 'city'. Earlier usage of the concept of the city was seen among North American federal scholars,[15] who were aware of how limited the power of cities was, given that the latter were traditionally conceived of as mere 'creatures of the State'.[16] These scholars on one side observed the potential of subsidiarity in having gone further than federalism in foreseeing more city power within states' internal organisation.[17] On the other side, they also anticipated that cities would grow in importance to become independent international actors beyond nation states within a framework of 'international local government law'.[18] Notably, for example, it was proposed that, in order to recognise and increase city power in the American system of government, the traditional federal emphasis on the vertical allocation of powers should shift to a focus on horizontal inter-city relationships,[19] so that cities could build more participatory forms of societal organisation (both internally and externally with other cities) and hence be better able to resist centralised control.[20] However, it was only much more recently that the term 'city', as used in contradistinction to other local government entities, acquired a more specific meaning and value.[21] This was in no small part due to a ground-breaking awakening within constitutional law scholarship that shed light on the city as an autonomous legal entity.[22] Even so, these developments have antecedents in the distant past. It was originally in the work of Althusius, the

[13] Y Blank, 'Federalism, Subsidiarity, and the Role of Local Governments in an Age of Global Multilevel Governance' (2010) 37 *Fordham Urban Law Journal* 509, 545.

[14] C Panara and M Varney, *Local Government in Europe: The 'Fourth Level' in the EU Multilayered System of Governance* (Routledge 2013) (see also ch 1, section II). As previously seen, however, this recognition has arguably occurred only on paper (as claimed by M Finck, 'Challenging the Subnational Dimension of Subsidiarity in EU Law' (2015) 8 *European Journal of Legal Studies* 5).

[15] See, inter alia, Blank (n 13); GE Frug, 'Empowering Cities in a Federal System' (1987) 19 *The Urban Lawyer* 553.

[16] GE Frug, 'The City as a Legal Concept' (1980) 93 *Harvard Law Review* 1057, 1063.

[17] Blank (n 13).

[18] GE Frug and DJ Barron, 'International Local Government Law' (2006) 38 *The Urban Lawyer* 1, 11 argue that 'there is a role for the international local government law in shaping the future of urban life' (62).

[19] Frug, 'Empowering Cities' (n 15) 565.

[20] Frug argues that city powerlessness also prevents the realisation of 'public freedom', which is conceived as 'the ability to participate actively in the basic societal decisions that affect one's life': Frug, 'The City as a Legal Concept' (n 16) 1068. It should be noted, however, that Frug uses the term 'city' interchangeably with 'town', 'neighbourhood', and 'regional government' (1061).

[21] E Arban, *Cities in Federal Constitutional Theory* (Oxford University Press 2022).

[22] R Hirschl, *City, State: Constitutionalism and the Megacity* (Oxford University Press 2020).

forerunner of subsidiarity and federalism in the European space, that fundamental importance was given to the city as one of the multiple layers of society, alongside the family (conceived as the primordial form of association among individuals), the collegium, the province, and the commonwealth.[23] Althusius described the city as a *civitas* 'in the broadest sense, [as] a body of many and diverse associations', a community conceived of as 'an association formed by fixed laws and composed of many families and collegia living in the same place'. He defined the city itself as 'a community of citizens dwelling in the same urban area (*urbs*), and content with the same communication and government (*jus imperii*)'.[24] The urban community settled in the city is distinguished by Althusius from the rural community (usually a hamlet, village or town), and accordingly is meant to have its autonomous powers and governing bodies. The political and economic relevance of the city as such was therefore recognised in an overall vision of cities as autonomous subjects within a multilayered society.[25]

Althusius is thus acknowledged as a pioneer in federal scholarship on the status of cities. In turn, contemporary federal constitutional theory is increasingly cognisant of the importance of cities (and their networks) within the context of rising urbanisation.[26] Against this backdrop, a much-debated and as yet unresolved overarching question is whether or not the city should be constitutionalised as an autonomous level of government,[27] and if so, whether it is about time that federalism went beyond its usual dual structure to accommodate a three-tiered system.[28] At the same time, federal scholarship is also engaged with the challenge of defining the city – a crucial issue in constitutional and public legal thought. The city could be understood in multiple ways: among other things: (a) as a short-hand term for urbanisation, in relation to the concentration of people and economic

[23] Identified by Althusius in his work *Politica*: see FC Carney (trans), *The Politics of Johannes Althusius* (Beacon Press 1964).

[24] ibid 34 ff.

[25] For an overview of Althusius's understanding of the city, see E Arban, 'An Intellectual History of Federalism: The City and the "Unit" Question' in E Arban (ed), *Cities in Federal Constitutional Theory* (Oxford University Press 2022).

[26] B Petkova, 'Federalism in 2030' (2022) Graz Law Working Paper Series No 1. She describes 'horizontal federalism' as an emergent trend in city networks and traditional vertical (or top-down) federalism as on the decline. Her view is thus that the future of federalism involves a shift to horizontal forms of federal cooperation.

[27] Hirschl strongly supports constitutional entrenchment of cities, arguing in Hirschl, *City, State* (n 22) that it would empower cities with meaningful regulatory autonomy. Arban echoes this view, asserting that this would facilitate experimentation in 'new modes of governance for the urban area in constitutional law as opposed to local governments' (E Arban, 'Constitutional Law, Federalism and the City as a Unique Socio-Economic and Political Space' in E Hirsch Ballin et al (eds), *European Yearbook of Constitutional Law 2020: The City in Constitutional Law* (Springer 2020) 323). A more sceptical position is taken by Saunders and Arban (n 3) where they observe that 'constitutionalization is not necessarily a panacea. On the contrary, whether constitutionalized or not, local government is often treated as something of a poor cousin in federations across the world'.

[28] As emerges from the edited volume, Arban, *Cities in Federal Constitutional Theory* (n 21), as well as more clearly, in R Schragger, 'Conclusion: The City in the Future of Federalism' in E Arban (ed), *Cities in Federal Constitutional Theory* (Oxford University Press 2022). The author claims that cities are disadvantaged by state-based federalism but represent the future of federalism.

activities; (b) as a jurisdiction, referring to a precise level of government; (c) as a proprietary or regulatory entity; and (d) as a polity, referring to a democratic political community.[29] A broad definition of the city sees it as a unique socio-economic and political space that deserves its powers and autonomy, a space which 'is strategic for building new modes of governance and reconcil[ing] diversity and social cohesion'.[30] That said, efforts among the academic community to reach a shared definition of the city within federal theory are still ongoing. Yet even so, and notwithstanding the lack of such a definition, federal scholarship has made crucial contributions to the advancement of local-level government through its work focused on the development of 'city' as a legal category.

In this theorisation of the local level the concept of polycentricity[31] comes second. Whereas the predominant conceptualisation of federalism looks at the local level from a government (or institutional) perspective, polycentricity involves looking at the local level from a governance (or societal) perspective. In keeping with our understanding of democracy as a system of both government and governance,[32] these two perspectives are complementary, and in what follows, we present a general overview of this theory in so far as it could contribute to a wider recognition of the local level of government. The link between federalism as a theory of government and polycentricity as a theory of governance was originally made decades ago in American political science scholarship.[33] The scholars in question regarded (American) federalism not from the perspective of administrative decentralisation, but rather from that of polycentric governance. This is a perspective in which the idea of the active participation of individuals in a variety of associations led to a conception of federalism as 'a principle of association'.[34] Introduced in 1961[35] in relation to the debate on the problem of government in metropolitan areas,[36] the concept

[29] Categories elaborated upon in Schragger (n 28).

[30] Arban, 'Constitutional Law, Federalism and the City' (n 27).

[31] The debate on polycentricity is broad and interdisciplinary. Here, it is examined in relation to local government and is understood as 'a descriptive theory of governance' in accordance with J van Zeben and A Bobić (eds), *Polycentricity in the European Union* (Cambridge University Press 2019) 2.

[32] See ch 1, section IV.

[33] It was Vincent Ostrom who drew a connection between these two theories in order to explore their contribution to local democracy. He first engaged with the concept of polycentricity in V Ostrom et al, 'The Organization of Government in Metropolitan Areas: A Theoretical Inquiry' (1961) 55 *American Political Science Review* 831. An even earlier mention of the term is found in M Polanyi, *The Logic of Liberty* (University of Chicago Press 1951). However, although these two works are often discussed together, they have somewhat different understandings of polycentricity. For Ostrom et al, it refers to 'the adoption of a society-wide, systematic approach, focusing on the provision of public goods within communities'; for Polanyi, it refers to 'a professional organization within which people are motivated by professional duties, not membership of a broader society or community' (see further, J van Zeben, 'Polycentricity as a Theory of Governance' in J van Zeben and A Bobić (eds), *Polycentricity in the European Union* (Cambridge University Press 2019) 12 ff).

[34] RE Wagner, 'Self-Governance, Polycentrism, and Federalism: Recurring Themes in Vincent Ostrom's Scholarly Oeuvre' (2005) 57 *Journal of Economic Behaviour & Organization* 173, 184.

[35] Ostrom et al (n 33).

[36] Indeed, under the US federal system, metropolitan areas do not constitute a legal entity.

of polycentricity (also referred to as 'polycentric governance') refers to the existence of 'many centres of decision-making which are formally independent of each other',[37] a situation in which there is 'a complex combination of multiple levels and diverse types of organizations drawn from the public, private, and voluntary sectors that have overlapping realms of responsibility and functional capacities'.[38] Accordingly, American metropolitan areas were defined as 'polycentric political systems' (where 'political' stands for 'government')[39] with widely distributed decision-making powers that actively foster citizen participation, self-governance and local democracy. In addition, polycentricity was perceived as capable of facilitating co-production[40] of public services by governmental authorities and citizens, with citizens seen as active contributors to democracy acting within their communities according to the principle of self-responsibility.[41] Individual capacity for self-governance in polycentric systems also provided the basis on which the fundamental theory relating to the governance of the commons was elaborated.[42] This claimed that natural resource systems can be governed by communities of individuals in ways that safeguard these resources and prevent their degradation more effectively than a central governmental authority or a market actor would.[43] In polycentric systems, every centre of decision-making enjoys some degree of autonomy, but no one has ultimate authority for making all collective decisions. This notion suggests that strengthening individuals' capacity for self-governance is the only way, according to polycentric theory,[44] to counteract the autocratic directions in which democracies are in danger of heading. The idea of self-governing democracy thus attaches central priority to the need to have responsible citizens capable of carrying out self-organised collective action for resolving community problems.

[37] Ostrom et al (n 33) 831.

[38] MD McGinnis and E Ostrom, 'Reflections on Vincent Ostrom, Public Administration, and Polycentricity' (2012) 72 *Public Administration Review* 15. According to them, polycentricity, as conceived of by Ostrom, is 'a natural outgrowth of the intrinsic human capacity to work with others' (23).

[39] V Ostrom, 'Polycentricity' in MD McGinnis (ed), *Polycentricity and Local Public Economies: Readings from the Workshop in Political Theory and Policy Analysis* (University of Michigan Press 1999).

[40] 'Co-production implies that citizens can play an active role in producing public goods and services of consequence to them' (E Ostrom, 'Crossing the Great Divide: Coproduction, Synergy, and Development' (1996) 24 *World Development* 1073).

[41] 'I have come to the conclusion, however, that democratic societies are necessarily placed at risk when people conceive of their relationships as being grounded on principles of command and control rather than on principles of self-responsibility in self-governing communities of relationships': V Ostrom, *The Meaning of Democracy and the Vulnerability of Democracies: A Response to Tocqueville's Challenge* (University of Michigan Press 1997) 4.

[42] E Ostrom, *Governing the Commons: The Evolution of Institutions for Collective Actions* (Cambridge University Press 1990).

[43] On the commons, see further Parts III and IV.

[44] The thesis advanced by V Ostrom, *The Meaning of American Federalism: Constituting a Self-Governing Society* (Institute for Contemporary Studies 1991).

This is where the importance of the local level comes into play. While federalism is traditionally more concerned with vertical rather than horizontal relationships (that is, with relations between the national and subnational levels),[45] polycentricity puts horizontal relationships among diverse actors at its core. As a result, the local level represents an additional fundamental level of government that must find a place on a par with the national and subnational levels.[46] Furthermore, the local level is best positioned to enable citizen participation – both by fostering awareness of collective challenges and by empowering communities to take direct action, rather than deferring responsibility to higher levels of government. In democratic societies, indeed, 'governments only exercise a complement of authority that is necessary for taking collective decisions pertaining collective goods',[47] while primary responsibility for governing is spontaneously assumed by individuals who, in their effort of self-governance, need to be supported by public authorities[48] and, above all, by the local level of government. The capacity of polycentric systems to support individuals' self-governance also leads to higher levels of individual liberty, through recognition and support.

This governmental support of individuals goes back to what we called the 'forgotten meaning of subsidiarity'[49] in the EU, a meaning which relates to the horizontal dimension of subsidiarity not towards public actors but societal ones. Given how closely it is to the concept of polycentricity, this horizontal dimension has also been referred to as 'polycentric subsidiarity'.[50] This refers to an interpretation of the subsidiarity principle which, in contrast to the focus on its vertical dimension, emphasises the relationship between self-governance and the horizontal distribution of power;[51] as such, the concept provides a lens through which one can look at individuals, intermediary bodies, and states at all their levels with

[45] Ostrom argues that American federalism has long misinterpreted its founding documents by focusing solely on the vertical delegation of power to state and federal governments. He contends that the 1787 Constitutional Convention of Philadelphia also aimed to embed a direct role for individuals within the federal design. See further, K Nicolaïdis and J van Zeben, 'Polycentric Subsidiarity' in J van Zeben and A Bobić (eds), *Polycentricity in the European Union* (Cambridge University Press 2019) 92. For a recent reflection to explore federalism beyond institutional frameworks, with greater attention to its societal dimensions, see NP Alessi and C Salati, 'Federalism beyond Government: Thinking Outside the (Institutional) Box through the Commons' (forthcoming 2026).

[46] eg, F Cheneval, '*Demoicratic* Self-Government in the European Union's Polycentric System: Theoretical Remarks' in J van Zeben and A Bobić (eds), *Polycentricity in the European Union* (Cambridge University Press 2019) 70, reports that studies have successfully tested polycentric theory with regard to local government and the provision of public goods. See also M McGinnis (ed), *Polycentricity and Local Public Economies: Readings from the Workshop in Political Theory and Policy Analysis* (University of Michigan Press 1999).

[47] V Ostrom, *The Meaning of Democracy* (n 41) 48.

[48] 'Public officials are potential allies and teachers in the process of self-governance by supporting communities to identify and solve common problems' (J van Zeben, 'Policentricity' in B Hudson et al (eds), *Routledge Handbook of the Study of the Commons* (Routledge 2019).

[49] See ch 3, section II.C.

[50] Nicolaïdis and van Zeben, 'Polycentric Subsidiarity' (n 45).

[51] ibid 81. In arguing for the need to redefine the principle of subsidiarity in the EU, the authors contend that 'horizontality in our normative debates around levels of governance … is undertheorized' (81).

the aim to 'facilitate the organic development of self-governing collective[s] and individuals'.[52]

In the light of these various theoretical and doctrinal considerations, it emerges that, from both a government and governance perspective within state theory, federalism and polycentric theory are key to our understanding of the local level of government as an increasingly important player. From a government perspective, the debate on federalism has the merit of recognising the local level – and in particular cities – as the third level of government; from a governance perspective, polycentricity has the merit of recognising the local level of government for its potential to better support and facilitate the self-governance of individuals and communities under an overarching system of shared rules. If we apply all of this to the EU context, it is possible to recognise the potential that these two theoretical perspectives hold for shedding new light on the role of the local level of government in regard to, on the one hand, higher levels of government and, on the other, associated or individual persons. The combined contribution of federalism and polycentricity stands to go beyond even the well-known EU conceptual category of multi-level governance (MLG) – an idea which has been used to explain EU institutional development, but which so far has not proven relevant in galvanising recognition of the local level.[53]

II. The EU Institutional Contribution: From Local to Urban

In looking at the local level of democracy within the European legal space, the main terms used so far are 'local governments' and 'local authorities'. However, as is evident in recent literature on federalism, there is mounting interest both among scholars and institutions not only in the local level of government per se beyond the wider subnational (regional) level, but also in the city as a particular

[52] ibid 106.

[53] On MLG, see ch 1, section IV. According to McGinnis and Ostrom (n 38) 18, the EU concept of MLG closely resembles the American concept of polycentricity, but at the same time the two differ from each other in several respects. Among other things, polycentricity encompasses all arenas of society rather than only the political. See M Stephan et al, 'An Introduction to Polycentricity and Governance' in A Thiel et al (eds), *Governing Complexity: Analyzing and Applying Polycentricity* (Cambridge University Press 2019); J van Zeben, 'Polycentric Features of the European Union' in J van Zeben and A Bobić (eds), *Polycentricity in the European Union* (Cambridge University Press 2019) 38. With regard to the potentially fundamental contribution that polycentricity could make to the EU, see van Zeben, 'Polycentric Features of the European Union', ibid, 32: 'As compared to federalism, polycentricity allows for an additional dimension of crosscutting, overlapping "issue-specific" jurisdictions and envisages an explicit role for non-governmental bodies, such as private and community-based organisations. This role is particularly important in the light of the EU's sui generis approach to governance and government, which allows for private actors to shape and enforce rules and incorporate new forms of governance.' As seen in ch 1, section IV, the EU is indeed a unique system of both government and governance.

unit separate from other local governments. This is so despite the lack of a shared definition within the EU of what a city is from a legal perspective. In addition, the category of 'local government' itself is heterogeneous, as the meaning assigned to it depends on each EU Member State's internal constitutional framework.[54] The concept of 'local government' serves as a mere collective noun invoking a broad variety of entities that differ in size, shape and function (it may well then be more appropriate to use the plural common noun, 'local governments').[55] Indeed, if one tries to specify what exists exactly at the local level in the EU, what stands out is that a wide variety of forms of local government, each with different historical paths, qualify as the 'local level' of democracy, ranging from 'municipalities' to 'provinces', 'metropolitan cities', 'towns', 'communities', 'counties': these are but a few of the terms used for public entities that are considered as belonging to the local level of government.[56] 'Municipality' is perhaps the term that recurs most frequently in all the Member States' legal orders,[57] as it refers to a basic administrative unit that 'may coincide with a town, a city, or even a village'.[58] The de facto situation in the EU, however, reveals a disconnect between law and policies when it comes to the local level. While European constitutional contributions mainly use the term 'local' (in regard to governments or authorities) without providing a legal definition of it (or, for that matter, of the term 'municipality', which belongs to the legal traditions of nation states), on the part of EU institutions there is a growing tendency to use the terms 'urban' and 'city' in defining policy goals to be achieved within a governance perspective. It is precisely this development in terminology which is explored below. The EU has long led the way in urban policy efforts, even though the EU Treaties do not grant it explicit legal competence in this area. In as early as 1997, the EU Commission paved the way for an EU Urban Agenda[59] with a view to forging a common framework for addressing urban issues affecting EU cities. The Commission understood the importance of creating a common vision

[54] Ch 3, section I.

[55] N Steytler, *Local Government and Metropolitan Regions in Federal Systems* (McGill-Queen's University Press 2009), writes that the 'local government' 'is merely a collective noun for a wide variety of governance institutions that come in all shapes and sizes and that perform widely divergent functions. They range from mammoth metropolitan municipalities of mega-cities to small rural entities … It would, therefore, be more appropriate to refer to local governments, in the plural. What they do have in common is that there is no order of government between them and the communities they serve. This is also their strength and democratic claim; they are the government closest to the people' (4).

[56] For a comparative overview of which public entities qualify as local governments across EU Member States, see B Brezovnik et al (eds), *Local Self-Government in Europe* (Lex Localis 2021). See also the declarations attached to the instruments of ratification under Article 13 of the CoE European Charter of Local Self-Government, where each State designates its recognised categories of 'local authorities' (full list available at: www.coe.int/en/web/conventions/full-list?module=declarations-by-treaty&numSte=122&codeNature=0).

[57] See A Ladner, N Keuffer and A Bastianen, *Local Autonomy Index in the EU, Council of Europe and OECD countries (1990–2020), Release 2.0* (European Commission 2021). In particular, see the table at pp 10–12 for a comparison of EU Member States' most important elements of local government.

[58] Panara and Varney (n 14) 371.

[59] European Commission, 'Communication Towards an Urban Agenda in the European Union' COM(1997) 197 final.

for placing focus on towns and cities as self-standing entities beyond the three other levels of government (supranational, national, regional). This was in keeping with developments at the international level relating to urban issues, among them the strong attention which the United Nations (UN) began to give to the worldwide phenomenon of rapid urbanisation through the UN-Habitat Conferences (Habitat I, Vancouver 1976; Habitat II, Istanbul 1996; Habitat III, Quito 2016) and the creation in 1977 of a programme on human settlements and sustainable urban development (the United Nations Human Settlements Programme – UN-Habitat). Also thanks to such initiatives at the international level, the EU Commission acknowledged the progressive urbanisation of European society and the need to play a complementary role with nation states in addressing urban issues, given that its policies indirectly affect cities and towns. This was to be achieved not through the request for additional supranational power but within a governance perspective, that is, by promoting policy coordination and taking advantage of opportunities at the European level for espousing and facilitating potential solutions.[60]

The increasing importance attached internationally to cities is also reflected in the usage of the terms 'urban', 'city' and 'cities', which have often prevailed over 'local governments' or 'local authorities'.[61] In this regard, the Urban Agenda promoted by the EU Commission in 1997[62] was the first initiative aimed at creating a common vision on urban matters for the EU. It has not been the only one, though: since then, this vision has come to be shared by other actors in EU institutions (inter alia, the Council, European Parliament, European Economic and Social Committee, and European Committee of the Regions),[63] as well as by national representatives (at informal meetings of ministers responsible for territorial cohesion and/or urban development).[64]

[60] ibid 3.

[61] See, eg, 'Cities and urban development' among the topics of the EU Commission (ec.europa.eu/info/eu-regional-and-urban-development/topics/cities-and-urban-development_en).

[62] European Commission, 'Communication Towards an Urban Agenda in the European Union' COM(1997) 197 final. Other important documents of the Commission are: European Commission, 'Communication from the Commission on the Urban Dimension of EU Policies – Key Features of an EU Urban Agenda' COM(2014) 490 (18 July 2014); European Commission Joint Research Centre, *The Future of Cities Report* (2019).

[63] Among the other acts, see, for example, the Council of the European Union, *Council Conclusions on the Urban Agenda for the EU* (adopted 24 June 2016); European Parliament, 'Resolution of 3 July 2018 on the Role of Cities in the Institutional Framework of the Union' (2017/2037(INI)); European Committee of the Regions, 'Opinion – Implementation Assessment of the Urban Agenda for the EU' (adopted 5 July 2018); European Economic and Social Committee, 'Opinion on the Renewed Territorial Agenda of the EU; Leipzig Charter and the Urban Agenda for the EU' (18 September 2020).

[64] See, eg, the *European Spatial Development Perspective – Towards Balanced and Sustainable Development of the Territory of the European Union*, adopted at the Informal Council of Ministers responsible for Territorial Cohesion, Potsdam, May 1999 (as the first declaration calling for an EU urban policy); the *Lille Action Programme*, adopted at the Informal Council of Ministers responsible for Urban Development (Lille, 3 November 2000) (and introducing the urban issue in the *acquis communautaire*); the '*Urban Acquis*' adopted at the Informal Council of Ministers responsible for urban development held in Rotterdam on 29 November 2004; the Bristol Accord adopted at the Informal Council of Ministers responsible for urban development held in Bristol on 6–7 December 2005 (which introduced the term 'sustainable communities'); the Leipzig Charter on Sustainable European Cities,

Of the initiatives undertaken at the EU level, perhaps the most important is the 2016 Urban Agenda for the EU, which was launched as part of the Pact of Amsterdam agreed upon at an informal meeting of ministers on urban matters.[65] To this day, it is still the reference point for EU urban policy, with its achievement made possible thanks to the common commitment of diverse actors at the EU level. The Pact was also preceded by a large number of other declarations and related documents.[66] Among these, the 2007 Leipzig Charter on Sustainable European Cities merits special mention as a milestone on the EU urban development path, with its aim being to promote integrated, sustainable urban development and thereby improve living conditions in deprived neighbourhoods in European cities.[67] The 2016 Urban Agenda for the EU is regarded as an innovative framework for all urban policies (serving as an umbrella framework for all these initiatives), one which was able to apply the principle of multi-level governance to cities.[68] Its aspiration was to increase urban authorities' involvement in the European decision-making process. This was later reinforced by the New Leipzig Charter, adopted in 2020 by the informal meeting of ministers on urban matters, which provided for a renewed overarching framework on urban policies post-2020. The latter is premised on five key 'good urban governance' principles: (1) an urban policy for the common good; (2) an integrated approach; (3) participation and

adopted at the Informal Council of Ministers responsible for urban development and territorial cohesion held in Leipzig on 24–25 May 2007 (which was a milestone towards the 2016 Urban Agenda); the 'Declaration of Ministers towards the EU Urban Agenda' (the Riga Declaration), adopted at the Informal Council of Ministers responsible for territorial cohesion and urban development held in Riga on 10 June 2015 (which links the Urban Agenda with 'better regulation'); the 'Urban Agenda for the EU – Pact of Amsterdam', adopted at the Informal Council of Ministers responsible for urban development held in Amsterdam, 30 May 2016; the Bucharest Declaration ('Towards a Common Framework for Urban Development in the European Union') adopted at the Informal Council of Ministers responsible for urban development held in Bucharest on 14 June 2019; and the 'New Leipzig Charter: The Transformative Power of Cities for the Common Good' adopted by the EU Ministers responsible for urban matters on 30 November 2020 in Leipzig; the Ljubljana Agreement and its Multiannual Working Programme adopted by EU Ministers responsible for Urban Matters on 26 November 2021.

[65] For an overall analysis of the 2016 Urban Agenda, see S Pazos-Vidal, *Subsidiarity and EU Multilevel Governance: Actors, Networks and Agendas* (Routledge 2019) 168 ff.

[66] See above (nn 64 and 65).

[67] The 2007 Leipzig Charter states: 'We increasingly need holistic strategies and coordinated action by all persons and institutions involved in the urban development process which reach beyond the boundaries of individual cities. Every level of government – local, regional, national and European – has a responsibility for the future of our cities. To make this multi-level government really effective, we must improve the coordination of the sectoral policy areas and develop a new sense of responsibility for integrated urban development policy' (2), available at: territorialagenda.eu/wp-content/uploads/leipzig_charter_2007.pdf.

[68] 'The Urban Agenda for the EU … has enabled cities, Member States, the European Commission and other key stakeholders to come together to jointly tackle pressing urban matters and deliver concrete outputs for the benefit of EU citizens': European Commission, 'Urban Agenda for the EU (UAEU): Multi-Level Governance in Action 2021 Update' (November 2021). The three overarching objectives of the 2016 Pact of Amsterdam are 'better regulation' (aimed at making European legislation more city-friendly in design); 'better funding' (concerning funding opportunities); and 'better knowledge' (aimed at encouraging knowledge-sharing). To this end, 14 thematic partnerships on topics related to urban issues were established – see further the Urban Agenda at: futurium.ec.europa.eu/en/urban-agenda/library/pact-amsterdam.

co-creation by citizens to strengthen local democracy; (4) multi-level governance (involving, inter alia, civil society and the private sector, alongside the local level and upper levels); and (5) a place-based approach.

Alongside the Urban Agenda and related policies,[69] the EU Commission, which is playing a leading role among European actors, has undertaken many other initiatives[70] and funding decisions focusing on cities.[71] However, acknowledging that 'there is an increasing mismatch between cities as administrative entities and the reality of modern urban life',[72] and that, like capitals and bigger cities, small and medium-sized cities[73] should also be given recognition, the Commission recently made a commitment to develop a global, people-based definition of 'cities' within its leadership of other international organisations.[74] It is indeed well known that to date there is a lack of a common EU (or European) definition of what a 'city' is, let alone a global definition of it. Definitions vary from country to country depending on the criteria that are considered pertinent (for example, administrative boundaries, population size, density, history, competencies, and rights) and on the methodologies employed to measure compliance with these criteria. Nonetheless, within the context of the EU, two key institutions – the Commission and the European Parliament – took decisive steps to address this gap. The Commission, in partnership with the Organisation for Economic Co-operation and Development (OECD), produced two landmark reports in 2012 and 2020,[75] introducing a common definition of 'city' based on grid cells as used for statistical purposes.[76]

The most recent definition – the one articulated in the 2020 report – is people-based and founded purely on density and total population: it uses so-called 'population grid cells'[77] as a form of measurement for ensuring that settlements

[69] While the Urban Agenda provides the main framework for EU urban policy, other Commission policies also address urban challenges. Notably, the Cohesion Policy – rooted in Article 174 TFEU – is managed by the Directorate-General for Regional and Urban Policy (DG-REGIO: ec.europa.eu/regional_policy/home_en).

[70] eg, initiatives relating to the European capital of culture, the European capital of innovation, and the European green capital; the Community of Practice on Cities; the Covenant of Mayors for Climate and Energy. For a full list, see: ec.europa.eu/info/eu-regional-and-urban-development/topics/cities-and-urban-development/city-initiatives_en.

[71] eg, Urban Innovative Actions (UIA), URBACT, and Horizon 2020.

[72] European Commission, 'Urban Agenda for the EU (UAEU): Multi-Level Governance in Action 2021 Update (November 2021) 22.

[73] ibid 23.

[74] The OECD, World Bank, Food and Agriculture Organization (FAO); International Labour Organization (ILO); and UN-HABITAT. The commitment was formally undertaken at the Habitat III Conference in 2016.

[75] European Commission and OECD, *Cities in Europe: The New OECD-EC Definition* (2012); and OECD and European Commission, *Cities in the World: A New Perspective on Urbanisation* (2020): www.oecd.org/publications/cities-in-the-world-d0efcbda-en.htm.

[76] Data collection for city statistics in the EU is undertaken jointly by the National Statistical Institutes, the Directorate-General for Regional and Urban Policy (DG-REGIO), and Eurostat. See: ec.europa.eu/eurostat/web/cities/background.

[77] Population grid cells are a means used to describe the spatial distribution of the population for statistical purposes.

of the same size are classified in the same way. In this regard, 'cities consist of contiguous grid cells that have a density of at least 1500 inhabitants per km^2 or are at least 50% built up. They must have a population of at least 50.000'. The tripartite classification of settlements – into cities, towns and semi-dense areas,[78] and rural areas[79] – was based on the 'degree of urbanisation' method (approved by the UN Statistical Commission in March 2020); this method is designed to reflect the urban–rural continuum so as to overcome the problem posed by dividing the territory into only two parts, namely city or rural areas. In addition, the same report makes a further distinction, that between a 'city' and its 'functional urban area', which is also termed as 'metropolitan area'. A 'functional urban area' consists of the city and its 'commuting zones' (the city's surrounding zones), and as such captures the full economic functioning of a city by reflecting its level of travel-to-work flow.[80] The Commission has thus made commendable progress in developing a shared, concrete definition within the EU (but also beyond it) of what a 'city' is.[81] Although the EU COM-OECD definition takes a statistical approach to defining the city, this may well be relevant to a legal approach to the same issue.

A different path is the one taken by the European Parliament, whose contribution to defining a city can be traced to a 2018 resolution on the 'role of cities in the institutional framework of the Union'.[82] It duly recognises that 'there is no single definition of what constitutes the city in terms of population, area, function or level of autonomy' and that 'each Member State, therefore, may and will have a different approach to the term'; at the same time, it proposes a general definition of cities in which they are 'understood as towns, cities and urban and metropolitan areas, as well as small and medium-sized cities'.[83] This means in effect that all forms of settlement which are not rural are considered as cities. The Parliament showed awareness of the fact that, since more than 70 per cent of the European population lives in urban areas, most EU policies and legislation are implemented primarily at the local level, even though the EU has no competence in that regard.

[78] Towns and semi-dense areas were also split into three categories: dense towns; semi-dense towns; and suburban or peri-urban areas. See further OECD and European Commission, *Cities in the World: A New Perspective on Urbanisation* (2020) 32. For a critical perspective on the issue of defining what a 'town' is and on how small and medium-sized towns (SMSTs) have been neglected by urban research even though about 27 per cent of the EU population live in SMSTs, see L Servillo et al, 'Small and Medium-Sized Towns in Europe: Conceptual, Methodological and Policy Issues' (2017) 108 *Tijdschrift Voor Economische En Sociale Geografie* 365 (366 for the percentage reported).

[79] Rural areas were split into three categories: villages; dispersed rural areas; and mostly uninhabited areas. See further, OECD and European Commission, *Cities in the World: A New Perspective on Urbanisation* (2020) 32.

[80] ibid 10. The latter finds that 'local units in the commuting zones in OECD-EC's sphere of work have at least 15% of their working population commuting to the city for work' (23).

[81] See also European Commission, *The Future of Government 2030+* (2019); Eurostat, *Applying the Degree of Urbanisation: A Methodological Manual to Define Cities, Towns and Rural Areas for International Comparisons* (2021); Eurostat, *Urban Europe: Statistics on Cities, Towns and Suburbs* (2016).

[82] European Parliament, 'Resolution of 3 July 2018 on the Role of Cities in the Institutional Framework of the Union' (2017/2037(INI)) [2020] OJ C 118, 2 ff.

[83] ibid 5.

In addition, it recognised that cities are the level of politics best understood by the public and hold strong potential as spaces for the exercise of active citizenship. Consequently, cities, understood in a broad sense, should be better involved in EU decision-making, particularly in respect of legislation that affects them directly. It should be noted that, like the Commission's acts, this parliamentary resolution is a non-binding soft law[84] instrument which therefore is used only 'to seek commitments from the other EU institutions'.

In addition to the EU Commission and Parliament, a variety of organisations and networks have begun to act as advocates for the interests of European cities.[85] Among them is the CoE, which has long been involved in the development of a shared understanding of the urban space and the city itself as an autonomous subject functioning in tandem with other local authorities.[86] In the first place, EU cities – in their capacity as local authorities – receive constitutional coverage in the European Charter of Local Self-Government. In addition, the CoE developed a specific 'European Urban Charter' in 1992,[87] which evolved into the 'Manifesto for a New Urbanity. European Urban Charter II' in 2008[88] and, eventually, the 'European Urban Charter III: Urban living in the era of transformations', adopted by the Congress of Local and Regional authorities at its October 2023 plenary session.[89] While the 1992 Charter represents a milestone in Europe for its recognition of the urban phenomenon and its inclusion of a 'European Declaration of Urban rights', its content was revised in the 2008 Manifesto to establish a set of common principles and priorities enabling 'towns and cities' to meet the current challenges of urban societies and to rely on a common European urban blueprint based on 'humanist values, individual freedom, economic prosperity, social solidarity, care for the planet and living culture'.[90] As for the Urban Charter III,

[84] See ch 1, section IV.

[85] Some examples are Eurocities; United Cities and Local Governments (UCLG); the Council of European Municipalities and Regions (CEMR); Intercultural Cities; Energy Cities; Local Governments for Sustainability (ICLEI); and Human Rights Cities. City networks, however, extend far beyond European cities and are a growing phenomenon worldwide. See, for example, the C40 network on the climate crisis and the Sharing Cities Action on the platform economy.

[86] For a critical perspective on the (over)emphasis on the 'urban' (as compared to the 'rural'), see Council of Europe Congress of Local and Regional Authorities, *Developing Urban-Rural Interplay* (2020): rm.coe.int/developing-urban-rural-interplay-governance-committee-co-rapporteurs-w/1680a0628b. The report highlights the critical need to strengthen connections between urban, rural and suburban areas to achieve territorial cohesion, drive sustainable development, and prevent fragmentation (1).

[87] For the text of the Charter, see: rm.coe.int/168071923d. The Charter was adopted by the CoE's Standing Conference of Local and Regional Authorities of Europe (CLRAE) on 18 March 1992, a session held during the annual plenary session of the CLRAE (17–19 March 1992, Strasbourg).

[88] For the text of the Charter, see: rm.coe.int/urban-charter-ii-manifesto-for-a-new-urbanity-publication-a5-58-pages-/168095e1d5.

[89] For the text of the Charter, see: rm.coe.int/cg-2023-45-20-prov-draft-report-european-urban-charter-iii-en-rapporte/1680acca9f.

[90] Council of Europe, Congress of Local and Regional Authorities, *Manifesto for a New Urbanity: European Urban Charter II* (2008) 34.

it serves as a sort of urban constitution for local authorities and outlines a catalogue of principles for modern urban living which towns and cities should aim to apply in their urban policies, programmes and actions. In a nutshell, the contribution of the CoE has aimed to highlight principles seen as common to all European cities and to provide the basis for future developments on urban rights. However, a concrete definition of a city has not yet been included in its work. It is again important to note that the CoE's urban charters are instruments of soft law and, as such, are not legally binding.

In conclusion, the EU and other European institutions have significantly advanced local government, primarily through policies and initiatives that frame issues in terms of 'urban' and 'city' rather than just 'local government'. While the Commission and Parliament have proposed a shared EU definition of the city, it remains limited to statistical use and lacks legal force. This gap offers a creative opportunity for law developments that would define what constitutes a city within the EU.

III. The Rising Role of Cities and their Challenge to European Public Law

Given the ongoing urban turn in institutional actions and the absence of a shared EU legal definition of 'city', public law scholarship offers essential insights. The city has emerged as a central focus in discussions about transformations in this area of law,[91] driven by the rise of a globally recognised 'new urban age',[92] already extensively explored across other disciplines.[93] From a strictly legal point of view, this trend can be seen first in international law, where cities are increasingly becoming protagonists in a new world order,[94] one in which the leading actors are no longer only nation states as defined in the post-Westphalian order, but also cities as non-state actors, together with non-governmental organisations. Also, this trend is evident in European (supranational) and domestic public law, where constitutional and administrative law scholars have begun to examine the city as

[91] See, eg, the topic of the first Austrian ICON.S Chapter Conference: 'Public Law and the Cities' (Vienna, 10–11 September 2024). For a discussion of the emerging role of the city as seen within the context of changes in public law, see G Della Cananea, 'Jean-Bernard Auby e Lo Ius Publicum Europeum' in G Della Cananea and Js Ziller (eds), *Il Nuovo Diritto Pubblico Europeo: Scritti in Onore Di Jean-Bernard Auby* (Giappichelli 2019). The latter highlights that, with the emergence of a European public law that extends beyond nation states, the city is coming to play an increasingly key role as a political community.

[92] M Bloomberg, 'City Century: Why Municipalities Are the Key to Fighting Climate Change' (October 2015) *Foreign Affairs* 116, 117.

[93] See ch 3, section I.

[94] As observed by international lawyers. See, for example, CF Swiney, 'The Urbanization of International Law and International Relations: The Rising Soft Power of Cities in Global Governance' (2020) 41 *Michigan Journal of International Law* 227, 275 ff.

an autonomous legal category. The debate turns in essence around a single fundamental issue: whether the city as an autonomous subject in relation to other local authorities is emerging as a new category of law – a 'city law' field – and to what extent this could also be delineated beyond constitutional/administrative disciplinary divisions and traditional administrative/nation-state borders. This is relevant first and foremost for understanding the role and power of cities concerning the innovation of (local) democracy from both a domestic and European perspective, and their reach in supporting citizen participation.

Among the first reflections within public law on the city as an autonomous unit was a landmark study in 2013 by Jean-Bernard Auby. This argued for a '*droit de la ville*'[95] in view of the political and economic 'renaissance of cities,[96] a situation calling for an all-encompassing approach referred to as 'the law of cities',[97] which would be applicable to the various dimensions of how cities function (urban law, local government law, and administrative law). This *droit de la ville*, it was argued, should thus be conceived of as a general designation covering three aspects of the city:[98] (1) the physical aspect of its infrastructure and private as well as public spaces; (2) its dynamics relating to land use, urban planning, economic activities, and sustainable development; and (3) its politics, including its government (along with citizen participation), the public services it provides, and the so-called 'right to the city'.[99]

Auby maintains that a new transversal categorisation[100] is necessary because current municipal boundaries are inadequate both for managing urban areas that have expanded far beyond mere administrative boundaries,[101] and for addressing diverse challenges (demographic, economic, cultural, social, climatic, fiscal) that require interdisciplinary expertise as well as a rethinking of legal categories. This is

[95] See, in particular, J-B Auby, *Droit de la Ville: Du Fonctionnement Juridique des Villes au Droit à la Ville* (LexisNexis 2013). For discussion of how this idea has evolved in recent years, see J-B Auby, 'Droit de La Ville: An Introduction' (2013) 5 *Italian Journal of Public Law* 302.

[96] Auby, 'Droit de La Ville: An Introduction' (n 95) 303.

[97] The designation of this field is still a work in progress. See ibid 305.

[98] These are the three different areas of a city's legal regulation that, according to Auby, should be included under the term 'droit de la ville'.

[99] H Lefebvre, 'Le Droit à La Ville' (1967) 6 *L'Homme et La Société* 29. The 'right to the city' affirms that access to core urban amenities – housing, safety and services – is a basic human right. It frames the city as a political space of struggle and transformation. Building on this, the notion of a 'right through the city' captures how global protests use urban space – public squares and streets – to demand rights and political change. See also W Nicholls and F Vermeulen, 'Rights *through* the City: The Urban Basis of Immigrant Rights Struggles in Paris and Amsterdam' in MP Smith and M McQuarrie (eds), *Remaking Urban Citizenship: Organizations, Institutions, and the Right to the City* (Transactions Publishers 2012). The right to the city also became the core of the World Charter on the Right to the City adopted by the World Social Forum initiative in 2005 (text available at: www.right2city.org/wp-content/uploads/2019/09/A1.2_World-Charter-for-the-Right-to-the-City.pdf).

[100] 'The law of cities can be simply apprehended as the law applicable to various essential dimensions of cities functioning … and it is possible to go through these various issues without too much wondering whether you are in the field of constitutional law, administrative law, planning law or whatever' (Auby, 'Droit de La Ville: An Introduction' (n 95) 303).

[101] ibid 304 argues that there is 'insufficient institutional match'. In the EU space, this relates to the need for the EU Commission to develop the new concept of the Functional Urban Area (FUA), as discussed in section II.

in line with the growing need to define 'the city beyond the municipality'[102] – not as an attempt to institute a new law aimed at replacing the different legal fields already in existence, but rather as an effort to articulate a broader approach, and introduce additional tools, for addressing societal challenges in urban areas.

The 'city beyond the municipality' is a notion that seeks to capture the many flows and networks that pass through cities in the form of people, services, production, ideas, policies, capital and goods. This notion encompasses not only the residents of the municipality but all those who live there as a community, such as foreigners or commuters (in other words, those who enjoy what has been called 'urban citizenship').[103] Moreover, the city is, on the one hand, a place where different legal orders coexist, and where legal acts passed by other higher levels of government find their concrete and ultimate application; on the other hand, it is also a place where citizens' experiences of informality could be recognised and supported by the public side from a governance perspective. This is what has been defined as 'informal public law'[104] in recognition of the social origin of law and in reference to the many rules that are created in the city even in the absence of an explicit link to formal legality. In short, if we look at a city as a quintessential form of human settlement, we cannot avoid noticing that the *civitas* has gone far beyond the borders of the *urbs*, in the sense that the political community of the city – with its problems and challenges – nowadays increasingly exceeds the borders of the city's physical environment as defined for decades by states. In fact, the concept of the 'city' long predates the idea of the State itself or of any international or supranational order.[105] The city's contemporary renaissance seems to reawaken its original vocation as a political community beyond its constriction within state superstructures.

Indeed, there is debate and scholarship not only about 'the city beyond the municipality', but also about 'cities beyond the State'.[106] Here, cities are considered from an

[102] F Giglioni, 'Verso Un Diritto Delle Città. Le Città Oltre Il Comune' in E Carloni and F Cortese (eds), *Diritto Delle Autonomie Territoriali* (Cedam 2020); F Cortese, 'Il Nuovo Diritto Delle Città: Alla Ricerca Di Un Legittimo Spazio Operativo' in GF Ferrari (ed), *Smart City: L'evoluzione Di Un'idea* (Mimesis 2020). Cortese sees the city itself as being capable of creating law thanks to its local autonomy (90). Additionally, R Cavallo Perin, 'Beyond the Municipality: The City, Its Rights and Its Rites' (2013) 5 *Italian Journal of Public Law* 307.

[103] On the concept of 'urban citizenship', see ch 3 (n 21).

[104] On the city as a place of informal public law ('diritto pubblico informale'), see the landmark contribution of Fabio Giglioni, whose work on Italian cities will be of great use in Part III. He claims that experiences of informal public law serve as the concrete basis on which cities exercise their autonomy and pave the way for a law of cities. See F Giglioni, 'Order without Law in the Experience of Italian Cities' (2017) 9 *Italian Journal of Public Law* 291.

[105] Ch 3, section I.

[106] See the recent work of an Italian research group of public law scholars (Gruppo Progetto Città, University of Padova) who are studying cities as emerging subjects of law: F Pizzolato et al (eds), *La Città Oltre Lo Stato* (Giappichelli 2021). See also Filippo Pizzolato et al (eds), *La Città e La Partecipazione Tra Diritto e Politica* (Giappichelli 2019). Some preliminary considerations at the foundation of this book were published as part of this project: see C Salati, 'La Libertà Dei Cittadini Attivi Oltre Lo Stato: Prime Considerazioni Sull'amministrazione Condivisa in Unione Europea' in F Pizzolato et al (eds), *La Città Oltre Lo Stato* (Giappichelli 2022).

international or supranational European perspective. On the one hand, this involves looking at their capacity to form horizontal networks[107] and engage in a new method of governance that complements the one by nation states and responds to global as well as local challenges; on the other hand, the idea of 'cities beyond the State' entails advocating for their greater autonomy. This awakening brings new issues not only with concern to the practical organisation of the city, but also about a concrete and shared legal definition and perspective of constitutionalisation within domestic as well as supranational law. While the former constitutes the object of study of administrative lawyers, the latter is the perspective of constitutional scholars.

In the light of urban transformation and the organisational issues that accompany it, scholars of constitutional law have begun considering the city as an autonomous legal subject. Those who advocate for this way of seeing cities are essentially concerned with empowering cities through their recognition in constitutions.[108] Sometimes the focus is solely on the recognition of 'megacities' (or metropolitan cities), but more generally it is on whatever might qualify as a 'city' irrespective of its size.[109] This is especially pertinent in the EU context, given that the vast majority of EU cities are medium sized rather than 'megacities' on the scale of those in other parts of the world such as the Global South.[110] Within the European legal space, it is thanks largely to the CoE 1985 European Charter of Local Self-Government that the city – together with other local authorities – has received constitutional recognition from a European perspective, in particular with regard to its political autonomy.[111] Nevertheless, the city is recognised as an independent legal subject by European constitutional law only in so far as this is determined within the domestic legal order of each Member State,[112] since an

[107] Generally, see L Bobbio, 'Invece Dello Stato: Reti' (2005) 34 *Parolechiave* 33, who describes the EU as based on reticular governance, and nation states on pyramidal governance.

[108] See Hirschl, *City, State* (n 22).

[109] Cities, therefore, are considered as distinct from other local governments. See, as a starting point, M De Visser, 'Constitutionalizing Cities: Realizing Government Agendas or Sites for Denizen Engagement?' in A Flynn et al (eds), *Cities and the Constitution: Giving Local Governments in Canada the Power they Need* (McGill-Queen's University Press 2024); E Hirsch Ballin et al (eds), *European Yearbook of Constitutional Law 2020: The City in Constitutional Law* (Springer 2020); M De Visser et al, 'Introduction: The City as a Multifaceted and Dynamic Constitutional Entity' in E Hirsch Ballin et al (eds), *European Yearbook of Constitutional Law 2020: The City in Constitutional Law* (TMC Asser Press 2020); Saunders and Arban (n 3); J Shaw and I Štiks, 'The Constitutionalisation of Cities and the Future of Global Society' (2021) *Identities* 295.

[110] For a critical review of Hirschl, *City, State* (n 22), see E Arban, 'City, State: Reflecting on Cities in (Comparative) Constitutional Law' (2021) 19 *ICON* 343. The main points of relevance that Arban raises are, first, that European cities are not megacities, so further research would need to be done specifically on cities within the European legal space; and, secondly, that no definitions of 'city' and 'megacity' are provided for constitutional purposes.

[111] In addition, the Charter 'provides some basis to believe that European cities may be better off than their counterparts in the United States, Canada, or Australia … It protects the basic prerogatives of local government' (Hirschl, *City, State* (n 22) 87).

[112] Even if nation-state constitutions clearly define them as separate from other local authorities, cities are in most cases still regarded 'as creatures of the state, fully submerged within a Westphalian constitutional framework and assigned limited administrative local governance authority' (Hirschl, *City, State* (n 22) 10).

EU or shared European legal definition of the city does not yet exist. In terms of the 1985 Charter, therefore, the city in the European legal space is but one among other local authorities and without a clear and legally binding definition. As to the question, then, of whether to constitutionalise the city as such within nation-state constitutions, the debate is still open. Although many scholars lean towards a positive answer, there are drawbacks to be considered, such as the risk of introducing unnecessary complications in multi-level government, overburdening bureaucracies, and deepening the divide between urban and rural areas.[113] That being said, the constitutional entrenchment (be it at a domestic or a EU and European level) of cities as separate subjects from municipalities and other local governments may also have positive effects. Perhaps the most relevant is that legal recognition of the city as a political community consisting both of democratic government and governance with citizens would accord it a greater degree of autonomy in dealing with contemporary challenges. At the moment, though, the prospect of constitutionalisation is utopian, and it is not even certain that it is desirable. Whatever the case, without any consensus as to what a 'city' is, the debate remains premature.

Instead, what seems the most important contribution of constitutional law to the increasing role of cities is the rediscovery of the principle of subsidiarity.[114] In fact, the European principle of subsidiarity seems to be capable of providing guidance across all three dimensions[115] of city relationships, namely relationships with international or supranational (European) institutions, with other institutions within the national constitutional architecture, and with inhabitants. Some have put forward options for attaining a greater degree of city autonomy[116] by utilising the principle of subsidiarity (a) in relation to international institutions and organisation, so as to 'globalise the city at the extra-constitutional level' (the idea being to free cities from their dependency on the State); (b) in relation to other institutions within the national constitutional architecture, so as to 'institutionalise the city at the constitutional level' (meaning to entrench the city constitutionally as a political community); and (c) in relation to the city's inhabitants, so as to 'to democratise the city at the sub-constitutional level' (which entails fostering 'citizen participation in democratic processes'). The latter is of particular interest: it concerns the potential innovation that subsidiarity could bring to the relationship between the city and its inhabitants.[117] The idea of subsidiarity-as-democracy is very much in line with the horizontal dimension of subsidiarity, as a consequence of its recognition of the capacity of cities to support their citizens in practical action of general interest. This democratic reading of the European principle of subsidiarity has

[113] Arban, 'City, State' (n 110).

[114] For two starting-points, see De Visser 'Constitutionalizing Cities' (n 109); and M Cahill and G O'Sullivan, 'Subsidiarity and the City: The Case for Mutual Strengthening' in E Arban (ed), *Cities in Federal Constitutional Theory* (Oxford University Press 2022).

[115] Three categories defined in De Visser et al, 'Introduction: The City' (n 109).

[116] Cahill and O'Sullivan (n 114).

[117] This is what is termed a 'denizen-centric approach' in De Visser et al, 'Introduction: The City' (n 109) 9.

already found application in many Italian cities, as we will see in Part III. All in all, subsidiarity may offer hope to city scholars because, as it has been claimed,[118] it 'provides a paradigm … for greater autonomy'. More specifically, the European principle of subsidiarity could constitute the paradigm for claiming wider autonomy for EU cities.

What emerges, in sum, is the clear growth of the city's importance as a place of democracy and, consequently, of citizen participation. Looking at them from a realistic perspective, it can be observed that cities – considered as human settlements that have their own identity and instil a sense of belonging that transcends administrative borders – can vary significantly in terms of territorial and population size; can contribute to economic prosperity, generate ideas and innovation, and promote policies capable of overcoming the State's immobility on certain issues; and are a vital place for supporting citizen participation in regard to practical daily matters. In short, 'cities beyond the municipality' constitute the strategic laboratory where problem-solving is the object not only of a government elected at the closest level by citizens, but also of the informal governance practised by public authorities together with their inhabitants. The city, that is to say, is the urban area where local democracy is best placed for experimenting with innovative forms of participation, some of which may be informal in nature. Cities have long predated states as strategic places for citizen participation within a political community in the European territory, and the local level remains the level of government best suited for pushing the boundaries of participation even further. Considering the European turn towards the discourse on cities and the urban, one can regard European cities as places for local democracy from a transnational perspective. This does not mean that local democracy and participatory practices cannot also be found in rural areas, for example.[119] Simply put, cities are key because they face more complex problems and challenges.

A last point that should be made about the city as a political community founded on democratic government and governance relates to the concerns that surround the top-down implementation of the so-called 'smart city' paradigm.[120] Envisaged as a means of addressing urban issues through the transformation of technological infrastructure, the smart city was born essentially as a top-down project implemented by corporations, even though citizen participation is a core

[118] Cahill and O'Sullivan (n 114). The authors argue that, to strengthen the project of city autonomy, scholars would have to define the concepts of both 'city' and 'autonomy'.

[119] For an understanding of cities as urban areas in contrast to rural areas, see the (few) considerations contained in the European Parliament Resolution of 3 July 2018 on the Role of Cities in the Institutional Framework of the Union (2017/2037(INI)) [2020] OJ C 118, 2 ff. For an introduction to the relationship between urban and rural areas and the constitutional silence around it, see R Hirschl, 'Constitutional Design and the Urban/Rural Divide' (2022) 16 *Law & Ethics of Human Rights* 1.

[120] For an introduction to the smart city from a public law perspective, see S Ranchordás, 'Smart Cities, Artificial Intelligence and Public Law: An Unchained Melody' in A Quintavalla and J Temperman (eds), *Artificial Intelligence and Human Rights* (Oxford University Press 2023).

element of smart city governance. It is only recently that a new bottom-up push has placed citizens back at the centre as participants in its democratic governance.[121] Citizen participation in the context of the smart city has focused so far mainly on the ownership and management of data.[122] However, recently the topic of citizen participation in city governance has also started to be debated, on the basis of the recognition of the city as a political community beyond mere smart city technology, that as such should find ways to support bottom-up inputs of active citizenship.[123] It must be stressed that the issue of democratic participation in the smart city remains unresolved and that the focus should be on valuing citizens' creative, spontaneous initiatives and channelling these through democratic instruments.

All things considered, the rising phenomenon of urbanisation is increasingly recognised by EU institutions, mainly through policies, as well as in public law scholarship, with growing interest seen among federal, constitutional and administrative legal scholars. Despite the lack of any legally binding definition, this is occurring within the general overarching framework of European constitutional principles, among which are subsidiarity and local self-government. Even though EU law is blind to cities, EU policies are not, and are already reaching out to cities, primarily through funding opportunities.

IV. Core Elements of a City Definition in the EU

Despite legal and institutional complexity, core elements for defining EU cities are emerging. Some may argue such a definition is unnecessary, citing conceptual ambiguity, city diversity, constitutional silence, and limited awareness of the CoE 1985 Charter. However, as urbanisation accelerates, European public law must meet the challenge with clarity and commitment.

Some of the main challenges in doing so relate to the idea of urban citizenship, the smart city as an emerging paradigm, the growing role of soft law and city networks, the possibility of constitutional reforms, the interdisciplinarity and diversity of research methods, and finally innovations concerning citizen participation and democracy itself. That being said, given the countless number of definitions in the literature or policy reports, and within international and

[121] C Ratti and M Claudel, *The City of Tomorrow: Sensors, Networks, Hackers, and the Future of Urban Life* (Yale University Press 2016).

[122] E Morozov and F Bria, *Rethinking the Smart City: Democratizing Urban Technologies* (Rosa Luxemburg Stiftung 2018). In essence, they advocate for citizen-led technological sovereignty in smart cities, in terms of which resources such as urban data would be owned, controlled and managed as commons.

[123] E Keymolen and A Voorwinden, 'Can We Negotiate? Trust and the Rule of Law in the Smart City Paradigm' (2019) 34 *International Review of Law, Computers & Technology* 233. The authors argue for negotiation as a method of opening the city to contributions by an active citizenry.

supranational institutions and organisations' acts, the city in relation to democracy could be defined in terms of certain foundational propositions. These are as follows:

- The city in the EU is the place where transformations of democracy are concretely taking place from the perspective of both government and governance.
- The city is the place where citizen participation is more common, and where democratic innovations may be designed and more flexibly applied.
- As a local authority, the city is also the place for local self-government within urban areas, as distinct from local authorities in rural areas.
- The city can rely on the subsidiarity principle in its vertical dimension as the European constitutional paradigm to advocate for more autonomy.
- The city as a public autonomy has the capacity to support civic individual autonomies in pursuing the general interest of their communities thanks to the horizontal dimension of subsidiarity.

In conclusion, the network of local democracy in cities in the EU could contribute to the renewal of democracy in the EU, thanks to both subsidiarity and local self-government principles. Whereas under EU law cities and other local authorities are considered not as active subjects but passive receivers[124] EU soft law is, by contrast, increasingly reaching out to cities and relying upon their democratic role and potential as political communities.[125] The city is, therefore, the site of a crucial intersection of government and governance, in addition to which subsidiarity – thanks to both its vertical and horizontal dimensions – could come to constitute the archetypal European principle. Neither fully legal nor fully political, the city inhabits the intersection of these two dynamics.

Local self-government and subsidiarity, the core principles of EU local democracy, are vividly reflected in cities' push for greater autonomy and responsiveness to grass-roots participation beyond representative channels. Considered in its earliest historic desire for autonomy untied from subsequent nation-state structures, the city in the EU now stands as a vital laboratory for transforming local democracy: this can occur through participatory forms together with its inhabitants thanks to the basis provided by the European principle of subsidiarity and local self-government.

[124] J Van Zeben, 'Local Governments as Subjects and Objects of EU Law: Legitimate Limits?' in S Bardutzky and E Fahey (eds), *Framing the Subjects and Objects of Contemporary EU Law* (Edward Elgar Publishing 2017) 138.

[125] M De Visser, 'The Future Is Urban: The Progressive Renaissance of The City in EU Law' (2020) 7 *Journal of International and Comparative Law* 389. She states that cities are 'democracy enhancers' and thus argues that 'soft law should systematically be included when researching Europe's cities'.

PART III

Civic Participation Through the Commons (CPC) in the Case of Italian Cities

5

The Constitutional Roots of the Italian Case

I. Shared Administration of the Commons as a Democratic Innovation in Italian Cities

Given the challenges that democracy is facing, especially in its participatory form and at the local level, three key insights from Parts I–II guide our research: (1) an action-oriented form of participation – as the frontier of this principle – enabling citizens to contribute through concrete actions beyond decision-making; (2) a horizontal view of subsidiarity, rooted in EU constitutional debates but largely overlooked; and (3) the growing role of cities as autonomous subjects among other local authorities, challenging nation-state structures and redefining the *civitas* beyond administrative borders. These points show a great potential still unexplored contained in the European constitutional principles in recognising and providing cover for a broad variety of experiences aimed at renewing democracy starting from the local level. Part III (chapters five and six) explores how horizontal subsidiarity is applied in Italian cities, through the provision of constitutional support for local participation through the 'commons' (or 'common goods'). As previously mentioned, this book terms this 'civic participation through the commons' (CPC). The case of Italian cities implementing horizontal subsidiarity ('the Italian case') is in fact central to this book, since it offers a clear organisational model – *shared administration* – and specific legal tools like the *regulation on the commons* and the *collaboration pact*, through which CPC can take place. In this way, shared administration of the commons in Italian cities constitutes a democratic innovation as explained in chapter two, where the commons constitute the concrete ground upon which a new type of collaborative governance can take place. The principle of subsidiarity in its horizontal dimension constitutes the constitutional anchorage of this democratic innovation.

The Italian experience constitutes a pioneering case for three main reasons. First, because the Italian Constitution explicitly outlines – uniquely across the EU – subsidiarity in a horizontal dimension, providing for a description of that. Second, because this theoretical inclusion in the constitutional text has found a practical application through the organisational model of shared administration that an increasing number of cities and other local authorities – starting from the year 2014 – have adopted for innovating their relationship with citizens. Third, because the model of shared administration of the commons has become increasingly institutionalised to the point of drawing the contours of a form of CPC that has no equal in other experiences on the commons in the EU.[1] It exemplifies what we called 'the forgotten meaning of subsidiarity' (in chapter three), by enabling cities to promote an action-oriented idea of participation based on the commons. Aligning with the EU and Council of Europe (CoE) legal orders, this horizontal view of subsidiarity could inspire similar models in other European cities facing commons-related challenges. As a first step in this exploration, the case of Italian cities stands out as a unique phenomenon, offering lessons of universal significance that transcend national boundaries.

In conclusion, two clarifications: references to 'the Italian case' or 'the case of Italian cities' mean the application of horizontal subsidiarity in Italian cities. Also, all mentions of the Constitution or constitutional principles in Part III refer to the Italian Constitution, not European constitutional principles.

II. From Participation in Deciding to Participation in Doing: A Necessary Premise

The concept of participation is key for approaching the Italian case.[2] Participation encompasses various meanings and practices, and reflects the broader challenges representative democracies face, both in Italy and across the EU and beyond.[3] In public law, participation broadly means involving those outside formal roles in decision-making, complementing official processes. On one side, therefore, we have the State in its organisational structure, and on the other we have society with its pluralism. With participation, both the State and society are going towards each other to include 'more society within the State', and 'more State within the society':[4] this process requires an organisational framework regarding the subjects, the spaces and the interests of participation, and it is up to legal scholars to define it.

Alongside administrative and political participation – the two traditional forms of participation – a third form has emerged in Italy:[5] shared administration.[6] This

[1] See further ch 6. On shared administration as a democratic innovation see also C Salati, 'L'Amministrazione Condivisa come Innovvazione Democratica' (2025) Labsus: www.labsus.org/2025/10/lamministrazione-condivisa-come-innovazione-democratica/.

[2] M Nigro, 'Il nodo della partecipazione' [1980] *Rivista Trimestrale di Diritto e Procedura Civile* 225.

[3] In ch 1, section III.

[4] In the wording of Nigro (n 2) 230 ff.

[5] On this third form of participation, see G Arena, 'Amministrazione e Società. Il Nuovo Cittadino' (2017) 1 *Rivista Trimestrale di Diritto Pubblico* 43, 50; A Valastro, 'La Partecipazione Alla Prova Dei Territori: Dal "Decidere" al "Fare"' (2016) *Labsus*: www.labsus.org/2016/08/la-partecipazione-alla-prova-dei-territori-dal-decidere-al-fare/.

[6] G Arena, 'Introduzione All'amministrazione Condivisa' *Studi Parlamentari e Di Politica Costituzionale* (1997) 29. See also E Rocca, 'The City, Between *Innen* and *Aussen*: The Revolution of the Horizontal Subsidiarity Principle in Italy' (2017) 5 *Birkbeck Law Review* 135.

constitutes an organisation model which enables individual as well as associated citizens to collaborate equally with the State in managing resources and addressing issues of general interest. Doctrinal contributions gave a meaningful label to this new form of participation: that is 'partecipazione al fare', which means participation in doing, as it stands in parallel with 'partecipazione al decidere' that means participation in deciding.[7] While the idea of participation in deciding refers to the involvement of citizens in having their own say in the decision-making process, the concept of participation in doing is trying to capture those types of citizens' participation aimed at practically doing something and solving problems for the general interest of the community.

This new understanding of participation marks a paradigm shift[8] in the relationship between individuals and public authority.[9] Traditionally, public law followed a bipolar model,[10] setting citizens and the State in opposition: authority guided the State, while citizens relied on individuals' fundamental rights to limit that authority. The result was a clear divide between those who govern and those who are governed. In the most recent decades, however, what starts to emerge is the development of a new modality of relation between the two: from the bipolar paradigm where citizens are considered as users or consumers, the new trend is going towards a more collaborative and equivalent relationship where citizens become allies of public authorities, defining a new public law paradigm that has been defined as the 'subsidiarity paradigm'.[11] This new public law paradigm, anchored in Article 118(4) of the Italian Constitution, embodies citizens' participation in doing, where individuals are not only bearers of needs and demands,

[7] On the distinction, see A Valastro, 'La Democrazia Partecipativa Alla Prova Dei Territori: Il Ruolo Delle Amministrazioni Locali Nell'epoca Delle Fragilità' in A Valastro (ed), *Le Regole Locali Della Democrazia Partecipativa. Tendenze e Prospettive Dei Regolamenti Comunali* (Jovene 2016) 30; A Valastro, 'La Democrazia Partecipativa Alla Prova Dei Territori: Tendenze e Prospettive Dei Regolamenti Comunali' (2016) 3 *Osservatorio Sulle Fonti* 14; G Cotturri, 'Storia del principio di sussidiarietà in costituzione' in G Arena and G Cotturri (eds), *Il Valore Aggiunto: Come La Sussidiarietà Può Cambiare l'Italia* (Carocci 2010). Also F Pizzolato, 'Il Civismo e Le Autonomie Territoriali' in F Bassanini et al (eds), *Il Mostro Effimero. Democrazia, Economia e Corpi Intermedi* (Il Mulino 2019) 73, talks about this dualism of participation in deciding and in doing.

[8] In the sense expressed by T Kuhn, *The Structure of Scientific Revolutions* (University of Chicago Press 1962). A paradigm shift is foreseen by the scholar Feliciano Benvenuti with regard to the form of the State: from a state based on the opposition between the State itself and its citizens, to a collaboration between the two where a broad autonomy is granted to all the levels of government. The democratic state, for the scholar, should be referred to the broadest participation of citizens to the administrative functions of the State, allowing therefore new forms of participation to emerge beyond the elections. Civic participation is seen, in this paradigm shift, as the core of the new dimension of the State. See F Benvenuti, 'Il Ruolo Dell'amministrazione Nello Stato Democratico Contemporaneo' in G Marongiu and G Candido De Martin (eds), *Democrazia e Amministrazione. In Ricordo Di Vittorio Bachelet* (Giuffrè Editore 1992).

[9] G Arena, 'User, Customers, Allies: New Perspectives in Relations Between Citizens and Public Administrations' in G Arena and M Chiti (eds), *Public Administration, Competitiveness and Sustainable Development* (Firenze University Press 2003).

[10] The term comes from S Cassese, 'L'arena Pubblica. Nuovi Paradigmi per Lo Stato' (2001) 3 *Rivista Trimestrale di Diritto Pubblico* 601.

[11] D Donati, *Il Paradigma Sussidiario: Interpretazioni, Estensione, Garanzie* (Il Mulino 2014).

but also of capabilities that can contribute to the general interest of a community. It is, indeed, this shift from the question 'which rights does a person have?' to the question 'what can a person be and what can they do?'[12] that captures the spark for citizens' spontaneous activation in practically *doing* something instead of only participating in the decision-making process. This shift reflects the capabilities approach,[13] focusing on what individuals can actually do and their potential to contribute freely and responsibly to society.

The idea of participation in doing redefines, therefore, participation as an enabler for the spontaneous exercise of an active freedom[14] by all those active citizens[15] willing to contribute to the constitutional duty of solidarity[16] with practical actions towards the general interest of society.

III. The Novelty of Horizontal Subsidiarity in Article 118(4) of the Italian Constitution

This new idea of participation has found strong support in Article 118(4) of the Italian Constitution on the principle of subsidiarity in its horizontal dimension: in contrast with the principle of vertical subsidiarity (Article 118(1)) on the division of administrative functions between the different levels of government,[17] horizontal subsidiarity looks at the relationship between the State and the community.[18] At the same time, while vertical subsidiarity works as a guarantee of institutional pluralism, horizontal subsidiarity reflects societal pluralism.[19]

In recent years, subsidiarity has been conceptualised by scholars, courts and institutions in a variety of ways – extending beyond its predominant vertical interpretation to include its often overlooked horizontal dimension. The dominant, vertical understanding includes labels such as 'global', 'active', 'transversal', 'static/dynamic' and 'ascending/descending' subsidiarity. In contrast, the horizontal or societal reading encompasses labels such as 'circular', 'polycentric', 'functional', 'networked/diagonal' and 'fiscal' subsidiarity. Interestingly, despite these diverse formulations, they can generally be traced back to the same two foundational

[12] Valastro, 'La Democrazia Partecipativa Alla Prova Dei Territori: Il Ruolo' (n 7) 15 f.

[13] The reference goes to economic and philosophical theories on capabilities and the capability approach developed by Amartya Sen and Martha Nussbaum.

[14] F Benvenuti, *Il Nuovo Cittadino: Tra Libertà Garantita e Libertà Attiva* (Marsilio 1994).

[15] G Arena, *Cittadini Attivi* (Laterza 2006).

[16] S Rodotà, *Solidarietà: Un'utopia Necessaria* (Laterza 2014).

[17] TE Frosini, 'Sussidiarietà (Principio Di) (Dir.Cost.)' *Enciclopedia Del Diritto* (2008) 1134, 1135 f; U Rescigno, 'Principio Di Sussidiarietà Orizzontale e Diritti Sociali' (2002) 1 *Diritto Pubblico* 5, 17 ff.

[18] 'Horizontal subsidiarity' is a doctrinal category introduced in the literature by the scholar Antonio d'Atena in 1996: see A D'Atena, 'Sussidiarietà e proporzionalità nelle dinamiche multilivello e nelle relazioni pubblico–privato' (2022) 4 *Federalismi.it* 339. Since then it has been widely used and constitutes the ordinary label used for referring to Article 118(4).

[19] ibid 341 f.

dimensions – vertical and horizontal – thus reinforcing the view that subsidiarity inherently bridges both institutional and societal spheres.[20]

Despite having been explicitly introduced in the constitutional text only in 2001, the principle of subsidiarity finds its roots many decades before, outside the juridical and scientific debate.[21] Referred to as one of the strongest ideas of contemporary constitutionalism, it was considered as a principle with a disruptive relevance equal to the principle of separation of powers at the time it was introduced.[22] Its origin in the Italian legal order as a relation between the State and the community is usually said to date back to Christian social doctrine.[23] However, its explicit introduction in the Italian Constitution in 2001 was not a consequence of the elaboration of this principle from the Catholic Church nor from the legal scholarship,[24] but rather a direct consequence of its introduction in EU law by the Maastricht Treaty at Article 3 B (today's Article 5 of the Treaty on European Union), and to a lesser extent of the provision of Article 4(3) of the European Charter of Local self-government. Unlike the EU and the CoE, however, the introduction of subsidiarity in the Italian Constitution includes not only its vertical dimension but also its horizontal one. The meaning of subsidiarity as the support given by the State to autonomous initiatives of individuals as active members of their community is explicitly written and described, among the European constitutions, only[25] in the post-2001 Italian Constitution in

[20] For a comparative analysis of all these labels, see further C Salati and E Arban, 'Sussidiarietà, Pluralismo e Autonomie: Un Canale Aggiuntivo Alla Partecipazione' in C Salati and E Alber (eds), *Partecipazione e innovazioni democratiche in Italia. Una prospettiva multidisciplinare e multilivello* (forthcoming 2026).

[21] A D'Atena, 'Costituzione e principio di sussidiarietà' (2001) 1 *Quaderni Costituzionali* 13. See also I Massa Pinto, *Il principio di sussidiarietà: profili storici e costituzionali* (Jovene 2003) (in particular, 52 ff and 135 ff). For a study on subsidiarity as a principle of political philosophy, see C Millon-Delson, *Le principe de subsidiarité* (Presses Universitaires de France 1993). On the original ambiguity of the principle, see S Cassese, 'L'aquila e le mosche. Principio di sussidiarietà e diritti amministrativi nell'area europea' (1995) 118 *Il Foro Italiano* 373. For some essential references on the horizontal dimension of subsidiarity, see A Albanese, 'Il principio di sussidiarietà orizzontale: autonomia sociale e compiti pubblici' (2002) 1 *Diritto Pubblico* 51; P Duret, 'La sussidiarietà "orizzontale": le radici e le suggestioni di un concetto' (2000) 1 *Jus Online* 95; G Arena, 'Il principio di sussidiarietà orizzontale nell'art. 118, u.c. della Costituzione' (*Astrid Online*, 2003).

[22] For this idea, A D'Atena, 'Il principio di sussidiarietà nella Costituzione italiana' [1997] *Rivista Italiana di Diritto Pubblico Comunitario* 603, 627.

[23] See ch 3, section II.A.

[24] As Antonio D'Atena claims, the Italian legal scholarship demonstrated a belated interest in the principle of subsidiarity, in comparison to the German legal scholarship where the debate among scholars has been wider: see D'Atena, 'Il principio di sussidiarietà' (n 22). As also highlighted by the author, the only prominent exception is to be found in the jurist Egidio Tosato: his perspective – rooted in the Christian social doctrine – was the only one also recognising the legal dimension of the principle of subsidiarity, with the centrality of the person with their freedom to actively participate in the general interest of the society, and the promotional role of the State towards individuals. See E Tosato, 'Sul principio di sussidiarietà dell'intervento statale' in *Nuova Antologia* (1959) (Now in *Persona, Società Intermedie e Stato*, Giuffrè Editore, Milano, 1989).

[25] Some EU countries have an explicit mention of subsidiarity – in its vertical meaning – in their constitutions: for example, Austria, France, Germany, Portugal, Switzerland. See ch 3 (n 104) and the subsequent ones for implicit traces of the horizontal dimension of subsidiarity in other legal orders.

Article 118(4),[26] which has been defined as 'horizontal subsidiarity' (or 'social subsidiarity').[27] The text agreed for Article 118(4) in the constitutional reform states that: 'the State, regions, metropolitan cities, provinces and municipalities shall promote the autonomous initiatives of citizens, both as individuals and as members of associations, relating to activities of general interest, on the basis of the principle of subsidiarity'. It is thanks to those few lines that the centrality of the person was explicitly recognised in its social and relational dimension as included in the works of the Constituent Assembly[28] and as promoted by Christian social doctrine, and its practical implementation through the organisational model of *Shared administration* permitted. In the following sections (III.A, III.B, III.C) we will analyse the three main pillars of horizontal subsidiarity: its subjects, its objects, the action.

Importantly, the new form of civic participation enabled by horizontal subsidiarity is also taking form in accordance with other constitutional principles. Among others, first, with Article 1(2) on individuals' sovereignty, by empowering citizens to take actions of general interest and in this way exercising their sovereignty. Second, with Article 2 on societal pluralism, by recognising citizens' contributions, both individually and within intermediate communities. Third, with Article 3(2), by recognising individuals' full development through their societal participation. Fourth, with Article 4(2) on civic duties, by recognising citizens' duties to contribute to societal development in accordance with their capabilities and free will. Fifth, with Article 5 on local autonomy, by recognising local authorities'

[26] However, some authors already foresaw the implicit existence of the principle in the Italian Constitution before its introduction in 2001: see J Luther, 'Il principio di sussidiarietà: un "principio speranza" per il diritto costituzionale comune europeo?' (1996) 119 *Il Foro Italiano* 184.

[27] 'Horizontal subsidiarity' has also been defined as 'social subsidiarity', while 'vertical subsidiarity' as 'institutional subsidiarity' in G Pastori, 'Sussidiarietà e diritto alla salute' (2002) 1 *Diritto Pubblico* 85. Traces of subsidiarity in its vertical and horizontal dimensions are also to be found in: (a) the work of the 1997 Bicameral Committee for the reform of the second part of the Italian Constitution (*Bicamerale D'Alema*) at Article 56 (whose work eventually did not succeed); (b) law no 59/1997 (also known as '*legge Bassanini*', named after the then Minister of the public function Franco Bassanini, who initiated a process of reform known as 'administrative federalism') on the reform of the public administration at Article 4, III, a) attributing to public authorities the role to support families, associations and communities in functions and activities of social importance; (c) law no 328/2000 at article 5(1) on social services. See Cotturri (n 7).

[28] During the Italian Constituent Assembly (1946–48), Giorgio La Pira's report in the First subcommittee on rights and duties of citizens emphasised the priority of the person over the State and linked the person to their natural communities (family, religious, work, local, etc), opposing individualist and totalitarian views. Also Giuseppe Dossetti's contribution recognised, despite ideological differences, the need to support individuals' rights in a societal dimension of solidarity, where the person finds their realisation within the different communities ('comunità intermedia') where their relationships take place, and only in case of incapacity should the State intervene. See Commissione per la Costituzione, Prima sottocommissione, *Resoconto sommario della seduta di lunedì 9 settembre 1946*: www.camera.it/_dati/costituente/lavori/I_Sottocommissione/sed003/sed003.pdf. For an overview of the traces of the principle of horizontal subsidiarity in the Constitutional Assembly debate, see V Cerulli Irelli and R Cameli, 'Il Principio di Sussidiarietà Orizzontale nei Lavori dell'Assemblea Costituente' (*Astrid Online*): www.astrid-online.it. For a historical understanding of the role of the intermediate communities, see P Grossi, *Le Comunità Intermedie Tra Moderno e Post-Moderno* (Marinetti 2015), and M Rosboch, *Le Comunità Intermedie e l'avventura Costituzionale* (Heritage Club 2017).

self-government. Sixth, with Article 117(6) on the regulatory autonomy of local authorities. Horizontal subsidiarity, therefore, is providing for an essential reference point for shared administration of the commons – as we will see in chapter six – within a wider constitutional framework.

A. The Subjects: The State and the Citizens

The State and the citizens are the two subjects envisioned by horizontal subsidiarity. On the side of the State, according to Article 118(4), the subsidiarity paradigm refers to the 'State, regions, metropolitan cities, provinces and municipalities' as the actors designed to support citizens' activities of general interest. They hold a role of support, promotion, facilitation and enablement towards citizens.[29] The vertical subsidiarity principle assigns primary responsibility to local governments due to their closeness to citizens, with higher levels intervening only if lower levels cannot fulfil their tasks (Article 118(1)) and in accordance with the division of competences between levels of government (Article 117).

In addition to the State, the Constitution refers to 'citizens, both as individuals and as members of associations' as the other subject. Subsidiarity is a principle capable of extending the legal *status* of citizenship, also encompassing all those individuals who are willing to get involved in activities of general interest, but do not have Italian legal citizenship.[30] The core rationale behind that lies in the support given by horizontal subsidiarity to individual freedom exercised as a social commitment:[31] individual freedom is at the centre of the promotional role of the State at all its levels, as long as it is aimed at the benefit of society. The term active freedom ('libertà attiva')[32] predates its constitutional formulation and views individuals as bearers of capabilities willing to serve their community. It expresses a contemporary idea of liberty – one that involves active participation in public life not only for private interest, but out of a personal commitment to the constitutional duty of solidarity (Article 2).

[29] The committment of the State at all its levels towards citizens' initiatives through the principle of horizontal subsidiarity has been brought back to the concept of promotional law ('diritto promozionale') in F Giglioni, 'Le Città Come Ordinamento Giuridico' (2018) 1 *Istituzioni Del Federalismo* 29.

[30] F Giglioni, 'Forme Di Cittadinanza Legittimate Dal Principio Di Sussidiarietà' (2016) 2 *Diritto e Società* 305; G Arena, 'Immigrazione e Cittadinanze' in R Acciai and F Giglioni (eds), *Poteri Pubblici e Laicità Delle Istituzioni: Studi in Onore Di Sergio Lariccia* (Aracne editrice 2007) 113 ff; F Giglioni, 'La Sussidiarietà Orizzontale Nella Giurisprudenza' in G Arena and G Cotturri (eds), *Il Valore Aggiunto: Come La Sussidiarietà Può Cambiare l'Italia* (Carocci 2010) 164. With regard to the recognition of a wider concept of administrative citizenship ('cittadinanza di residenza') aimed at also including migrants in actions of care, regeneration, management of the commons, see judgment no 119/2015 of the Constitutional Court.

[31] A Sen, 'Individual Freedom as Social Commitment' (Winter/Spring 1998/99) 25(4)–26(1) *India International Centre Quarterly* 53.

[32] Benvenuti, *Il Nuovo Cittadino* (n 14).

The exercise of this active freedom – which is based on a civic autonomy[33] – is the distinctive feature of a new model of citizen that has been defined within the Italian legal scholarship as active citizen,[34] and has found its legal foundation in the model of citizen portrayed in Article 118(4) of the Constitution. Active citizens ('cittadini attivi') refers to all those individuals who spontaneously decide to take responsibility within a limited action of care. Simply belonging to a community does not make one a citizen; active citizenship means freely exercising individual sovereignty through participation, beyond traditional representative delegation.[35] Active citizens are normal citizens that at some point in lives decide to take up an autonomous initiative: it is a model of practised citizenship ('cittadinanza praticata')[36] where the spontaneous and autonomous activation of citizens is aimed at contributing to solving problems of general interest[37] in collaboration with public authorities.

The Constitution defines citizens as both individuals and members of associations. Typically, volunteers and third-sector members[38] handle general interest actions. Yet, under subsidiarity (Article 118(4)), even individuals without formal status or legitimation[39] can contribute to their communities. The mention of citizens as members of associations relates to third-sector organisations[40] promoting

[33] In parallel to public autonomy, Benvenuti clarifies a distinction between two forms of individual autonomy: private autonomy ('autonomia privata'), when the exercise of an individual freedom is meant to bring an advantage to the individual themselves; civic autonomy ('autonomia civile'), referring to all those individuals willing to exercise their active freedom on an equal level with public authorities. In the author's ideal future scenario of democracy, the so-called *demarchia*, citizens first hand participate through an exercise of their active freedom in putting into practice their constitutional duty of solidarity, therefore becoming themselves participants in the production of the legal system as members of the *polis*. Benvenuti, *Il Nuovo Cittadino* (n 14) 60 ff and 80.

[34] On the concept of *active citizens* ('cittadini attivi') see Arena, *Cittadini Attivi* (n 15).

[35] On the distinction between 'citizenship as belonging' and 'citizenship as participation' within the Constitution, see G Arena, 'La Cittadinanza Attiva Nella Costituzione' in F Cortese et al (eds), *Dallo Status Di Cittadino Ai Diritti Di Cittadinanza* (Editoriale Scientifica 2014).

[36] For this concept, see Giglioni, 'Forme Di Cittadinanza' (n 30) 313 ff.

[37] On the 'general interest', see further, section III.B.

[38] The term 'third sector' was coined in A Etzioni, 'The Third Sector and Domestic Missions' (1973) 33 *Public Administration Review* 314, for referring to a third alternative between the two dominant state (public) and the market (private) sectors. For the Italian constitutional debate relating to the third sector, see further L Gori, *Terzo Settore e Costituzione* (Giappichelli 2022).

[39] L Gori, 'La Disciplina del volontariato individuale, ovvero dell'applicazione diretta dell'art.118, ultimo comma, Cost.' (2018) 1 *Associazione Italiana Dei Costituzionalisti* 1.

[40] With the introduction of the Code of the Third Sector (CTS) with Legislative Decree No 117 of 3 July 2017, a common label was given for not-for-profit organisations such as voluntary organisations, associations for social promotion, philanthropic entities, social enterprises (including social cooperatives), associative networks and mutual associations, recognised and not recognised associations, foundations and other private entities different from for-profit companies: all of them are now considered as Entities of the Third Sector (ETS), and registered in a national register (*Registro unico nazionale del Terzo settore*). For an introduction on the relation between the principle of horizontal subsidiarity and the third sector, see L Gori, 'La "Saga" Della Sussidiarietà Orizzontale. La Tortuosa Vicenda Dei Rapporti Fra Terzo Settore e P.A.' *Federalismi.It* (2020); and G Arena, 'Sussidiarietà Orizzontale Ed Enti Del Terzo Settore' in A Fici et al (eds), *I Rapporti Tra Pubbliche Amministrazioni Ed Enti Del Terzo Settore. Dopo La Sentenza Della Corte Costituzionale n. 131 Del 2020* (Editoriale Scientifica 2020).

solidarity and social benefits through accountable activities. Cooperation between them and public authorities for activities of general interest usually happens through co-planning and co-design to identify needs and implement solutions. Since 2001, the novelty of horizontal subsidiarity is that it includes not only associated citizens, but also individual ones.[41] This requires the State at all levels to also support initiatives from citizens outside third-sector organisations, such as individuals, informal groups and neighborhood committees.

The 2001 constitutional reform, therefore, introduced the pursuit of the general interest as a role not just for the State but also for private individuals and associations to contribute autonomously. Importantly, citizens' initiatives are not privatisation efforts transferring public services to private enterprises. Instead, horizontal subsidiarity fosters a new alliance between the State and citizens, based on free, autonomous action – their active freedom – aimed at the community's general interest, not private economic gain.[42]

In this paradigm shift, a debate arises on whether profit-making private enterprises can also become active citizens by implementing horizontal subsidiarity without seeking profit. This has been termed 'corporate active citizenship' ('cittadinanza attiva d'impresa').[43] Supporters argue these enterprises can aid public institutions by sharing their organisational, human, economic resources, fostering collaboration rather than competition[44] according to the subsidiarity paradigm. This signals a transformation of civil society.

B. The Object: The Activities of General Interest

The object of initiatives of horizontal subsidiarity is vaguely defined as *activities of general interest*, meaning actions benefiting the majority in a community. In the Italian context, private interest refers to individual goals, while public interest relates to state responsibilities fulfilled by public authorities. Unlike public interest, general interest can be pursued jointly by public authorities and private subjects – individually or through associations – according to the new paradigm defined by the principle of horizontal subsidiarity.[45]

Private individuals' actions respond to a free choice of contributing to their community, and not to an obligation established by law. The general interest often

[41] E Rossi and L Gori (eds), *Ridefinire Il Volontariato* (Pisa University Press 2020).

[42] See section III.B for the difference between general interest, public interest, private interest.

[43] G Arena, *I Custodi Della Bellezza* (Touring 2020) 55 f.

[44] In favour, see F Ozzola, 'Dal Dire al Fare. La Sussidiarietà Orizzontale in Pratica' in G Arena and G Cotturri (eds), *Il Valore Aggiunto: Come La Sussidiarietà Può Salvare l'Italia* (Carocci 2010). Arena, *Cittadini Attivi* (n 15) 132 ff; Gori, 'La Disciplina del volontariato individuale' (n 39) 6; Giglioni, 'Forme Di Cittadinanza' (n 30) 318. Against see, for example, the judgment of Consiglio di Stato n.1440/2003.

[45] It is important to note that the Italian concept of public interest (*interesse pubblico*) referring to the interest pursued by the public administration as a body serving the State and not the community, does not coincide with the Anglo-Saxon tradition of 'public interest' nor with the ancient Roman law concept of *res publica*. For this explanation, see Arena, *Cittadini Attivi* (n 15) 110.

overlaps with public interest but can also include private actions that generate positive externalities.[46] It is broader than both, representing situations where there is a common goal and collaboration between private and public sectors.

The activities of general interest do not coincide with the administrative functions strictly considered,[47] which compete with public authorities, but can coincide with public functions in the way that citizens can also participate in the State's activity.[48] The general interest recognises the possibility for citizens to take action in a responsible and supportive way towards others, instead of just for personal interest. General interest, therefore, excludes private profit initiatives and public administration duties, focusing on services benefiting individuals and the community.

After many (conflicting) judgments trying to give a more precise content to the general interest,[49] Constitutional Court judgment no.131/2020 clarified (see further chapter six, section III) that general interest activities are non-profit efforts by citizens that pursue civic and supportive aims of social utility. Thanks to Article 118(4) of the Constitution, the State is no longer the only actor designed for pursuing the interest of the community, but can be complemented by autonomous activities of private citizens. The Court underlined that such activities can be implemented not only by citizens associated within third sector organisations, but also by individual or not associated citizens.

In addition to that, and in exclusive relation to third-sector organisations, a great contribution in the definition of activities of general interest came in 2017 with the third Sector Code (legislative decree no.117/2017), that outlines in Article 5 a detailed list of all those activities that such organisations can pursue. Among these, for example, we can find activities relating to: social actions; healthcare services; education; environment protection; cultural heritage; inclusion in the job-market of disadvantaged workers; humanitarian aid and social integration of migrants; social agriculture; charity; promotion of legality and peace; promotion and safeguard of human rights; civil protection; and requalification of assets seized from organised crime.

[46] Rescigno (n 17) 29; Arena, 'Introduzione All'amministrazione Condivisa' (n 6) 58. A common example of private interest aligning with general interest is a citizen caring for a neglected public flower-bed near their home, despite it being the public administration's responsibility. This citizen's private interest in tidiness at the same time benefits the general interest of the wider community, illustrating how active citizens can freely support public maintenance. It is correct to say that while the State (through the public administration) maintains the flower-bed, active citizens can exercise their freedom by taking care of that flower-bed. Article 118(4) of the Italian Constitution mandates state support for such spontaneous initiatives within a collaborative framework between the State and its citizens.

[47] In this way, V Cerulli Irelli, 'Sussidiarietà (Diritto Amministrativo)' (2003) *Enciclopedia Giuridica*, Treccani, 5. See also Rescigno (n 17), who claims that horizontal subsidiarity can never refer to powers of command, but only services and goods distribution, and activities relating to social rights (23).

[48] Of this idea Nigro (n 2) 235. See also Benvenuti, *Il Nuovo Cittadino* (n 14); G Pastori, 'L'insegnamento di un maestro' (2017) 1 *Rivista Trimestrale Di Diritto Pubblico* 143, 149.

[49] For a detailed overview, see S Pellizzari, 'Il Principio Di Sussidiarietà Orizzontale Nella Giurisprudenza Del Giudice Amministrativo: Problemi Di Giustiziabilità e Prospettive Di Attuazione' (2011) 3 *Istituzioni Del Federalismo* 593; Giglioni, 'La Sussidiarietà Orizzontale Nella Giurisprudenza' (n 30) 159 ff.

C. The Action: The Support for Autonomous Initiatives

With concern to the action, both citizens and the State (at all its levels) have their own role. The Constitution affirms that the State, regions, metropolitan cities, provinces and municipalities 'shall promote the autonomous initiatives' of citizens: we will first explore what these initiatives mean, then examine the State's role.

Horizontal subsidiarity can take place only if active citizens take action:[50] citizens are the only ones who can bring the principle to life, as its effects depend on their spontaneous initiative, and not on a decision of public authorities.[51] The initiatives should be autonomous, meaning that the full self-determination of citizens (as long as it is in line with the general interest) is legitimated and given value by the Constitution. The autonomous aspect of the initiative means that no salary can be corresponded,[52] while only some assistance could be given by public authorities as a support for the freely exercised action of citizens. Citizens' actions, however, cannot expect to always be upheld: the power to decide whether an action is in line with the general interest or not remains on the public authorities, and for this reason the principle of horizontal subsidiarity defines a collaboration among the two parts, and not a substitution. Additionally, the support for an autonomous initiative cannot create a disadvantage for others: because of that, concurring initiatives should always be considered by public authorities, which need to also guarantee third parties' needs.[53]

The collaboration between the two parts drawn in Article 118(4) envisages a relationship between two autonomous parts: public autonomy and private (civic)[54] autonomy. The principle of horizontal subsidiarity therefore consists of an equal relationship between autonomies, based on what has been defined a relational autonomy ('autonomia relazionale').[55] This concept looks at autonomy not only as the guiding principle to safeguard and recognise local authorities against a centralised power (that in the Italian Constitution is granted in Article 5), but also as the underlying principle in a pluralist society for an equal relationship between different private and public interests.

The paradigm shift from a bipolar to a subsidiarity paradigm[56] enables a new relationship between public authority and individual freedom. Citizens' autonomous initiatives under Article 118(4) represent in this sense a new form of

[50] Arena, 'Il principio di sussidiarietà orizzontale nell'art.118' (n 21) 3; Arena, *Cittadini Attivi* (n 15) 63 f.

[51] It must be noted, however, that the autonomous initiative of citizens sometimes could come as a consequence of a public call: in this case, there would be an invitation by public authorities to present spontaneous initiatives for the general interest that would eventually be supported by them.

[52] F Giglioni, 'Sussidiarietà Orizzontale e Terzo Settore' (*Astrid Online*, 2002) 2: www.astrid-online.it/static/upload/protected/Gigl/Giglioni-SO-e-III-settore.pdf.

[53] Giglioni, 'Forme Di Cittadinanza' (n 30) 332.

[54] See above (n 33).

[55] G Arena, 'Le Diverse Finalità Della Trasparenza Amministrativa' in F Merloni (ed), *La Trasparenza Amministrativa* (Giuffrè 2008) 22.

[56] See above (n 11).

liberty – so-called social liberties ('libertà sociali')[57] – developed through Constitutional Court case law. Within the subsidiarity paradigm, this relationship between public[58] and civic autonomy is forming a new legal space[59] for collaborations based on the exercise of social liberties in the general interest. A very first mention of that occurred in 1998,[60] when the principle of social liberty was invented[61] by the Constitutional Court with reference to all those activities that take place occasionally and without seeking profit. At that time, relationships based on social solidarity as an exercise of one's individual freedom were already recognised by the Court[62] as a constitutional legitimation of the different forms of solidarity put in practice by volunteers. A second mention of the term occurred with judgment no.300/2003 where banking foundations were considered among those subjects or legal entities entitled to the 'organization of social liberties' according to Article 118(4).[63] A third mention came with judgment no.185/2018 when the Court acknowledged the autonomous capacity of third-sector organisations (as private bodies), to exercise their social liberties as granted by Article 2 of the Constitution to implement actions of social solidarity.[64] The latest recognition of this new type of liberty came with judgment no.131/2020. This can be considered a ground-breaking judgment under different perspectives, but the one relevant here is the connection established by the Court between Article 118(4) of the Constitution and social liberties. In fact, according to the Court, the principle of horizontal subsidiarity represents a new framework for social liberties not dependent on the State or on the market, but on all those forms of social solidarity freely and autonomously exercised by citizens.[65] The Court states that horizontal subsidiarity gives value to the social

[57] Not to be confused with social rights. See G Tiberi, 'La Dimensione Costituzionale Del Terzo Settore' (*Astrid Online*, 2008) 7; S La Porta, *L'organizzazione Delle Libertà Sociali* (Giuffrè 2004) 27.

[58] On the concept of public autonomy, see F Merloni, 'Le Autonomie Nella Costituzione Repubblicana' (2010 108(3) *Astrid Rassegna*): www.astrid-online.it/static/upload/protected/Merl/Merloni_Le-autonomie-nella-Costituzione-repubblicana.pdf; A Police, 'Le Autonomie Pubbliche Come Ordinamenti Giuridici' in R Cavallo Perin et al (eds), *Attualità e Necessità Del Pensiero Di Santi Romano* (Editoriale Scientifica 2019).

[59] Giglioni, 'Forme Di Cittadinanza' (n 30) 323, where this new legal space is regarded as a '*zona franca*'.

[60] Constitutional Court judgment no.50/1998.

[61] A Pace, 'Violazione della "libertà sociale" o, piuttosto, restrizione della "libertà individuale"?' (1998) 2 *Giurisprudenza Costituzionale* 584.

[62] Constitutional Court judgment no.75/1992. Individuals' freedom to put in practice the principle of social solidarity was later reaffirmed in Constitutional Court judgment no.309/2013.

[63] Constitutional Court judgment no.300/2003.

[64] Constitutional Court judgment no.185/2018.

[65] See further, ch 6, section III. See further, S Pellizzari and C Borzaga, *Terzo Settore e Pubblica Amministrazione: La Svolta Della Corte Costituzionale* (Euricse 2020) 36: '*Si è identificato così un ambito di organizzazione delle "libertà sociali" (sentenze n. 185 del 2018 e n. 300 del 2003) non riconducibile* né allo Stato, né al mercato, ma a quelle "forme di solidarietà" che, in quanto espressive di una relazione di reciprocità, devono essere ricomprese "tra i valori fondanti dell'ordinamento giuridico, riconosciuti, insieme ai diritti inviolabili dell'uomo, come base della convivenza sociale normativamente prefigurata dal Costituente" (sentenza n. 309 del 2013)'.

and responsible use of citizens' active freedom,[66] not only through third-sector organisations and their volunteers, but also as private individuals. As addressed in the previous section, on the practical level, citizens' autonomous initiatives consist in activities of general interest referred to the production of goods or services for the community, or to complement public authorities in guaranteeing social rights.

In parallel to citizens' autonomous initiatives, the second aspect of the provision under study is the role of the State, regions, metropolitan cities, provinces, municipalities: the Constitution states that they shall promote ('favoriscono') those initiatives. The verb used in the constitutional provision is key to understanding the dynamic of the relationship. The true innovation of the 2001 constitutional reform lies in introducing an obligation[67] on all state levels to support citizens' autonomous initiatives – when these serve the general interest as defined in Article 118(4).

Public authorities then should play a supportive role,[68] either by backing citizens after action or by enabling conditions for action through transparency and the promotion of participation. Though sometimes associated[69] with the enabling state model,[70] the subsidiarity paradigm differs: it emphasises non-profit, solidarity-driven civic initiatives, not market-based ones. While the enabling state shifts public responsibility in social welfare to citizens, horizontal subsidiarity fosters equal collaboration, with citizens freely complementing public roles through their social liberty. Private citizens acting for the general interest, in fact, do not do that for receiving a profit. This marks a new, balanced relationship between State and citizens: for citizens' free choice to contribute to their community with an assumption of responsibility, there is a parallel supportive role of the State.[71]

[66] See above (n 32).

[67] Rescigno (n 17) 29 ff.

[68] L Violini, 'Il principio di sussidiarietà' in G Vittadini (ed), *Sussidiarietà: La riforma possibile* (Milano 1998); Frosini (n 17) 1136 and 1140 f.

[69] M Chiti, 'La Rigenerazione Di Spazi e Beni Pubblici: Una Nuova Funzione Amministrative?' in F Di Lascio and F Giglioni (eds), *La Rigenerazione Di Beni e Spazi Urbani. Contributo al Diritto Delle Città* (Il Mulino 2017); F Gaspari, 'Città intelligenti e intervento pubblico' (2019) 98 *Il diritto dell'economia* 71, 79 ff.

[70] The enabling state, first defined in the US, represents a shift from the welfare model to a market-oriented approach where public support backs private responsibility for financing and producing social welfare. See N Gilbert and B Gilbert, *The Enabling State: Modern Welfare Capitalism in America* (Oxford University Press 1989) 163 ff, and N Gilbert, *Transformation of the Welfare State: The Silent Surrender of Public Responsibility* (Oxford University Press 2002), where the author warns of the risk of 'a silent surrender of public responsibility' (193). For the distinction between the welfare state, the regulatory state, and the enabling state, see S Cassese, 'The Administrative State in Europe' in A von Bogdandy et al (eds), *The Max Planck Handbooks in European Public Law: The Administrative State* (Oxford University Press 2017) 76 f.

[71] Recent Constitutional Court rulings, especially judgment no.52/2021 (paragraph 6.4), clarify that the State at all its levels must actively support citizens' initiatives – particularly from the Third Sector – under Article 118(4). This duty goes beyond mere passive permission and non-obstruction and requires instead for regions to promote and involve civic actors recognising their key role in civil society.

IV. The General Interest Applied to the Commons

Within the constitutional formulation of horizontal subsidiarity, the concept of general interest has notably provided for a constitutional ground to the commons. In fact, beyond the production of goods or services and the fulfilment of social rights,[72] Article 118(4) may also support other types of activities of general interest: namely, autonomous and responsible initiatives of shared governance of common goods.[73] Between its constitutional recognition in 2001 and the 2017 definition of general interest activities, in fact, the concept of general interest was shaped by the idea of 'common goods' or 'commons' ('beni comuni')[74] and allowed for the spread of commons-based initiatives around Italy.

Although research on this concept is still evolving across disciplines[75] (law, economics, political science, among others), the most advanced legal theory on commons has emerged in the Italian context.[76] Here, common goods are seen as a legal category and administrative practice involving tangible, intangible, and digital assets – of public or private property – that support individual and collective wellbeing, with governance that may be either collaborative or conflictual. The common goods refer to many ground-level disjointed experiences that started to appear at the boundaries of law, and that are still needed for a clear legal and constitutional framework. Within this context, the principle of horizontal subsidiarity has so far been the only constitutional principle able to serve as a reference point for all those bottom-up experiences of care, regeneration and shared governance[77] of the commons implemented by active citizens, and able to provide them with a clear and legal organisational framework rooted in the Constitution. Horizontal subsidiarity was indeed able to intercept a phenomenon taking place in society, connecting that within a constitutional and legal framework.

The reference point for the global academic debate on the commons dates back to 1968, when the biologist Garrett Hardin denounced the 'tragedy of the commons', with reference to the problem of the free access to resources, that leads

[72] Rescigno (n 17) 23.

[73] The original academic contribution of the scholar Gregorio Arena and the work of the network *Labsus-laboratiorio per la sussidiarietà* represent the reference point in Italy for this interpretation of Article 118(4) of the Constitution and for its on the ground implementation in hundreds of Italian local authorities through the organisational model *shared administration* of the commons (www.labsus.org/).

[74] See further, chs 6, 7 and 8.

[75] C Micciché, *Beni comuni: risorse per lo sviluppo sostenibile* (Editoriale Scientifica 2018) 11 ff; V Cerulli Irelli and L De Lucia, 'Beni Comuni e Diritti Collettivi' (2014) 1 *Politica del Diritto* 3.

[76] F Cortese, 'I Beni Mutanti. Fisiologia e Sfide Del Dibattito Sui Beni Comuni' (2018) 1 *Munera* 13, 17.

[77] The three terms 'care', 'regeneration' and 'shared governance' refer to the three terms 'cura', 'rigenerazione' and 'gestione condivisa' used by the first Bologna Regulation in 2014 for referring to the three types of collaboration activities between active citizens and public authorities. See further, ch 6, section II.

to over-exploitation of a good that eventually becomes unavailable for future generations.[78] Later, an attempt to answer this dilemma came from the Nobel prize winning scholar Elinor Ostrom:[79] her economic contribution to the construction of a theory of the commons represents a reference point not only for economic and social studies worldwide, but also for the legal scholars in Italy who are taking part in the elaboration of a commons theory within a constitutional and legal framework. Trying to search for a third way to go beyond the two solutions given by economists until then of privatisation or enforcement imposed by outside force (the dualism between a governance of the State or of the market), Ostrom's theory led the way towards community self-organisation and self-governance of the commons, through the elaboration of eight design principles.[80] It is interesting to note the specific importance given by Ostrom to the community: in fact, she emphasises the advantage of cooperative behaviours, and the necessity of participatory democracy and of an organised civil society. While in economic theory the commons are defined as non-excludable and rival goods in their consumption, the category seems to be much more complex and undefined than that, as many of the terms related to that show:[81] among others, commons, common pool resources, global commons, new commons, tangible common goods, intangible common goods, digital common goods, social goods, public goods, collective properties, rights of civic uses. The economic classification and definition reflect only one aspect of the concept:[82] from here the need for legal scholars to contribute to the category rooting the concept within legal traditions.[83]

In the Italian context, one of the earliest intuitions regarding the connection between the principle of horizontal subsidiarity and the common goods came in 2004 with the Charter of Subsidiarity[84] elaborated by Labsus-Laboratorio per

[78] 'Therein is the tragedy. Each man is locked into a system that compels him to increase his herd without limit – in a world that is limited. Ruin is the destination toward which all men rush, each pursuing his own best interest in a society that believes in the freedom of the commons. Freedom in a commons brings ruin to all … Every new enclosure of the commons involves the infringement of somebody's personal liberty': G Hardin, 'The Tragedy of the Commons' (1968) 162 *Science* 1244, 1248.

[79] E Ostrom, *Governing the Commons: The Evolution of Institutions for Collective Actions* (Cambridge University Press 1990).

[80] The eight design principles are: '1) Clearly defined boundaries [of the CPR, for individuals who have the rights to withdraw resources unit from it]; 2) Congruence between appropriation and provision rules and local conditions; 3) Collective-choice arrangements; 4) Monitoring; 5) Graduated sanctions [for those who violate operational use]; 6) Conflict-resolution mechanisms; 7) Minimal recognition of rights to organize [external government authorities should not challenge CPR institutions]; 8) Nested enterprises. Appropriation, provision, monitoring, enforcement, conflict resolution, and governance activities are organized in multiple layers of nested enterprises', ibid 90.

[81] Miccichè (n 75) 32.

[82] ibid 37 ff.

[83] See further, ch 6 and 7.

[84] The Charter was approved by the First national Convention on subsidiarity, that took place in Rome on 12 March 2004. For its clarity and foresight, the whole text is worth being consulted at: www.labsus.org/la-carta-della-sussidiarieta/. Deserving specific attention are points 5, 6, 7 and 9, that will be translated into English here. Point 5: Activities of citizens aimed at the production, care and valorisation of common goods, carried out on a non-profit basis in compliance with the principles of solidarity, responsibility, equality and legality, are in the general interest. Common goods are those

la sussidiarietà, a research collective devoted to the study of the on the ground application of the principle of horizontal subsidiarity. The concept of general interest was in this way translated into practical actions of care, regeneration and management of the common goods, putting at the core (active) citizens and their capabilities exercised through autonomous initiatives.[85] The category of common goods – used in a legal meaning – was in this way used in order to promote a new model of society, based not on opposition, but on collaboration between public authorities and individuals' active freedom. The official recognition of this interpretation came with the first municipal Regulation for the Shared administration of the urban commons adopted by the municipality of Bologna in 2014. For the very first time in Italy – and within the international context – a clear legal framework on the care, regeneration and shared governance of the commons as a collaboration between citizens and public authorities was elaborated, also creating an unprecedented model for other local authorities, as we will see further.

In conclusion, in the Italian context, horizontal subsidiarity offers constitutional grounding for citizens' practical collaboration with public authorities. Interpreting general interest as the basis for recognising and promoting citizen-led care, regeneration and governance of commons supports a bottom-up new democratic model of civic participation through the commons where citizens are supported in their practical actions of participation in doing.

goods, tangible and intangible, for which citizens by their free choice share the responsibility of care with the administration. Point 6: Citizens through the care of the commons create the conditions for the full development of each human being and first and foremost of themselves, implementing together with the institutions the constitutional principle of equal opportunities for all. Point 7: Enterprises realise forms of active corporate citizenship both by supporting citizens' autonomous initiatives and by directly taking care of common goods. Point 9: Active citizenship and participation are complementary but distinct, as active citizenship entails not only participation in consultative and decision-making processes and public policy-making, but also a direct and autonomous contribution to the care of the commons.

[85] For understanding how this match between the concept of general interest and practical actions on the commons took place see G Arena, 'Beni Comuni. Un Nuovo Punto Di Vista' (*Labsus*, 2010), and G Arena and P Bonasora, 'Il Vertice Di Labsus Cambia per Fare Spazio a Nuove Energie!' (*Labsus*, 2021), where Arena recalls the original reasons for the connection among the two concepts.

6

The Organisational Model of Shared Administration of the Commons

I. The Italian Legal Contribution to the Commons Theory

Italy represents the first juridical culture questioning itself on the classification and on the governance of the commons/common goods ('beni comuni'),[1] therefore constituting an interesting forerunner for other EU countries.[2] Despite the fact that the reference point in Italian legal debate is the work of Elinor Ostrom,[3] more concurring meanings attributed to the concept of commons have developed in the past years, leading to the impossibility of reaching one shared definition, given the broadness and diversity of interpretations.[4] The Italian legal debate is also shaped by the historical significance given by legal scholars in previous centuries to the concept of 'common', from the ancient Roman law (with the *res communes omnium*)[5]

[1] In Part III and in our overall work, the two English terms 'commons' and 'common goods' are used as synonyms for translating the Italian concept of 'beni comuni', as a consequence of the fact that Italian legal scholars have been translating 'beni comuni' with both the English terms mentioned.

[2] The first attempt to come to a classification was initiated by a group of scholars in a conference on 6 June 2006 that took place at the Accademia Nazionale dei Lincei, with the aim of rethinking public property in relation to their social utility: works collected in U Mattei et al, *Invertire la rotta: idee per una riforma della proprietà pubblica* (Il Mulino 2007). In particular, for the reflection of the need for including a third type of goods – the commons – between private and public goods, see S Rodotà, 'Linee guida per un nuovo codice dei beni pubblici' in U Mattei et al (eds), *Invertire la rotta: idee per una riforma della proprietà pubblica* (Il Mulino 2007) 361.

[3] E Ostrom, *Governing the Commons: The Evolution of Institutions for Collective Action* (Cambridge University Press 1990).

[4] MB Vanni, 'Understanding the commons: the reception of Elinor Ostrom's work in Italian legal scholarship' [2014] *Ius Publicum* 1, 2. The author offers an outline of the Italian legal reception of the work of Elinor Ostrom on the commons in Italy.

[5] Originally, the concept of common goods could be traced back to the Roman law of the second and third centuries AD with the term *res communes omnium*. The reference goes to the jurist Marciano, who elaborated this category in addition to the *res publicae* (public goods): his text can be found in Justinian's codification, the *Corpus Iuris Civilis* (in Institutiones 2.1. and 2.1.1; Digest 1.8.2.). The *res communes omnium* consist of those goods that are in common to everyone and that cannot be classified within private goods nor within public goods and therefore do not belong to anyone in particular (rivers, air, the sea, the seashore). For further on this point, see Vanni, ibid, 10 ff, and M Talamanca, *Istituzioni di diritto romano* (Giuffrè 1990) 382. However, while the *res communes omnium* were referred

to medieval institutes (with the experiences of civic uses, *usi civici*).[6] Understanding the broader Italian debate on the commons helps contextualise the development of the Shared Administration model and its diverse influences.

The present concurring doctrinal approaches and interpretations of the Italian concept of 'beni comuni' could essentially be divided into two branches:[7] the first focused on the ownership of the commons; the second concerned with their governance, not depending on their legal status. The first position is represented by those scholars who challenge the governance of the commons because it is too oriented towards privatisations, globalisation and a neoliberal agenda. They contest the capacity of the state to safeguard and guarantee public goods for future generations, and therefore advocate for a new legal category referring to common goods to be introduced in addition to the two earlier categories of public goods and private goods.[8] They see commons as a new form of ownership and seek a legal definition through Civil Code reform. The second approach, rooted in public law, focuses on governance solutions in the absence of specific legislation,[9] prioritising procedures over the definition of the goods themselves.[10]

Despite the fact that an existing problem of definition still exists nowadays, throughout the years these two doctrinal approaches have contributed to the effort of defining what the common goods are. Even if today a legally binding definition is still missing at the constitutional and legislative level, we have two major well-known contributions that are being used as reference points in the Italian legal debate: namely the draft law elaborated by the Rodotà Commission in 2007 (headed by the jurist Stefano Rodotà),[11] and the definition provided by the first 'Municipal Regulation for the collaboration between citizens and the public administration for the care and regeneration of the urban commons' designed by the municipality of Bologna with the support of the research collective Labsus-Laboratorio per la sussidiarietà in 2014 (also referred to as the Bologna

to abundant resources, today's meaning of common goods refers to goods that are either scarce or problematic in their management (C Micciché, *Beni comuni: risorse per lo sviluppo sostenibile* (Editoriale Scientifica 2018) 17 f).

[6] The medieval practice of *civic uses* ('usi civici') broadly refers to collective rights of use of goods over lands and pastures to communities, mainly developed in rural and mountain contexts. The very first attempt at regulation dates back to Law no.1776/1927, while the latest came in 2017 with Law no.168 '*Norme in materia di domini collettivi*'. See G Genio, 'Gli usi civici nella legge n. 168 del 2017 sui domini collettivi: sintonie e distonie attraverso la giurisprudenza costituzionale e il dibattito in sede costituente' (2018) *Federalismi.It.*

[7] See F Cortese, 'What Are Common Goods (Beni Comuni)? Pictures from the Italian Debate' (2017) 11(2) *Polemos* 417.

[8] U Mattei, *Beni comuni. Un manifesto* (Laterza 2011); M Rosaria Marella, 'The Commons as a Legal Concept' (2016) 28 *Law Critique* 61. Most scholars with this approach come from private law, focusing on property rights, though exceptions exists (like public law scholar Lucarelli).

[9] This approach essentially embraces a public law perspective, mainly constitutional and administrative law. G Arena and C Iaione, *L'Italia Dei Beni Comuni* (Carocci 2012).

[10] F Cortese, 'I Beni Mutanti. Fisiologia e Sfide Del Dibattito Sui Beni Comuni' (2018) 1 *Munera* 13.

[11] *Commissione Rodotà – per la modifica delle norme del codice civile in materia di beni pubblici* (14 June 2007).

Regulation).[12] Appointed by the Minister of Justice on 21 June 2007 with the aim of drafting a bill to delegate the government to reform the Civil Code concerning the discipline on public goods, the Rodotà Commission came up with a division of assets into three categories: public goods, private goods, and common goods ('beni comuni'). Within this new classification, common goods were referred to as all those goods that express a functional benefit to the exercise of constitutionally protected fundamental rights[13] as well as to the autonomous development of the person. According to the definition provided by the Commission, they have to be upheld and safeguarded by the legal system, also for the benefit of future generations, and their owners can be both private persons and public legal entities; notwithstanding their title, their collective fruition must be safeguarded according to the law. Specific commons listed are rivers, torrents and their springs; lakes and other waterways; the air; parks as defined by law; forests and woodlands; high altitude mountains; glaciers and snowlines; shores and coastlines declared natural reserves; protected flora and fauna; and archaeological, cultural, environmental goods and other protected landscaped areas.[14] Two important innovative aspects of the Commission were the introduction of the possibility for assets to be not only tangible, but also intangible; and the classification of goods not depending on their property regime, but on their social utility, in relation to the fundamental rights of individuals outlined by the Constitution. With the fall of the government in 2008, a few months after the presentation of the draft, the proposal, however, did not have any follow-up.[15]

[12] *Comune di Bologna 2014 Regolamento*: www.comune.bologna.it/sites/default/files/documenti/REGOLAMENTO%20BENI%20COMUNI.pdf. For the English translation, see: www.comune.bologna.it/media/files/bolognaregulation.pdf. The research group and its socio-legal online journal can be found at: www.labsus.org. The regulation was revised in 2023: www.comune.bologna.it/amministrazione/documenti-e-dati/regolamenti/regolamento-collaborazione-soggetti-civici-amministrazione-beni-comuni-urbani.

[13] On this shift from the economic analysis of goods to the constitutional theorisation of the commons as linked to fundamental rights, see Q Camerlengo, 'Città e Cittadini: Uno Spazio per i Beni Comuni?' in B Biscotti et al (eds), *Città, Cittadini, Conflitti* (Giappichelli 2020) 84 ff.

[14] Art.1, c.3 c) Commissione Rodotà – per la modifica delle norme del codice civile in materia di beni pubblici (14 giugno 2007) – Proposta di articolato: 'beni comuni, ossia delle cose che esprimono utilità funzionali all' esercizio dei diritti fondamentali nonché al libero sviluppo della persona. I beni comuni devono essere tutelati e salvaguardati dall' ordinamento giuridico, anche a beneficio delle generazioni future. Titolari di beni comuni possono essere persone giuridiche pubbliche o privati. In ogni caso deve essere garantita la loro fruizione collettiva, nei limiti e secondo le modalità fissati dalla legge … Sono beni comuni, tra gli altri: i fiumi i torrenti e le loro sorgenti; i laghi e le altre acque; l'aria; i parchi come definiti dalla legge, le foreste e le zone boschive; le zone montane di alta quota, i ghiacciai e le nevi perenni; i lidi e i tratti di costa dichiarati riserva ambientale; la fauna selvatica e la flora tutelata; i beni archeologici, culturali, ambientali e le altre zone paesaggistiche tutelate'. Works of the Commission available at: www.giustizia.it/giustizia/it/mg_1_12_1.wp?previsiousPage=mg_1_12&contentId=SPS47624.

[15] The draft law was presented to the Senate again a few months later by the Regional Council of Piedmont, with no follow-up (*Disegno di Legge n.2031 (24-feb-2010) Delega al Governo per la modifica del codice civile in materia di beni pubblici*). Three other draft laws on the reform of public goods and the introduction of a category of the commons were presented in 2019, also without any consequence (proposals by members of Parliament D'Ippolito, Nugnes, Fassina): the draft laws can be found at: www.commissionepopolarebenicomuni.it/materiali-di-lavoro/.

The second major reference point in the Italian commons debate is the definition in Bologna's 2014 municipal regulation, later adopted by many other local authorities.[16] The work carried out for reaching this innovative regulation came up with a definition of the 'urban commons', constituting a true innovation in the global arena on the commons. According to the Bologna Regulation, the urban commons are all those tangible, intangible and digital goods that citizens and public authorities – also through participative and deliberative procedures – recognise to be functional to the individual and collective wellbeing, and for which together they share the responsibility for their care or regeneration. Contrary to the first interpretation, the definition contained in this special regulation does not aim at giving a legal classification to some goods (the commons), but rather to creating a label for some goods to be governed differently in a functional way.[17] Accordingly, it is the role of the community around a specific good that becomes essential for the recognition and transformation of a public or private good into a commons. The common goods, therefore, do not represent a *tertium genus* between private goods and public goods, but a qualification to be added to them:[18] in line with this perspective, the commons have been associated with the constitutional principle of horizontal subsidiarity,[19] deriving the legitimation of their *shared administration* (or co-management)[20] from Article 118(4) of the Constitution.[21] The Constitution's direct legitimation of the municipal regulation enables grass-roots governance of the commons, applying horizontal subsidiarity without waiting for new property law.[22] It is important to note that this second perspective on the commons also draws on the definition offered by the Rodotà Commission, linking the commons with the fulfilment of the fundamental needs of human beings, in line with the Constitution. In sum, commons are resources around which community relations take form: they are functional to guaranteeing the satisfaction of the community's needs; and they require open access, shared governance, and preservation for the future. This

[16] The up-to-date number of local authorities that have adopted the same type of regulation (or a similar one) can be found at: www.labsus.org/i-regolamenti-per-lamministrazione-condivisa-dei-beni-comuni/. It is important to clarify that while the Bologna Regulation represents the original inspiration for its replication all around Italy, other cities have adjusted the Regulation according to local needs and peculiarities. The Regulation and its innovative model have also been further developed by the Co-City protocol, which is a methodology developed by *LabGov-the Laboratory for the Governance of the City as a Commons* (labgov.city/) based on five design principles. See further, ch 7 (n 17), and C Iaione, 'The Right to the Co-City' (2017) 15 *Italian Journal of Public Law* 80.

[17] Cortese, 'What Are Common Goods' (n 7) 423.

[18] F Giglioni, 'I Regolamenti Comunali per La Gestione Dei Beni Comuni Urbani Come Laboratorio per Un Nuovo Diritto Delle Città' (2016) 2 *Munus* 290.

[19] G Arena, *Cittadini Attivi* (Laterza 2006) 116.

[20] Cortese, 'What Are Common Goods (Beni Comuni)? (n 7) 423.

[21] G Pavani, 'European Sharing and Collaborative Cities: The Italian Way' (2022) 28 *European Public Law* 79, 98, 'on the theoretical level, the shared administration was supported by all the elements which compose the legal system: the legislative formant …; the jurisprudential formant …; the scholarly formant'.

[22] M Bombardelli, 'La Cura Dei Beni Comuni: Esperienze e Prospettive' (2018) 5 *Giornale Di Diritto Amministrativo* 559, 563.

approach challenges the State's exclusive role in taking care of the *res publica*, and traditional property norms, emphasising the community's active involvement regardless of legal ownership.[23]

Of great importance was the legitimation given by the Corte di cassazione in a landmark 2011 ruling,[24] offering the only high court definition of commons to date.[25] The Court defined commons as goods, regardless of legal status, that serve the community's general interest and which need specific governance. It emphasised two points: (1) prioritising functionality over ownership in identifying commons; and (2) the need for a public governance of commons. The Court urged a shift from a property-based view to a constitutional focus on fundamental rights. This definition has since been reaffirmed in later rulings.[26]

Before analysing the shared administration model used by Italian cities in this study, it is necessary to introduce another institutionalised approach to commons governance, understood as a case where communities secured formal collaboration or recognition from public authorities. Informal experiences are excluded from this work's scope. In fact, besides shared administration, *the* most notable institutionalised experience of governance of the commons in the Italian context is the unique 'Neapolitan way' developed in Naples.[27] Since 2011, Naples has adopted a definition of common goods aligned with the Rodotà Commission, included in its municipal statute.[28] To apply this locally, the traditional concept of 'civic use' was reimagined as urban civic and collective use ('uso civico e collettivo urbano'). This allowed for recognising collective rights over certain assets considered as common goods. The discipline of civic uses was therefore for the first time linked to the concept of urban commons.[29] In 2012,

[23] ibid 560 ff.

[24] Corte di Cassazione, Joint Chambers, 14 February 2011, no.3665. See F Cortese, 'Dalle Valli Di Pesca Ai Beni Comuni: La Cassazione Rilegge Lo Statuto Dei Beni Pubblici?' (2011) 11 *Giornale Di Diritto Amministrativo* 1170.

[25] While this is the only definition given by the jurisprudence, we can find references to the concept of common goods in many judgments, even though with no definitions: for an overview, see A Quarta, 'Beni Comuni, Uso Collettivo e Interessi Generali: Un Percorso Giurisprudenziale' (2019) 3 *Rassegna Di Diritto Civile* 933.

[26] Later judgments are: Corte di Cassazione, Joint Chambers, 16 February 2011, no. 3811; Corte di Cassazione, Joint Chambers, 16 February 2011, n. 3813; Corte di Cassazione, Joint Chambers, 18 February 2011 no. 3937; Corte di Cassazione, Joint Chambers, 18 February 2011, no. 3938.

[27] For the qualification of the experience of the 'Neapolitan way' as a 'radical democratic approach' in comparison to 'a public law school, the Bologna Model, which champions city regulations for urban commons with a constitutional anchor', see A Kioupkiolis, 'Transforming City Government: Italian Variants on Urban Commoning' (2022) 44(3) *Administrative Theory & Praxis* 186, 200.

[28] Municipal resolution no.24/2011 stated that: 'Il Comune di Napoli, anche al fine di tutelare le generazioni future, riconosce i beni comuni in quanto funzionali all'esercizio dei diritti fondamentali della persona nel suo contesto ecologico e ne garantisce il pieno godimento nell'ambito delle competenze comunali': www.comune.napoli.it/flex/files/9/b/8/D.5ce508de66d661496d2b/Deliberazione_di_c.c._n._24_del_22_settembre_2011.pdf. For an overview of the neapolitan experience, see MF De Tullio, 'Commons towards New Participatory Institutions. The Neapolitan Experience' in P Gielen and N Dockx (eds), *Exploring Commonism – A New Aesthetics of the Real* (Valiz 2018).

[29] RA Albanese, 'Usi Civici e Beni Comuni Urbani. Tra Presente e Passato, Tra Pubblico e Privato' in RA Albanese et al (eds), *Gestire i Beni Comuni Urbani Modelli e Prospettive* (Rubbettino 2020) 120.

the occupation of the former Asilo Filangieri (a publicly owned building) by cultural workers protesting precarious conditions marked the beginning of a practical experiment in urban commons. Declaring themselves 'commoners',[30] they drafted a Declaration of urban civic and collective use[31] and transformed the building into a self-governed cultural centre. This model was later officially recognised by the city through two council resolutions,[32] and paved the way for the official recognition in a similar way of many other public assets directly administered by people as commons. The Neapolitan example shows that the right to civic and collective use can exist without changing ownership, promoting self-governance.[33] It also illustrates how commons can be political spaces against privatisation[34] and for self-government of communities.[35] Naples continues to inspire similar initiatives across Italy.[36]

In conclusion, it is important to note some drawbacks of the Neapolitan model that could make it harder for citizens to have a positive impact in their communities, and for its replication in other contexts. Also because of that, this book understands the Italian case primarily according to the constitutional accommodation of commons-based initiatives through the model of shared administration, which has spread since 2014 to over 320 cities. First, the strong political connotation of many commons projects can alienate those with different beliefs, limiting inclusive participation and therefore failing in guaranteeing their constitutionally oriented mission. Second, these initiatives often begin as unauthorised occupations and rely heavily on local government recognition to gain legitimacy. This recognition may be delayed or denied if political views differ.[37] Even when support exists, formal approval can take years. Broader challenges – such as the lack of a category of positive law, the lack of dedicated municipal structures, and limited

[30] De Tullio (n 28).

[31] The Declaration can be found at: www.exasilofilangieri.it/regolamento-duso-civico/.

[32] Municipal resolutions no.400/2012 and no.893/2015. For an accurate perspective on the Neapolitan case from inside the local administration, see F Pascapè, 'Usi Collettivi Urbani e Rapporto Tra Il Membro Della Comunità e La Pubblica Amministrazione Locale Nell'esperienza Gestionale Del Comune Di Napoli' in RA Albanese et al (eds), *Gestire i Beni Comuni Urbani. Modelli e Prospettive. Atti Del Convegno Di Torino, 27–28 Febbraio 2019* (Rubbettino 2020). The author highlights the dilemma faced by local authorities when illegal occupations provided vital community services – like health, education and legal aid – that public authorities failed to offer.

[33] N Capone, 'Urbanistica e Beni Comuni Di Uso Civico e Collettivo. Considerazioni Preliminari' in F De Notaris (ed), *Avere Memoria, Costruire Il Futuro* (La scuola di Pitagora 2020) 105, 106.

[34] G Micciarelli, 'Le Teorie Dei Beni Comuni al Banco Di Prova Del Diritto La Soglia Di Un Nuovo Immaginario Istituzionale' (2014) 1 *Politica & Società* 123, 131; De Tullio (n 28) 307 f.

[35] Within the Italian legal debate, the self-government of the commons has been theorised as possible not only through the institute of civic uses, but also through the two private law instruments of the foundation and the trust: these are cases that have not or been little explored in Italy to date. See RA Albanese et al, *Gestire i Beni Comuni Urbani. Modelli e Prospettive. Atti Del Convegno Di Torino, 27–28 Febbraio 2019* (Rubbettino 2020), and in particular the contributions of Antonio Vercellone 'La fondazione' (87), and Annapaola Tonelli, 'Trust e beni pubblici: un nuovo ed efficiente percorso' (103).

[36] De Tullio (n 28) 307. In recent years, many bottom-up initiatives have promoted the commons and developed local solutions, in Naples and beyond. See the national network *Rete nazionale beni comuni emergenti e a uso civico* and its list of ongoing 'emerging common goods'at: www.retebenicomuni.it/.

[37] Also Pascapè (n 32) 174.

expertise – further hinder replication. A more robust institutional partnership between citizens and authorities is crucial to unlocking the full potential of the commons. All in all, and despite these issues, the case of Naples is relevant in so far as it demonstrates the capacity of commons to serve as laboratories of civic participation and grass-roots democracy, allowing citizens to take initiative without waiting for state action.

II. The Organisational Model of *Shared Administration* of the Commons

Commons theories have been described[38] as having a 'parasitic aptitude' – in their aim to introduce the legal category of the commons to redefine the relationship between citizens and the state. The most impactful interpretation links the commons to horizontal subsidiarity at Article 118(4) of the Constitution, leveraging local autonomy and regulation to lead the change. This shift is embodied in the shared administration model, developed in 1997[39] to foster collaboration between citizens and public administrations on matters of general interest. Originally rooted in administrative law as a response to the traditional bipolar paradigm between authority and liberty,[40] the model now supports a broader, constitutionally grounded public law paradigm. It emphasises equal partnerships, empowering local authorities and citizens to share resources and responsibilities, and lays the groundwork for a new form of civic participation and democratic governance.

Since 1997, the legal framework for this model has steadily strengthened. It is based on: (1) the constitutional principle of horizontal subsidiarity; (2) a prototype municipal regulation on the commons[41] that, since the 2014 Bologna Regulation, is allowing local authorities to apply this principle independently

[38] 'Common goods also represent a need for institutionalisation that tends to outgrow the confines of public property or administrative participation and relaunch a new concept of form of State, citizenship and the role of the public–private dichotomy … Common goods, basically, always presuppone a different State and administration from the existing ones', in Cortese, 'What Are Common Goods (Beni Comuni)? (n 7) 435.

[39] As a starting point, see G Arena, 'Introduzione All'amministrazione Condivisa' (1997) *Studi Parlamentari e Di Politica Costituzionale*; G Arena, 'User, Customers, Allies: New Perspectives in Relations Beween Citizens and Public Administrations' in G Arena and M Chiti (eds), *Public Administration, Competitiveness and Sustainable Development* (Firenze University Press 2003); G Arena and M Bombardelli (eds), *L'Amministrazione Condivisa* (Editoriale Scientifica 2022).

[40] See ch 5, section II.

[41] For the presentation of the Regulation see G Arena, 'Un Regolamento per La Cura Condivisa Dei Beni Comuni' (*Labsus*, 2014): www.labsus.org/2014/02/beni-comuni-un-regolamento-cittadini-attivi-piu-forti/. See also C Iaione and E de Nictolis, 'The City as a Commons Reloaded: From the Urban Commons to Co-Cities Empirical Evidence on the Bologna Regulation' in SR Foster and CF Swiney (eds), *The Cambridge Handbook of Commons Research Innovations* (Cambridge University Press 2022) 128 f.

under Article 117(6); and (3) the use of collaboration pacts ('patti di collaborazione') signed by citizens and public authorities. The model was later reinforced also thanks essentially to three initiatives: the national-level legislation on the third sector (the third-sector Code)[42] aimed at better defining the activities of general interest, co-planning and co-design relating to third-sector organisations, and thanks to some regional laws relating to a different extent to the shared governance of the commons or horizontal subsidiarity (regions of Lazio, Tuscany, Emilia-Romagna, Umbria, Piedmont, Molise, Apulia, Marche)[43] addressed to both single and associated citizens. Another important normative reference is to be found in law no.267/2000 on local authorities ('Testo Unico Entil Locali') that in Article 3(5) outlines that municipalities and provinces also perform their functions through activities that can be adequately exercised by the autonomous initiative of citizens and their social groups. Importantly, even though to date[44] no national law has been passed on the shared administration model of the commons, nevertheless many local authorities are reforming internally, and citizens are increasingly embracing their role under the constitutional principle of subsidiarity.

The strength of shared administration, therefore, lies in turning a constitutional principle into real-world practice. Also defined as collaborative governance,[45] the model of shared administration is designed to be a collaborative and not conflictual relationship.[46] It basically represents a relationship between two autonomies – the public autonomy, and the private (or civic)[47] autonomy – that is working for a caring society,[48] and that may even contribute to a reform of the form of the state. In this way, the organisational model of shared administration is granting an institutional structure for the creation of a new space at the boundaries between public law and private law, with the emergence of the general interest beyond the public and private ones. This space supports collaboration for the general interest, helping to build the 'Third Pillar' – the community – beyond

[42] 'Codice del terzo Settore', legislative decree no.117/2017. See ch 5 (n 40). For the model of shared administration and its relationship with third-sector organisations, see further S Sacchetti and G Salvatori, '"Shared Administration" as a New Relationship between the Public Sector and the Social Economy' (2023) 126 Euricse Working Paper Series.

[43] Emilia-Romagna regional law no.3/2023; Lazio regional law no.10/2019; Piedmont regional law no.5/2024; Tuscany regional law no.71/2020; Umbria regional law no.2/2023; Molise regional law no.21/2022; Apulia regional law no.11/2025; Marche regional law no.191/2025.

[44] As of August 2025.

[45] eg, in C Iaione, 'The Co-City: Sharing, Collaborating, Cooperating, and Commoning in the City' (2016) 75 *American Journal of Economics and Sociology* 415, 427.

[46] On the necessity for a shift for a state–citizens relation from an adversarial to a collaborative one based on trust, see G Arena, 'Le Diverse Finalità Della Trasparenza Amministrativa' in F Merloni (ed), *La Trasparenza Amministrativa* (Giuffrè 2008).

[47] See ch 5 (n 33).

[48] On the idea of a 'società della cura', see G Arena, 'La "Società Della Cura" e Il Valore Politico Dei Piccoli Gesti Quotidiani' (*Labsus*, 2018): www.labsus.org/2018/01/la-societa-della-cura-un-progetto-fondato-sullempatia/.

the state–market divide.[49] In shared administration, public authorities support citizens in caring for common goods. Its legal framework protects citizens' freedom to act for collective interests, including both third-sector groups and unaffiliated active citizens.

The significance of shared administration within a wider public law paradigm becomes clearer when trying to define the form of democracy emerging from this new type of collaborative relationship between citizens and the state (through the key role of local authorities). Interestingly, while shared administration is a form of participation in doing, it also includes decision-making.[50] Citizens act through co-design with public authorities, where both sides plan initiatives together under Article 118(4) of the Constitution. This model, alongside participatory democracy, helps transform local governance from the bottom up through active community involvement.

All in all, though shared administration began as a theoretical model in 1997, its practical adoption via the Bologna Regulation in 2014 has led to rapid growth and structured networking. It offers local authorities a clear legal basis and tools to support citizens' participation in doing. The concept of participation itself is strengthened by the principle of horizontal subsidiarity, including not only a participation in decision-making processes, but an action-oriented participation in problem solving. As the model spreads, local authorities play an increasingly key role in strengthening democracy from the ground up.

A. The Bologna Regulation and Beyond[51]

Since its first elaboration in the city of Bologna, the regulation on the commons has spread to over 320[52] local authorities, boosting local governments' role in civic participation and care for the common good under Article 118(4) of the Constitution. A municipal regulation was chosen being a simple, flexible tool to implement horizontal subsidiarity and enable easy replication by other local

[49] We are referring to the groundbreaking book by Raghuram Rajan, *The Third Pillar: How Markets and the State Leave the Community Behind* (Penguin 2019). On the role of the community as the third actor beyond the state and the market, and its role in pursuing a civil economy, see also the lifetime works of Stefano Zamagni. As an example, see further L Bruni and S Zamagni, *Civil Economy: Another Idea of the Market* (Agenda Publishing 2016).

[50] U Allegretti, 'La Partecipazione Come "Utopia Realistica"' in A Valastro (ed), *Le Regole Locali Della Democrazia Partecipativa: Tendenze e Prospettive Dei Regolamenti Comunali* (Jovene 2016) 246.

[51] For this section, see also C Salati, 'The Forgotten Meaning of the EU Principle of Subsidiarity – Horizontal Subsidiarity in Italian Local Governments' (2023) Diversity Governance Papers, and E Alber and C Salati, 'Coupling Social Innovation and Local Government: Shared Administration in Commons Governance' in K Kössler and et al (eds), *Public Participation in Local Governance: An Urban–Rural Perspective* (Palgrave Macmillan 2025).

[52] This number is updated to August 2025. For the up-to-date number of cities that have approved the same Regulation and that are trying to promote (with more or less success) the collaborative model of shared administration, see the dedicated page on the webite of *Labsus*: www.labsus.org/i-regolamenti-per-lamministrazione-condivisa-dei-beni-comuni/.

authorities. The Regulation also enforces regulatory autonomy (Article 117(6)), giving normative capacity to territorial autonomies without state intervention.[53]

The prototype regulation[54] is structured in seven parts.

(1) General provisions and definitions. This section anchors the Regulation in constitutional principles like horizontal subsidiarity (Article 118(4)) and regulatory autonomy of local authorities (Article 117(6)). It affirms public authorities' duty to support citizen-led initiatives – regardless of residency or citizenship – whether spontaneous or prompted by local authorities. It defines key terms (for example, urban commons, active citizens, collaboration pacts) and sets out guiding criteria for the collaboration between the civic and the state sides, such as mutual trust and responsibility, transparency, civic autonomy, inclusivity, sustainability and proportionality, children participation, informality in the relation between citizens and public authorities, proximity.

(2) Procedural provisions. Local authorities may establish a shared administration office to support collaboration pacts, which may be ordinary (small-scale) or complex (requiring more planning and resources).[55]

(3) Actions on commons. The Regulation permits collaboration pacts to include care, regeneration and shared governance of public spaces of different types. It also includes cultural heritage assets as well as assets confiscated from organised crime.

(4) State support. Public authorities can back citizens' initiatives with insurance, financial incentives (for example, free use of public assets, tax exemptions and benefits), simplified bureaucratic procedures, facilitation towards self-funding initiatives, and education for active citizenship – including school-based pacts between students, teachers and parents.

(5) Communication, transparency and evaluation. Authorities must publicise collaboration efforts to foster community awareness. Transparency is key for inclusivity and for the evaluation of the results and real impact.

[53] The absence of a national law that would serve as a strong enhancer of the model has been underlined as a critical point in I Carlotto, 'I Beni Comuni e i Regolamenti per l'amministrazione Condivisa' in R Realdon (ed), *La Sussidiarietà Orizzontale Nel Titolo V Della Costituzione e La Sussidiarietà Generativa* (Cedam 2018). An important endorsement, however, arrived in 2017 when the Court of Auditors (Corte dei Conti) ruling no.26/2017 (12 f) stated that the constitutional principle of horizontal subsidiarity must also be applied without legislative intermediation, therefore guaranteeing firm support for the regulations for the shared administration of the commons.

[54] Our analysis uses the *Labsus* prototype, the key reference most cities adapt to their local needs when approving the Regulation. For the latest update (February 2025) see: www.labsus.org/wp-content/uploads/2024/06/febbraio.2025.PROTOTIPO-LABSUS.-REGOLAMENTO-SULLA-COLLABORAZIONE-TRA-CITTADINI-E-AMMINISTRAZIONI.pdf. For its English version, see: www.labsus.org/wp-content/uploads/2024/06/June.2024.REGULATION-ON-COLLABORATION-BETWEEN-CITIZENS-AND-ADMINISTRATIONS-FOR-THE-CARE-OF-COMMON-GOODS-1.pdf.

[55] See further above (n 58).

(6) Responsibility. Citizens personally assume civil liability, though authorities may offer specific insurance. A reconciliation process is also provided for disputes.
(7) Final provisions. Interestingly, a closing clause favours interpretations that prioritize citizens' needs over institutional convenience.

B. The Collaboration Pact[56]

To put in practice the Regulation, the co-design of collaboration pacts is needed. Since the Bologna Regulation, more than 8,000 collaboration pacts have been signed across Italy.[57] The collaboration pact ('patto di collaborazione') is a legal tool that turns citizens' potential into concrete actions for caring, regenerating and co-managing the commons together with public authorities. Collaboration pacts are written agreements that constitute an innovative legal form based on horizontal subsidiarity. They are signed by two sides: public officials (political representatives as well as civil servants with a managerial role), and active citizens, individually or in groups. The object is one or more defined activities of general interest – often care, regeneration, or shared governance of tangible, intangible or digital commons. These pacts enable citizen-led local problem-solving and democratic innovation. While the public side has always one signatory on behalf of the public authority, the civic side may include many actors, with others able to join later: in this sense, the pact 'remains always open' also after its official signature. Civic initiative is seen not as charity, but as aligning private and public interest under a wider general interest. Pacts can be ordinary when they target small-claims actions (for example, gardening, social gathering, cultural or educational activities), or complex when they require more negotiation steps for their approval because the actions are more elaborated (for example, restoring buildings of historical or cultural importance).[58]

The implementation of a collaboration pact generally follows four key steps. The process begins with a proposal for a general interest activity, usually initiated by citizens under Article 118(4), or sometimes prompted by local authorities. Next comes the co-design phase – a dialogue between citizens and public authorities to negotiate the concrete terms of the action (or actions) on a commons and the general interest object of their collaboration. Each pact includes: the signatories; the aim of general interest; the commons involved; tasks, resources and responsibilities; support measures provided by the public authority, location, insurance (if any), and duration. The third step is formal signing. Finally, the monitoring phase of the pact implementation

[56] For this section, see further Salati 'The Forgotten Meaning' (n 51). Additionally, see Alber and Salati (n 51).
[57] Data from the 2024 *Labsus* annual report: www.labsus.org/rapporto-labsus-2024/.
[58] Bombardelli (n 22) 564.

starts. If disputes arise, the Regulation provides for a reconciliation committee with three members – one from each side and a jointly chosen third.

Figure 1 The four steps of a collaboration pact (author's elaboration)

Interesting data about the use of the collaboration pact are coming from a recent quantitative and qualitative survey on a national-level overview on the usage of this tool published in 2024.[59] On the basis of data collected for that study, the survey revealed that the majority of collaboration pacts (48.5 per cent) were signed in local authorities with more than 250,000 inhabitants, with a discrete number (33.3 per cent) also in local authorities with a number of inhabitants between 60,000 and 250,000. This accounts for more than 80 per cent of collaboration pacts signed in urbanised areas. The policy areas of such collaboration pacts spans across different fields: among others, environment (45.52 per cent); urban design and furniture (14.02 per cent); culture (8.81 per cent); social inclusion (11.20 per cent); education (5.34 per cent), as well as others like welfare, co-design of public services, or work-related activities. With regard to the signatories on the civic side, the major actors are: associations (44.19 per cent); followed by individual citizens (23.91 per cent); informal groups (11.76 per cent); for-profit enterprises (5.66 per cent); schools (4.83 per cent); social enterprises (3.62 per cent), followed in lower percentages also by ecclesiastical entities, foundations, other public entities, professionals and universities. The commons object of the collaboration pacts are mostly tangible (67.26 per cent): often there is a coexistence of tangible and intangible (25.02 per cent), while the number of the agreements signed on intangible (7.35 per cent) and digital (0.18 per cent) is very little. The physical spaces object of collaboration pacts are in the vast majority of cases green areas (44.19 per cent), but pacts also take place in public squares and streets (23.91 per cent); buildings (11.76 per cent); schools (5.66 per cent); cultural centres like theatres or cinemas (3.62 per cent) as well as, for example, in libraries, religious places, brownfields in smaller percentages. The average duration is between one and three years in the majority of cases (51 per cent), with some collaboration pacts also being signed for one year (10 per cent), or more than three years (30 per cent). Usually there is a possibility of renewal beyond the agreed duration. The last useful data to report are those relating to the forms of support provided by public authorities to the active citizens' side, since some kind of support is almost always provided. Accordingly, public authorities usually supply materials

[59] The survey aimed to provide an up-to-date national overview of the use of collaboration pacts. The analysis was challenged primarily by difficulties in retrieving data from local authority websites. Out of 312 local authorities with a regulation on the commons, 71 had active collaboration pacts as of 31 December 2023, totaling 1,115 ongoing pacts. The full report, including extensive data and graphs, is available at: www.labsus.org/rapporto-labsus-2024/.

(30.85 per cent); promote and publicise the collaboration pact initiatives (25.65 per cent); and provide for insurance cover (10.13 per cent); additional forms of support include tax benefits, technical support, a symbolic economic contribution bureaucratic simplification, free availability of spaces. Often several concessions are given at the same time. All in all, these data provide an interesting insight into the use of the tool but are only part of a phenomenon that is still difficult to map accurately.

The legal nature of this tool remains debated, creating challenges such as determining the appropriate court for disputes (civil or administrative).[60] Scholars mainly offer two views: one links it to private law contracts ('contratti'), the other to public law agreements ('accordi'),[61] both referencing Law no.241/1990 on administrative procedure – Article 1(1-bis) for the former, Article 11 for the latter.[62] A third view sees them as innovative public–private partnerships involving civic actors.[63] Given the lack of consensus, further legal clarification is needed, though some suggest this tool might evolve into an independent legal category of its own.[64]

One challenge of this legal tool – beyond classification – is its ability to engage citizens involved in protest, extra-institutional forms of actions, or indifference,[65] as well as its adaptability across diverse contexts and initiatives.

[60] To date, likely only one appeal case has arisen, involving a Bologna collaboration pact and the protection of excluded third parties. An administrative judge confirmed jurisdiction. See, on that, L Muzi, 'L'amministrazione Condivisa Dei Beni Comuni Urbani: Il Ruolo Dei Privati Nell'ottica Del Principio Di Sussidiarietà Orizzontale' in F Di Lascio and F Giglioni (eds), *La Rigenerazione Di Beni e Spazi Urbani* (Il Mulino 2017) 134.

[61] For the diverse interpretations of doctrine on the nature of the Collaboration pacts, an all-embracing analysis was carried out in F Giglioni, 'Le Città Come Ordinamento Giuridico' (2018) 1 *Istituzioni Del Federalismo* 29, 55 ff. For the most recognised positions, on the first interpretation linked to private law the reference goes to G Arena, 'Democrazia Partecipativa e Amministrazione Condivisa' in A Valastro (ed), *Le Regole Locali Della Democrazia Partecipativa. Tendenze e Prospettive Dei Regolamenti Comunali* (Jovene 2016) 235; of the same idea is V Cerulli Irelli, 'L'amministrazione Condivisa Nel Sistema Del Diritto Amministrativo' in G Arena and M Bombardelli (eds), *L'amministrazione Condivisa* (Editoriale Scientifica 2022) 29. On the opposite side, for the classification of the collaboration pacts as agreements of public law it is possible to refer to the observations on Article 11, law no.241/1990 as an archetype ('norma archetipo') in F Giglioni and A Nervi, *Gli Accordi Delle Pubbliche Amministrazioni* (Edizioni Scientifiche Italiane 2019) 33 ff, 272 ff. The two authors see the *accordo* of Article 11 (law no.241/1990) as a negotiation between public administrations and private subjects that, according to a hybrid system, would operate at the border between private law and public law: considered in this way, they see in the *accordo* a great innovative potential still unexplored, that could also include all those relationships grounded in Article 118(4) of the Constitution. More recently see F Giglioni, 'Forme e Strumenti Dell'amministrazione Condivisa' in G Arena and M Bombardelli (eds), *L'Amministrazione Condivisa* (Editoriale Scientifica 2022) 86 ff.

[62] This different perspective on the nature of the tool is also reflected in the texts of the municipal Regulations, each city defining them accordingly to Article 1 or Article 11 according to their own view.

[63] This is the position advanced in C Iaione and E de Nictolis, 'The Role of Law in Relation to the New Urban Agenda and the European Urban Agenda' in NM Davidson and G Tewari (eds), *Law and the New Urban Agenda* (Routledge 2020) 61. The two authors refer to what could be referred to as public–community partnerships.

[64] P Michiara, 'I Patti Di Collaborazione e Il Regolamento per La Cura e La Rigenerazione Dei Beni Comuni Urbani. L'esperienza Del Comune Di Bologna' (2016) 2 *Aedon* 16 f.

[65] R Bartoletti and F Faccioli, 'Public Engagement, Local Polities, Civic Collaborations' (2016) *Social Media + Society* 7.

III. The Recognition of the Model by the Constitutional Court

Judgment no.131/2020 of the Constitutional Court, already mentioned in relation to general interest and social liberties,[66] is emerging as a landmark judgment for the shared administration model. It followed a constitutional review of a regional law applying Article 55 of the Third Sector Code to community cooperatives without official mention of them in a national law.[67] The Court's reasoning explored key aspects of the case, including public-third sector relations, horizontal subsidiarity, general interest activities, social liberties, the shared administration model, and the relation with EU law.

Starting from the interpretation of Article 55 that states that public administrations have an obligation[68] to include third-sector organisations in the co-planning and co-design of activities of general interest, the Court said that this form of collaboration constitutes to date one of the most significant applications of the constitutional principle of horizontal subsidiarity. Since the publication of this judgment, third-sector organisations and public authorities, therefore, should favour a collaborative and not competitive relationship among them: this judgment constitutes the beginning of a constitutional law of the third sector,[69] with the third-sector organisations having been recognised as direct enhancers of the constitutional principle of horizontal subsidiarity. At the same time, the Court emphasised that Article 118(4) of the Constitution extends beyond the third sector, underlining how individuals' creativity for implementing actions of solidarity took many different forms throughout history. Horizontal subsidiarity allows citizens, not just public authorities, to act for the general interest. However, the Court noted the lack of specific legislation regulating such autonomous citizen initiatives, with Article 118(4) remaining the sole reference.[70] The clear recognition of active citizens' contributions to their community with activities of general interest should be seen, indeed, as the next frontier for development in the legislation and in the jurisprudence of the Court.

The second major point of reflection elaborated by the Court consists in the recognition of a channel of shared administration ('un canale di amministrazione condivisa') between public authorities and third-sector organisations, which is an alternative to the one of the market since it assumes a diverse model of action not founded on utilitarian exchanges, but on solidarity actions based on mutual

[66] See ch 5, section III.B and ch 5, section III.C.

[67] The question was eventually declared unfounded by the constitutional review of the Court, as community cooperatives ('cooperative di comunità') have to be included within social enterprises ('imprese sociali').

[68] E Rossi, 'Il Fondamento Del Terzo Settore è Nella Costituzione. Prime Osservazioni Sulla Sentenza n. 131 Del 2020 Della Corte Costituzionale' (2020) 3 *Forum Di Quaderni Costituzionali* 53.

[69] L Gori, 'Sentenza 131/2020: Sta Nascendo Un Diritto Costituzionale Del Terzo Settore' (2020) *Impresa Sociale*; Rossi (n 68).

[70] L Gori, 'Terzo Settore Come Protagonista Dell'attuazione Della Costituzione' in S Pellizzari and C Borzaga (eds), *Terzo Settore e Pubblica Amministrazione: La Svolta Della Corte Costituzionale* (Euricse 2020) 39.

exchanges. The area of application is therefore a new and unexplored one, paving the way for public–private relationships based on a logic of sharing and mutual consent.

A third key aspect of this case is the recognition of a 'third space' beyond state and market structures, where social liberties are organised to foster solidarity. The Court refers to EU law, highlighting that supranational law upholds not only the principle of competition, but also of solidarity. It asserts that Member States can design organisational models based on solidarity, especially for socially significant activities. Solidarity is thus a reference point in EU law for socially committed initiatives and, as such, strengthens the principle of horizontal subsidiarity.

One last aspect to note is that though the judgment never explicitly mentions 'common goods', nevertheless these should be considered as implicitly supported thanks to the reference to the model of shared administration. Since the Court traces this model back to the EU principle of solidarity, and since this model is realised through commons-based initiatives, it can be stated that the commons may have implicit constitutional support under EU law.

All in all, the key contribution of judgment no.131/2020 of the Italian Constitutional Court is to have anchored the Italian organisational model of shared administration not only to the Italian constitutional principle of subsidiarity in its horizontal dimension together with other constitutional principles, but also to the EU principle of solidarity that – according to the Court – has parallel value and importance with the EU principle of competition. Within the EU legal order, in fact, solidarity belongs to those principles that constitute the foundation of the EU construction and integration process and implies not only solidarity-based relations between states, but also between individuals. In this sense, EU solidarity has been suggested[71] as the ideal principle upon which to build a new European constitutional paradigm for creating an enabling environment for solidarity-based collaborations – among which are commons-related forms of civic participation.[72] This has been affirmed not only within EU primary law (primarily by Article 2 of the Treaty on European Union), but also through the rulings of the Court of Justice of the EU.[73]

IV. Civic Participation Through the Commons (CPC) in Italian Cities: Challenges and Innovative Pathways

The Bologna Regulation began as a pilot and has since become a model for other local authorities, each adapting it to their own context.[74] These authorities are

[71] S Rodotà, *Solidarietà. Un'utopia Necessaria* (Laterza 2014).

[72] S Rodotà, *Vivere La Democrazia* (Laterza 2018) 93 ff for the link between solidarity and the commons.

[73] See further on that, G Gotti, 'La Sussidiarietà Orizzontale Nello Spazio Costituzionale Europeo' (2025) *Associazione Italiana dei Costituzionalisti* 323. Additionally, see M Ross, 'Solidarity – A New Constitutional Paradigm for the EU?' in M Ross and Y Borgmann-Prebil (eds), *Promoting Solidarity in the European Union* (Oxford University Press 2010).

[74] C Salati, 'Città e Sussidiarietà Orizzontale: Orientamenti Dottrinali Dal Caso Italiano per l'Unione Europea' (2024) Italian Papers on Federalism.

pioneering horizontal subsidiarity, fostering collaboration between public and civic entities. This has led to the idea of 'informal public law',[75] which gives legal recognition to community-led practices like shared administration, previously considered outside formal positive law. Rather than ignoring these grass-roots efforts, informal public law brings them under legal cover. Although now also adopted by most metropolitan cities[76] and some local authorities' associations (mountain communities, and unions of municipalities),[77] the Regulation remains most common among municipalities. Still – in line with the more general trend also at the international and EU level – scholars and institutions increasingly refer to 'cities' and a 'law of cities' ('diritto delle città') that goes beyond mere administrative units, where cities are perceived as communities of citizens worth receiving autonomous attention by the legal doctrine.[78] In the Italian context, in fact, the use of the term 'cities' extends beyond the 14 Italian metropolitan areas defined by law.[79] 'Cities' is used to highlight their role as political communities, not just administrative units, building on the original distinction in Roman law between *urbs* (urban physical city) and *civitas* (term used for the exercise of citizenship rights by Roman citizens).[80] Unlike the exclusive Greek *polis* – which granted rights only to people of the same origin – the Roman *civitas* referred to a wider idea of city where people are subject to the same law. In this sense, Italian cities are evolving into laboratories for collaboration between citizens and public authorities, legitimising informal public law practices like CPC. This supports using the term 'cities' to highlight their role as political communities beyond administrative

[75] On the concept of informal public law ('diritto pubblico informale') see F Giglioni, 'Order without Law in the Experience of Italian Cities' (2017) 9 *Italian Journal of Public Law* 291, and F Giglioni, 'Il Diritto Pubblico Informale Alla Base Della Riscoperta Delle Città Come Ordinamento Giuridico' (2018) 2 *Rivista Giuridica Dell'edilizia* 3. See ch 4 (n 104).

[76] Torino, Milano, Genova, Bologna, Venezia, Firenze, Bari, Rome, Palermo, Reggio Calabria, Sassari. For the up-to-date list of metropolitan cities, see: temi.camera.it/leg19DIL/post/le-citt-metropolitane.html; for the up-to date-list of metropolitan cities and other local authorities that have adopted the regulation, see: www.labsus.org/i-regolamenti-per-lamministrazione-condivisa-dei-beni-comuni/.

[77] eg, the Unione della Romagna Faentina, and the XI Comunita' montana del Lazio (last update in August 2025).

[78] See ch 4, section III. Within the Italian legal debate see, for example, F Giglioni, 'Verso Un Diritto Delle Città. Le Città Oltre Il Comune' in E Carloni and F Cortese (eds), *Diritto Delle Autonomie Territoriali* (Cedam 2020); F Cortese, 'Che Cosa Succede in Città?' (2024) 3 *Munus*; F Pizzolato et al (eds), *La Città e La Partecipazione Tra Diritto e Politica* (Giappichelli 2019); R Cavallo Perin, 'Beyond the Municipality: The City, Its Rights and Its Rites' (2013) 5 *Italian Journal of Public Law* 307; G Pavani, 'From Smart to Sharing? Presente e Futuro Delle Città (al Di Là Delle Etichette)' (2019) 4 *Istituzioni Del Federalismo* 849; F Pizzolato et al (eds), *La Città Oltre Lo Stato* (Giappichelli 2021).

[79] We are referring to law no.56/2014 (*Legge 7 aprile 2014, n. 56, Disposizioni sulle città metropolitane, sulle province, sulle unioni e fusioni di comuni*). The metropolitan cities in Italy are Bari, Bologna, Cagliari, Catania, Firenze, Genova, Messina, Milano, Napoli, Palermo, Reggio Calabria, Roma Capitale, Sassari, Torino, Venezia. On the process of (failed) reforms of local government in urban areas in Italy and, in particular, on the confusing discipline of metropolitan cities, see R Medda, *Il Governo Locale Delle Aree Urbane in Italia* (Edizioni Scientifiche Italiane 2022). For another critical discussion, see E Longo, 'Local Governments and Metropolitan Cities' in E Arban et al (eds), *Federalism and Constitutional Law: The Italian Contribution to Comparative Regionalism* (Routledge 2021).

[80] Giglioni, 'Verso Un Diritto Delle Città' (n 78). See also, ch 1 (n 24).

or national classifications. Italian cities are the space of urban commons and are sometimes considered commons themselves.[81] The emerging field of the law of cities that is being experimented at the local level in Italy is proving cities to be at the frontier in the enhancement of democracy through the supportive and promotional role of legal instruments and of public authorities, which is taking place through the framework of shared administration. This collaboration redefines the relationship between state and citizens, transcending the formal borders between constitutional law, administrative law, urban law (and other disciplines), and highlighting the creative role of the law itself, of cities, and citizens for actions relating to the general interest of a community, in a wider dimension of (local) governance.

However, what is true is that there are still obscure and precarious aspects relating to the case of Italian cities. First, critics highlight cases of misapplication by public authorities, with some cities merely doing 'cutting and pasting' of the prototype regulation without adapting it to local contexts.[82] This shows a lack of understanding of the deeper paradigm shift. Second, some citizens also misuse the agreements for private gain, bypassing in this way fair procedures rather than embracing the subsidiarity principle. Third, this (subsidiarity) paradigm shift is likely to occur in social contexts that have certain favourable features and not in others, therefore raising the question of objective cultural difficulties. Fourth, the major precarious aspect is that the shared administration model is developing from the bottom up, without a dedicated national law – despite support from third-sector legislation, regional laws and Constitutional Court rulings. This may not be enough to secure its long-term stability and growth. Fifth, since it is not easy to have a concrete indication of its impact, the collaboration pact tool is sometimes criticised as being unnecessary in comparison to other already existing tools.[83] All these challenges highlight that the organisational model of shared administration is currently a niche innovation, still relatively new, and not yet predominant or fully established.

Notwithstanding that, Part III of this book captured the ongoing transformation in Italy driven by the constitutionalisation of horizontal subsidiarity and the growing engagement of public law scholars, who are rethinking legal paradigms in response to urban social dynamics and emerging phenomena. The Italian case illustrates how social practices can spark legal change, as seen in the development of the shared administration model, Constitutional Court judgment no.131/2020,

[81] On the idea of the *city as a commons* itself, see further C Iaione, 'Città e Beni Comuni' in G Arena and C Iaione (eds), *L'Italia Dei Beni Comuni* (Carocci 2012); C Iaione, 'La Città Come Bene Comune' (2013) 1 *Aedon* 31; G Arena, 'Le Città Come Beni Comuni' (*Labsus*, 2013); SR Foster and C Iaione, 'The City as a Commons' (2016) 34 *Yale Law & Policy Review* 281. See also further, ch 7 (n 17).

[82] As observed by SR Foster and C Iaione, 'Ostrom in the City. Design Principles and Practices for the Urban Commons' in B Hudson et al (eds), *Routledge Handbook of the Study of the Commons* (Routledge 2019) 246.

[83] Intrestingly, some scholars found that collaboration pacts effectively engage citizens who never undertook previous initiatives of civic participation: see C Iaione, I Pais and E de Nictolis, 'Valutare: La Valutazione Dei Patti Di Collaborazione' in R Paltrinieri (ed), *Culture e pratiche di partecipazione* (FrancoAngeli 2020).

and some regional laws. It is important to mention that, while the focus of this book is on cities due to urbanisation and concentrated challenges (as discussed in chapter four), the subsidiarity shift and shared administration model are also relevant to rural contexts.[84]

All in all, the collaboration pact has become a platform for bottom-up innovation – uniting people across divisions and ideologies around a shared general interest, and putting individuals' active liberty at the centre, backed by supportive public authorities. The Italian specificity is that, unlike other similar experiences which usually exist within mere projects, since 2001 civic initiatives are transformed into institutional practices through the collaboration pact tool and are rooted in the principle of horizontal subsidiarity.

In conclusion, while it is still too early to assess the full democratic impact of this new form of civic participation (CPC) rooted in horizontal subsidiarity, Part III has presented key data from the Italian context: over 320 cities have adopted the regulation for the shared administration of the commons, and thousands of collaboration pacts have been signed until now. From this framework, five core pillars emerge from the Italian case that can inform our research: (1) the principle of horizontal subsidiarity and its essential implementation through a supportive role of public authorities towards citizens' initiatives for the general interest; (2) the practical implementation of horizontal subsidiarity through the organisational model of shared administration (consisting of the regulation and collaboration pacts); (3) an action-oriented innovative form of civic participation supported by shared administration: namely, a civic participation through the commons (CPC); (4) the EU principle of solidarity as the reference point in EU law for this new type of collaboration occurring between public authorities and citizens based on shared administration; and (5) the emergence of the city as a legal category looking beyond administrative boundaries, where informal activities could be given legal value outside positive law, under the cover of an informal public law. With all its limitations, we consider the case of Italian cities paradigmatic for its ability to respond to new challenges and phenomena through, on the one hand, a solid anchoring to constitutional principles and, on the other, a creative use of law.

[84] The same consideration was given with regard to EU cities as urban local authorities in contrast to rural local authorities: see ch 4 (n 119).

PART IV

Facing the Commons Challenge in EU Cities

7

EU Cities as Laboratories for Civic Participation Through the Commons (CPC)

I. The Commons in the EU: Objective Difficulties of a Debate in the Making

Innovative forms of civic participation through the commons (CPC) is emerging across not only Italian, but also other EU cities. Italy stands out for institutionalising CPC via a constitutional and legal framework that fosters horizontal collaboration between cities and citizens, exemplified by the shared administration model. In addition to that, Italian legal scholarship also contributed significantly to the Rodotà Commission's 2007 draft law containing a constitutionally oriented definition of the commons, and Naples contributed with the declaration of urban civic and collective use of many common goods.[1] These developments place what we may call the 'Italian legal approach to the commons' at the forefront of legal innovation on the commons in and beyond Europe.[2] While CPC is gaining ground, the broader EU legal landscape remains unclear, making it difficult to provide a comprehensive overview: in this sense, the commons in the EU still constitute 'a debate in the making'. Nonetheless, this section offers an analytical review of major ongoing developments – still very fluid and mainly non-legal.

[1] As seen in ch 6, section I.

[2] This consideration draws on insights from interdisciplinary literature and leading commons activists, both in Europe and globally. For an overview of Italy's unique experiences and academic debate on the commons, see A Simonati, 'The (Draft) European Charter of the Commons – Between Opportunities and Challenges' (2018) 16(2) *Central European Public Administration Review* 91, 101. Additionally, it is interesting to report a reflection in C Vercellone et al, 'Managing the Commons in the Knowledge Economy' (d-cent Project, 2015), available at: shs.hal.science/halshs-01180341. The authors explain the uniqueness of the Italian legal contribution to the commons through the work of the Rodotà Commission and the municipal regulations on the commons (in addition to the grass-roots initiatives across the country of commoners) in this way: 'the historic inheritance of a tradition of decentralisation and local self-government that dates from the Revolution of the Comune in the 12th Century, the belated birth of a unified State and the fragility of its legitimacy, the intensity of social movements that have crisscrossed it since the crisis of Fordism, partly contribute to explaining why Italy is, in Europe, the place in which the same legal deliberation on common goods has been brought further ahead and faced in the most explicit way'.

To clarify this, it is important to first address some key considerations. First, the term 'commons' lacks a consistent definition across the EU, often used interchangeably with 'common goods' or 'common good'. This definitional ambiguity is present in both Italian[3] and broader international contexts, with numerous (non-legal) interpretations that risk leading to the conclusion that if everything is a commons, then nothing in fact is.[4] Language barriers and national differences further complicate consensus on a shared meaning of the commons in the EU.[5] Second, this difficulty in defining the boundaries of the commons as an object of study reflects two other challenges: interdisciplinarity, where the involvement of various academic disciplines sometimes leads to a terminological confusion that prevents from developing a shared language,[6] or to an incorrect appropriation of terms from other disciplinary contexts;[7] and transdisciplinarity,[8] which calls for integrating insights from both scholars and practitioners – especially the 'commoners'[9] directly engaged in experiences of 'commoning'. This confusion of approaches, knowledge and understandings leads us to a third problem, which is the one of classification. Many indeed have been the attempts at providing for taxonomies of the commons, often once again transplanted from one disciplinary field to another without taking into account the field of origin of a specific qualification. Among the others, the commons have been qualified as 'natural commons',[10] 'information

[3] Despite this, the definition in municipal regulations on the commons has become increasingly widespread and implemented. Notably, the Italian term *beni comuni* is used to translate both 'commons' and 'common goods' (see ch 6 (n 1)).

[4] Rodotà strongly warned about this risk: 'we must escape the temptation of the extension of the qualification as commons to every good or service. We are risking the inflation. We risk losing the specificity of the common. If all is a common, nothing is a common' (S Rodotà, 'Constituting the Commons in the Context of State, Law and Politics' in *Economics and the Common(s): From Seed Form to Core Paradigm* (2013), available at: boellblog.org/wp-content/uploads/2013/10/ECC-Rodota-keynote.pdf).

[5] On the relationship between law and language in the EU legal context and on the fact that, however, 'despite the lack of correspondence among EU categorical and conceptual structure, legal language, court enforcement and spirit of the people (social group), shared contexts of meanings within the EU and the national contexts are already flourishing', see further, E Ioriatti, 'Common Contexts of Meaning in the European Legal Setting: Opening Pandora's Box?' (2022) 36 *International Journal for the Semiotics of Law* 275.

[6] For some observations on interdisciplinarity when researching the commons, see LA Fennell, 'Ostrom's Law: Property Rights in the Commons' (2011) 5 *International Journal of the Commons* 9, 22 f.

[7] In Italy, for example, legal scholars often define 'beni comuni' using Elinor Ostrom's economic concept of the commons, appropriating a category that economists instead translate with another term ('beni collettivi'): on this mismatch, see G Gios, 'Beni Collettivi o Beni Comuni? Una Lettura Della Distinzione Tra Profili Dominicali e Modelli Di Gestione in Base Alla Teoria Economica' in M Bombardelli (ed), *Prendersi Cura Dei Beni Comuni per Uscire Dalla Crisi* (Editoriale Scientifica 2016). Additionally, see ch 6 (n 1).

[8] See further, C Rigolot, 'Transdisciplinarity as a Discipline and a Way of Being: Complementarities and Creative Tensions' (2020) 7 *Humanities and Social Sciences Communications* 100.

[9] 'Commoners' is the term generally used for referring to activists involved in commons initiatives. On commoners and 'the transformational language of the commons' as a result of larger collectives, see the introduction in D Bollier and S Helfrich, *The Wealth of the Commons: A World beyond Market and State* (The Commons Strategy Group 2013).

[10] Also considered as 'traditional commons', natural commons are for example communal lands, water reserves, fisheries, or forests: they constituted the object of research of Elinor Ostrom in E Ostrom,

and knowledge commons',[11] 'urban commons',[12] 'cultural commons',[13] 'global commons',[14] 'digital commons'.[15] The most well-known attempt at classifying different categories of commons so far has been the one that used the generic label of 'new commons'.[16] More and more categories are emerging and different authors like to introduce their own categories. Additionally, many concepts have been read under the lenses of commons, like for example 'the city as a commons',[17]

Governing the Commons: The Evolution of Institutions for Collective Actions (Cambridge University Press 1990). As it has been written, 'the traditional commons of North-West Europe, whether conceived of as lands or rights, are remnants of the premedieval land use systems where significant use rights were held jointly by the local population and managed by their customs': see E Berge, 'Protected Areas and Traditional Commons: Values and Institutions' (2005) 60 *Norsk Geografisk Tidsskrift/Norwegian Journal of Geography* 72.

[11] C Hess, 'The Unfolding of the Knowledge Commons' (2012) 8(1) *St Antony's International Review* 13, where knowledge is considered 'as all useful ideas, information, and data in whatever form in which it is expressed or obtained … whether indigenous, scientific, scholarly, or non-academic. It included creative works – music and the visual and theatrical art' (14 f). The author recognises that knowledge commons are also global commons (20). She also gives a general definition of the commons as 'a resource shared by a group of people that is subject to social dilemmas' (14).

[12] This term generally refers to commons in urban settings, though its scope – whether limited to tangible or also intangible goods – remains debated. Sheila R Foster first introduced the concept: see SR Foster, 'Collective Action and the Urban Commons' (2011) 87 *Notre Dame Law Review* 57. Italy adopted this term in the Bologna regulation (see ch 6). The first international conference on the topic took place in Bologna in 2015 (more information at: urbancommons.labgov.city/).

[13] They are defined as 'cultures expressed and shared by a community. Cultures can be generally recognized as systems of intellectual resources … Some examples include languages, the cultural atmosphere and image of cities, the type of a renowned wine such as Barolo, the traditional knowledge held by indigenous communities and the creativity expressed by a designers' community or an artistic movement' in E Bertacchini et al, 'Defining Cultural Commons' in E Bertacchini et al (eds), *Cultural Commons: A New Perspective on the Production and Evolution of Cultures* (Edward Elgar Publishing 2012) For a contribution advocating for a participatory governance of cultural heritage (considered as a commons) see C Iaione et al, 'Participatory Governance of Culture and Cultural Heritage: Policy, Legal, Economic Insights From Italy' (2022) 4 *Frontiers in Sustainable Cities*. For a recent contribution on the cultural commons as arenas of transformation (and with a claim towards EU institutions to support the commons through cultural policies) see R Cirillo and MF De Tullio (eds), *Healing Culture, Reclaiming Commons, Fostering Care: A Proposal for EU Cultural Policies* (Italian Institute for the Future 2021).

[14] Global commons are, for example, climate change, high seas, biodiversity, atmosphere, sustainability, globalisation, knowledge, the space. See C Hess, 'Mapping the New Commons' (Paper, 12th Biennial Conference of the International Association for the Study of the Commons, Governing Shared Resources: Connecting Local Experience to Global Challenges, 14–18 July 2008) 31.

[15] Knowledge, software and design are considered as digital commons in M Bauwens et al, *Peer to Peer: The Commons Manifesto* (University of Westminster Press 2019).

[16] Hess, 'Mapping the New Commons' (n 14). As she says, 'simply put, new commons (NC) are various types of shared resources that have recently evolved or have been recognized as commons. They are commons without pre-existing rules or clear institutional arrangements'. In order to capture the new types of commons, the author draws a map (13) according to which new commons include: cultural commons, knowledge commons, medical and health commons, neighbourhood commons, infrastructure commons, market as commons, traditional commons and global commons.

[17] For the city as a commons, see SR Foster and C Iaione, 'The City as a Commons' (2016) 34 *Yale Law & Policy Review* 281. According to this theory and starting from the definition given by Elinor Ostrom of the commons, cities themselves are identified as commons, as a consequence of the fact that they have a great variety of resources that are produced, used and managed in a shared way. The theory is based on a survey of experiences from all around the world carried out within a 5-year project and tries

'food as a commons',[18] 'the commons as a model of global governance'.[19] The literature offers many more definitions of commons, but no shared taxonomy exists, and the concept remains widely interpreted by scholars worldwide.[20]

Despite variations, the commons generally refer to resources whose governance is shared by a community, following rules distinct from market or state control.[21] This governance occurs in a space between private and public spheres, based on cooperative rather than competitive schemes. Recently, the concept has been summarised[22] by three keywords: 'community', 'commoning' (the practice) and 'common property', managed and owned outside traditional state or market frameworks.

II. The Commons and the EU Legal Order

The term 'commons' has become a buzz word, reflecting the complexity of this research field. This chapter focuses on potential legal contributions to the commons within EU primary law, highlighting a significant gap: no studies have yet connected the commons with European constitutional law or offered comparative analyses across the 27 Member States.[23] Therefore, this book aims to provide an initial framework to explore this intersection.

to put forward some design principles that collaborative cities should rely upon, namely: (1) collaborative governance; (2) an enabling state; (3) social and economic pooling; (4) legal experimentalism; and (5) technological justice. Together with a precise policy cycle, and some tools, their design principles constitute the so called 'Co-city Protocol', which has been used by the two authors throughout many contributions in order to theorise a policy framework that cities worldwide can adopt in their transition for becoming a collaborative city (indeed, a co-city). The website of the project is: commoning.city/. The most recent contribution to this theory is SR Foster and C Iaione, *Co-Cities* (MIT Press 2022).

[18] See further the recent work of JL Vivero-Pol et al, *Routledge Handbook of Food as a Commons* (Routledge 2019): the book contributes to understanding how food and food systems can be thought, interpreted and practised around the paradigms of commons and commoning.

[19] See further, M Deleixhe, 'Conclusion: Is the Governance of the Commons a Model for a New Global Governance?' in S Cogolati and J Wouters (eds), *The Commons and a New Global Governance* (2018).

[20] Even the two sources (online webpages) of the International Association for the study of the Commons (iasc-commons.org/) and the Digital library on the commons of Indiana University (dlc.dlib.indiana.edu/dlc/contentguidelines#information_commons) that are considered as among the reference points for scholars on commons worldwide do not provide for a clear understanding of how to properly classify the concept of commons.

[21] See the key contribution of Ostrom (n 10).

[22] D Bollier, *Think Like a Commoner: A Short Introduction to the Life of the Commons* (New Society Publishers 2011) as reported in M Bauwens and Y Onzia, *A Commons Transition Plan for the City of Ghent* (City of Ghent and P2P Foundation 2017) 8.

[23] It is interesting to mention that also the most recent and authoritative collective publications on the commons contain no contributions glancing at the European constitutional law in the EU legal context, nor at a comparative analysis among EU Member States. We are referring, for example, to B Hudson et al, *Routledge Handbook of the Study of the Commons* (Routledge 2019); and SR Foster and CF Swiney, *The Cambridge Handbook of Commons Research Innovations* (Cambridge University Press 2022).

According to our research, there seem to be seven main aspects and potential domains to consider for looking at the commons within the EU legal order: (a) property; (b) governance; (c) state aid; (d) public–private partnerships; (e) the social dimension of the EU; (f) services of general interest; and (g) human rights.[24]

(a) Property. Concerning property, the contribution of law has been primarily focused on the investigation concerning the definition and the legal regime of the commons. Since the problem of property was already contained in the economic debate on the commons,[25] it is natural that among legal scholars the first connection to the topic was found by property scholars, who therefore saw private law – and more precisely the field of property law – as the appropriate ground to use for giving a theoretical framework to the commons.[26] This also occurred within a wider critique to economic and political transformations determined by neoliberalism.[27] However, a more extensive debate about commons/common goods exists in domestic legal orders of single EU Member States,[28] and not in relation to the EU legal order for one fundamental reason which is contained in Article 345 of the Treaty on the Functioning of the European Union (TFEU): namely, the fact that 'the Treaties shall in no way prejudice the rules in Member States governing the system of property ownership'. The EU has, indeed, no competence on the system of property ownership.[29] Because of that, many scholars have long been advocating for a shift in approaching the commons looking not at their ownership, but at their governance (or management) together with the community around them.[30]

(b) Governance. The governance of the commons extends beyond property ownership, marking a second key aspect of a potential legal contribution. This shift in perspective aligns with Ostrom's ideas, emphasising the possibility of successful management of natural resources by communities. The idea that

[24] This outline is according to the main contributions that we have found in the literature. This, however, remains our perspective, and we therefore make no claim to generality. Additionally, it goes far beyond the aim of this work to go deeper into each one of these aspects: our intention within this chapter is limited to providing a general overview. In order to provide an in-depth account of all these identified aspects, further research should be carried out as a potential follow-up of this work.

[25] Fennell (n 6).

[26] This is very clearly illustrated in MR Marella, 'The Commons as a Legal Concept' (2016) 28 *Law Critique* 61.

[27] eg, see U Mattei and A Quarta, 'Right to the City or Urban Commoning? Thoughts on the Generative Transformation of Property Law' (2015) 1 *Italian Law Journal* 303.

[28] Analysing property law arrangements relating to the commons in EU Member States is clearly beyond the scope of this book; for that, see comparative legal studies such as M Spanò, 'Private Law Arrangements for the Commons: A New Comparative Perspective' in F Girard and C Frison (eds), *The Commons, Plant Breeding and Agricultural Research* (Routledge 2018).

[29] Very clear on that are F Giglioni, 'Beni Comuni e Autonomie Nella Prospettiva Europea: Città e Cittadinanze' in M Bombardelli (ed), *Prendersi Cura Dei Beni Comuni per Uscire Dalla Crisi* (Editoriale Scientifica 2016) 160 f, and S Cornella, 'Beni Comuni e Disciplina Europea Sugli Aiuti Di Stato' in M Bombardelli (ed), *Prendersi Cura Dei Beni Comuni per Uscire Dalla Crisi* (Editoriale Scientifica 2016).

[30] Among the others, Simonati (n 2) 94 writes that 'it may be useful changing the point of view: from the kind of ownership to the rules about the management of the commons, possibly with a direct involvement of the communities of users'.

it is possible to get out of the dualism between private property and public property leads, indeed, towards the issue of governance (or management) of commons notwithstanding their ownership regime. Often, the ownership of a good does not align with its use. In the EU context, this makes governance based on functionality more viable than on ownership. As an example, this shift constitutes the core aspect of the regulations on the commons that many Italian cities – as we saw – have adopted in order to deal with the grass-roots initiatives of care, regeneration and shared governance of the commons coming from active citizens. This shift looking at the functionality of a good and not at its ownership has allowed the model of shared administration to spread around the country notwithstanding the lack of a legally binding category of common goods in property law: on the other hand, it relied on the constitutional principles of horizontal subsidiarity, participation and regulatory autonomy of local governments which as we saw also have their correspondents among European constitutional principles. However, challenges remain – especially in determining who defines what counts as commons and who should govern them. Ultimately, unlike the private law focus on property, this governance approach stems from a public law perspective.

(c) State aid. The third aspect this book identifies in the search for legal domains in relation to the commons in the EU legal order is the one of state aid.[31] Addressed in Articles 107 and 108 TFEU, within the EU legal order state aid essentially constitutes 'any aid granted by a Member State or through State resources in any form whatsoever which distorts or threatens to distort competition by favouring certain undertakings or the production of certain goods …, in so far as it affects trade between Member States'. According to EU law, they 'shall … be incompatible with the internal market'.[32] As is usually the case with any rule, the Treaties provide for some exceptions[33] towards enterprises that contribute to the safeguarding or the promotion of goods that the doctrine has actually qualified as commons: this is the case, for example, of the possibility of state aid towards the promotion of culture and heritage conservation, and for environmental protection. The matter of state aid therefore may show that – despite the fact that it is occurring in an indirect way – the EU actually already provides for some support towards the commons.[34]

(d) Public–Private Partnerships. The fourth aspect that may be an indication of a potential contribution of EU law to the commons debate comes from the delivery of public services through public private partnerships (PPPs), within the wider EU law discipline of the regulation of public procurement, which

[31] Fundamental on this link is the contribution of Cornella (n 29).

[32] Article 107(1) TFEU.

[33] The exceptions are contained in Commission Regulation (EU) No 651/2014 of 17 June 2014 declaring certain categories of aid compatible with the internal market in application of Articles 107 and 108 of the Treaty Text with EEA relevance, OJ L187, 26 June 2014, at: eur-lex.europa.eu/legal-content/EN/TXT/?uri=OJ:L:2014:187:TOC.

[34] Cornella (n 29).

constitutes a key aspect of EU internal market integration.[35] Briefly speaking, some authors have argued[36] that within the broad discipline on PPPs it is possible to experiment newly conceived public partnerships not only with the private sector, but also with civil society and local communities. In particular, according to that there may be a chance to use this legal tool for defining collaborations on certain goods or services conceived as commons, so that new Public–Community partnerships (PCPs),[37] Public–Civic Partnerships (PCPs),[38] Public–Commons Partnership[39] (as they have been theorised) or other types of hybrid partnerships[40] could eventually be used for supporting initiatives on the commons. So far, however, it remains unclear how partnerships can be applied to the commons.

(e) Social dimension of the EU. The fifth aspect concerns the social dimension of the EU, and more precisely the development of a 'social market economy', for referring to the constitutionalisation within the Lisbon Treaty of a vision outlining the contours of an EU economic integration not only founded on the single market based on the principle of competition, but also complemented by a social solidarity dimension.[41] Grounded in Article 3(3) of the Treaty on European Union (TEU,)[42] the concept of social market economy has no concrete legal implication by itself, but nonetheless it constitutes the European constitutional reference point for the development of social policies in different fields. This is indeed the

[35] As an introduction on partnerships within public procurement we may refer further to the chapter 'Procurement and partnerships' in CH Bovis, *EU Public Procurement Law* (Edward Elgar Publishing 2012).

[36] C Iaione and E de Nictolis, 'The Role of Law in Relation to the New Urban Agenda and the European Urban Agenda' in NM Davidson and G Tewari (eds), *Law and the New Urban Agenda* (Routledge 2020) 58 ff.

[37] Also defined as Public–Private–People Partnerships (PPPPs) in ibid 59.

[38] D Ciaffi and T de Groot, *From the Netherlands the Idea of Public-Civic Partnership as a Declination of Sharing Administration* (*Labsus* 2021).

[39] This term was defined for proposing a tool for institutions to enable and empower the collective/social peer-creation of common value: see on that, Tommaso Fattori, *Public-Commons Partnership and the Commonification of that which is Public*: commonsblog.files.wordpress.com/2007/10/fattori-commonification-of-that-which-is-public.pdf. For an additional explanation of this idea, the work of the commoners community of the P2P Foundation could be consulted at: wiki.p2pfoundation.net/Public-Commons_Partnership.

[40] Beyond the partnerships already noted, scholars and practitioners have explored various innovative models – often using different terms for similar ideas – such as Public–Private–People Partnerships (PPPPs) (for example, see on that G Nesti, 'Defining and Assessing the Transformational Nature of Smart City Governance: Insights from Four European Cases' (2020) 86(1) *International Review of Administrative Sciences* 29); Public–Civil Partnerships (PCPs) (for example, see on that Dirk Holemans, *Introducing the Partner State: Public-Civil Partnerships for a Better City* (21 June 2019): www.nesta.org.uk/blog/introducing-partner-state-public-civil-partnerships-better-city/); Public–Private–Civic Partnerships (PPCPs) (C Iaione, *La Città Come Bene Comune* (Labsus 2011).

[41] To start, see the introduction in D Ferri and F Cortese (eds), *The EU Social Market Economy and the Law* (Routledge 2019).

[42] See additionally Article 9 TFEU: 'In defining and implementing its policies and activities, the Union shall take into account requirements linked to the promotion of a high level of employment, the guarantee of adequate social protection, the fight against social exclusion, and a high level of education, training and protection of human health.'

direction pursued by the EU Commission[43] in its work-in-progress commitment to the elaboration of an overarching framework for what goes under the name of 'social economy'. This term refers to all those entities providing for goods and services 'with different business and organizational models' operating in a large variety of economic sectors which share as main principles and features 'the primacy of people as well as social and/or environmental purpose over profit, the reinvestment of most of the profits and surpluses to carry out activities in the interest of members/users ("collective interest") or society at large ("general interest") and democratic and/ or participatory governance'.[44] According to the Commission, the main types of entities which are considered as belonging to the sector of social economy are cooperatives, foundations, associations (including charities), mutual benefit societies, and social enterprises; however, social economy actors can actually assume a multitude of legal forms. In a nutshell, it is possible to argue that the broad label of social economy is relevant to the commons in so far as it applies to sectors that are primarily organised on the basis of the solidarity principle, on which therefore EU competition rules do not apply in full. The commons, defined by community-based organisation beyond state and market logics, align with the EU's social economy by challenging the public–private dichotomy and promoting a new space grounded in social and solidarity logics.[45] For example, some evidence of this relation between the commons and, in particular, social enterprises is already coming from recent studies showing how informal activities of care of the commons can eventually develop in more structured entities of social economies, and how social enterprises can (and already are) contributing to the shared governance of the commons.[46] The commons, indeed, may be instrumental in starting social economy initiatives; and vice versa the further development of a framework for social economy could contribute to the further definition of the commons within the EU legal order.

[43] There is currently no overarching legal framework for the social economy due to its cross-sectoral nature, though the Commission is working on it: see Communication from the Commission to the European Parliament, the Council, the European Economic and Social Committee and the Committee of the Regions, 'Building an Economy That Works for People: An Action Plan for the Social Economy' (2021). Additionally, see European Economic and Social Committee, *Recent Evolutions of the Social Economy in the European Union* by JL Monzon and R Chaves (2017). More recently, see the Council of the European Union, Recommendation of 27 November 2023 on developing social economy framework conditions (C/2023/1344) that – following up upon a Commission's proposal – asks Member States to set out frameworks supporting the design and implementation of social economy strategies at the national level.

[44] Commission, Communication, 'Building an Economy That Works for People: An Action Plan for the Social Economy' COM(2021) 5.

[45] A Rieiro, 'The Commons and the Social and Solidarity Economy' in *Encyclopedia of the Social and Solidarity Economy* (Edward Elgar Publishing in partnership with United Nations Inter-Agency Task Force on Social and Solidarity Economy (UNTFSSE) 2023) 10.

[46] See the research conducted on communities cooperatives by C Burini and J Sforzi, 'Imprese di comunità e beni comuni. Un fenomeno in evoluzione' (Euricse 2020) 93. See further Silvia Sacchetti and Gianluca Salvatori, '"Shared Administration" as a New Relationship between the Public Sector and the Social Economy' (2023) *Euricse Working Paper Series*.

(f) Services of general interest. Strictly related to the topic of partnerships (within EU public procurements) and to the field of social economy is the concept of 'services of general (economic) interest' (SGIs) included in EU primary law at Article 14 TFEU, Article 106 TFEU, Protocol 26, and Article 36 of the Charter of fundamental rights of the European Union. Since the concept is not defined there, fundamental is the Quality Framework[47] elaborated by the Commission, where it is explained that SGIs are all those services that are considered by public authorities of the Member States as being of general interest (as they cannot be adequately supplied by market forces alone), and therefore subject to specific public service obligations. They could be economic as well as non-economic: while services of general economic interest (SGEIs) are subject to the rules on competition (Article 106 TFEU), non-economic services of general interest are not bound by internal market and competition rules but can be provided, commissioned, organised autonomously by Member States' domestic law (Article 2, Protocol 26). In the light of that, the relation[48] between SGIs and the commons lies, therefore, in the potential development of a governance framework for all those non-economic services of general interest that would consider themselves as commons, and therefore allow for an involvement of the community in their governance because of their very nature of general interest. A very clear example of this connection between the two is the Right2Water campaign, the first successful European Citizens Initiative in 2013: this started a transnational European water movement[49] advocating for a constitutional and legal recognition of water services as a commons against its liberalisation in accordance with the internal market rules, and as such was claiming for a more 'citizen-driven (rather than public/state) governance of public services'.[50]

(g) Human rights. The last among the aspects we identified in EU primary law that contributes to the debate on the commons is human rights, in so far as the commons – whether they are tangible or intangible – constitute the concrete ground on which many activists today claim rights they consider of primary importance: from the right to essential services to the right to housing; from the right to water to the right of association; from the right to participate to the right to the internet. Also the right to the city itself is related to the commons, in so far as the city may be considered as a commons itself.[51] These are obviously only a few among the rights which

[47] See the fundamental EU Commission, Communication, 'A Quality Framework for Services of General Interest in Europe' COM (2011) 3.

[48] In this connection, see the contribution of Cornella (n 29) 231 ff.

[49] See their website at: europeanwater.org/.

[50] P Blokker, 'Constitutional Mobilization and Contestation in the Transnational Sphere' (2018) 45(S1) *Journal of Law and Society* 52: 'The Right2Water claim for a legal redefinition of water as a public rather than a private good, … can be further read as part of a larger campaign that understands the future of Europe as an economic order based on the idea of the Commons, with an emphasis on civic participation and the local, bottom-up and citizen-driven (rather than public/state) governance of public services' (70).

[51] This is very clear in D Harvey, 'The Right to the City' (2003) 27 *International Journal of Urban and Regional Research* 939, where the author claims a right to the city is a 'new urban commons, a public sphere of active democratic participation' (941).

are claimed more and more by activists as well as by scholars. Above all, this inner connection between human rights and the commons has been made explicit within the EU legal context by the Italian draft law on the common goods elaborated by the Rodotà Commission that – as we already saw[52] – theorised the commons as all those things that express a functional utility for the exercise of fundamental rights and the free development of the person.[53]

In conclusion, EU primary law and legislation make no explicit reference to the commons. However, certain aspects of EU law may implicitly support future development of a clearer conceptualisation for the commons. All in all, the commons in the EU constitute a debate in the making first and foremost due to the current difficulties in providing for an overall understanding and institutionalisation of this concept for which a wide variety of actors have (and still are) contributing. With concern to the legal contribution to this debate, the legal aspects underlined here and linked somehow to EU primary law essentially lead us to the affirmation of an essential point, which is: despite the fact that EU primary law does not contain any explicit reference to the commons as such, it is possible to trace some indirect connections to fundamental legal aspects which are part of the EU legal order. This makes it possible to say that the Treaties to date contain a yet unexplored legal potential – which also goes beyond the seven aspects that we have emphasised – thanks to which more European constitutional hooks could be found for the commons in the future, even if currently the legal context is not yet mature enough to address the evolving challenges of the commons. The next step is to have a look at the complex developments in EU cities regarding the commons.

III. Commons Initiatives in EU Cities: A Complex Picture

Beyond the legal contribution to this commons debate in the making in the EU, contributions to this matter have also been of a different nature: from more political initiatives, to academic ones, to grass-roots initiatives, experiments and projects taking place in both urban and rural contexts. This book focuses on commons in urban settings, or 'urban commons', though the concept lacks a clear EU-wide definition. This section broadly reviews current urban commons developments across the EU.

[52] See ch 6, section I.

[53] All around the EU, the Italian jurist Stefano Rodotà is well known among commoners, and his legal contribution is widely considered as the pioneering contribution for the institutionalisation by legal means on the commons as a legal and constitutional category. See one of his international speeches on this topic: Rodotà, 'Constituting the Commons' (n 4).

Starting with political initiatives, the most relevant one was the EU Parliament's Intergroup on the Commons, established on 12 February 2015[54] and launched on 25 May of the same year.[55] Its goal was to build a shared understanding of the commons to influence Parliament's agenda. Though its work is not available online, it helped connect European commons actors and supported the first European Commons Assembly (held in Brussels, 15–16 November 2016).[56]

Concerning academic initiatives, one of the most relevant was the draft of a European Charter of the commons by a group of multidisciplinary scholars together with some activists as a result of a seminar held at the International University College of Turin in 2011.[57] Recognising that a closed catalogue of commons was impossible to define because of different perceptions on the commons, the authors provided for a wide definition outlining that commons consist of all those 'collective goods or services to which access is necessary for a balanced fulfilment of the fundamental needs of the people'.[58] What is interesting in the Charter is that what emerged was the need for an explicit protection of the commons at the constitutional level of EU primary law.[59]

Both initiatives were aimed at contributing to an institutionalisation of the commons: so far they have not, however, been followed up. Beyond legal, political and academic contributions, the commons phenomenon is taking shape through urban experiments across EU cities, where numerous local initiatives connect themselves to the commons and seek institutional recognition. Since there is no 'one size fits all' solution, every initiative on a commons needs to be contextualised in its own legal, social, political, cultural, geographical context and in accordance with the community around that specific commons.

Generally speaking, commons movements across the EU often stem from a shared critique[60] of existing legal and constitutional structures, especially the

[54] Brief report on that at: www.epsu.org/article/public-services-and-commons-intergroup-set.

[55] The opening contribution was from one of the Italian legal scholars, Stefano Rodotà, who drew attention to the need for a legal recognition of the commons also at the EU level, and in relation to individuals' fundamental needs. Report on that available at: www.epsu.org/sites/default/files/article/files/report_final_May_26th_COMMONS.pdf, and conference recording at: www.youtube.com/watch?v=2WYHEWTHDek.

[56] The idea of a European Commons Assembly originated in Villarceaux, France in May 2016 when 28 activists from 15 European countries met for 3 days to develop a shared agenda for the commons. Information on that can be found at: www.netcommons.eu/index.html%3Fq=news%252Feuropean-commons-assembly.html. A second European Commons Assembly was held in Madrid, 25–28 October 2017 (this time no longer in cooperation with the EUP Intergroup).

[57] For an exploration of the draft Charter, see Simonati (n 2).

[58] ibid 95.

[59] ibid 98: 'The invitation to the European legislator is formulated in very specific terms. Concerning its relationship with the Member States, "a Directive should be issued … to provide for the protection of the commons". As regards, instead, the European system itself, the draft states that the Commission should introduce "a new form of legitimate and democratic European Constitutional Law" and should "take all the necessary steps in order for the European Parliament … to be granted Constitutional Assembly Status in order to adopt a Constitution of the Commons'.

[60] For an introduction, see Paul Blokker, 'Commons, Constitutions and Critique'. *Lo Squaderno. Explorations in Space and Society*, 2014, available at: ssrn.com/abstract=2376431 and Rodotà (n 4). Notable contributions to the commons movement have also come from outside academia, especially

culmination of privatisation trends. This drive for change has taken two main paths. The first is an outlawed way, with activists and social movements occupying abandoned spaces, treating them as commons beyond public/private divides and beyond the logic of privatisation. These acts, rooted in civil disobedience, directly challenge existing property laws.[61] The second way has essentially taken place within the constituted legal and constitutional order through the creation of innovative experiences (whether self-managed, or through some kind of agreement with public or private entities). It is difficult to map all commons-related projects, practices and urban policies, or to reflect the diversity of actors involved – from scholars to activists, commons thinkers, local public authorities, social movements, or social economy actors. Publications are also limited due to the challenge of capturing these varied experiences.[62]

However, some projects on urban commons have created useful maps and networks of related initiatives, offering valuable data.[63] The most up-to-date source is the GeCo project, which aimed to fill this gap by mapping urban commons initiatives across EU cities.[64] This chapter uses its preliminary

through research collectives offering critical reflections on economic and social structures. Key figures include David Bollier and his blog (www.bollier.org/); Michel Bauwens, who developed the concept of *peer-to-peer* (P2P) to describe relational dynamics in distributed networks, promoted by the *P2P Foundation* and its hub *CommonsTransition* (p2pfoundation.net/, commonstransition.org/); and the P2P Lab, a research collective focused on open-source technologies and commons-based practices (www.p2plab.gr/en/). The collaboratory *Commons Network* (www.commonsnetwork.org/) also contributes by exploring commons-based models for economy and society (www.commonsnetwork.org/).

[61] As examples, see the experience of Italian property outlaws: A Quarta and T Ferrando, 'Italian Property Outlaws: From the Theory of the Commons to the Praxis of Occupation' (2015) 15 *Global Jurist* 261, and S Bailey and Ugo Mattei, 'Social Movements as Constituent Power: The Italian Struggle for the Commons' (2013) 20 *Indiana Journal of Global Legal Studies* 965. For squatters' experiences in commons-oriented spaces around the EU (essentially in Amsterdam and Berlin) see Jens Kimmel et al, *Urban Commons Shared Spaces* (*Commons Network and raumlaborberlin*, 2018), available at: www.commonsnetwork.org/wp-content/uploads/2018/11/SharedSpacesCommonsNetwork.pdf.

[62] This is also recognised in Alessandra Quarta and Antonio Vercellone, 'The Rise of Urban Commons in Europe' (*Blogdroiteuropeen*, 20 January 2021), available at: blogdroiteuropeen.com/2021/01/20/the-rise-of-urban-commons-in-the-europe-by-alessandra-quarta-and-antonio-vercellone/.

[63] We are referring to the data elaborated within two main projects: the GeCo project (funded by an EU Horizon 2020 programme) that came up with a map (bit.ly/3Gq6cvv) and a database (generative-commons.eu/database/) on urban commons around the EU, and the Co-Cities map (cocities.designforcommons.org/co-cities-map/) that constitutes the basis for the publication of the Co-cities open book (cocities.designforcommons.org/the-co-cities-open-book/) elaborated by the LabGov think tank (cocities.designforcommons.org/). Additionally, we may also include other maps on the commons that can be found online: the one elaborated by the city of Grenoble (umap.openstreetmap.fr/it/map/carto-des-communs-grenoble_451121#13/45.1806/5.7824), and the collection of commons initiatives in Italian cities (but also in a few other EU cities) on the website of the research collective *Labsus* (www.labsus.org/). Worth mentioning is also a recent study of the organisation Commons Network, that published a study on commons in the two cities of Amsterdam and Berlin while making references to a wide variety of other commons experiences throughout EU cities: Kimmel et al (n 61).

[64] Website available at: generative-commons.eu/. The database of GeCo includes 220 cases from 16 EU countries, according to data presented at the closing conference of the GeCo project, which can be found at: generative-commons.eu/ge-co-living-lab-final-event/. Started in February 2019, the project was concluded in February 2022. The last conference held within the GeCo project (namely 'The international conference on the urban commons') was held at the University of Turin, 21–22 June 2021: a summary has been published in M Elia, 'International Conference of Urban Commons' (2021) 21 *Global Jurist* 483.

casework to provide an overview. GeCo categorises commons initiatives into two main types: 'communities of citizens' (initiatives by formal/informal groups); and 'public initiatives' (policies by public institutions). This basic distinction helps make sense of the diverse landscape, though it remains broad. These findings suggest it is still too early to precisely define the commons in Europe, given the many ongoing and varied experiments. In fact, scrolling through the analysed cases and willing to summarise, among the 'communities of citizens' we can basically find: (a) the work of social and solidarity entities with a legal status like cooperatives, associations, NGOs; (b) bottom-up citizen initiatives without any formal legal structure, like communities creating open source technologies, mutual aid initiatives, activists occupying buildings or other spaces for reclaiming basic rights or for cultural initiatives, crowdfunding campaigns; and (c) communities sharing the governance of certain spaces (beyond the ownership of that asset)[65] within some sort of agreement with public or private entities or through the self-management of the space: for example, makers spaces, fab labs, green areas and urban forests, collaborative and multifunctional spaces, co-working spaces, art and cultural centres, community hub and social centres. On the other side, among municipalities' 'public initiatives' we can find a wide variety of ways[66] to promote or support activities that may be qualified as commons-oriented (sometimes also through the availability of public funds): for example, among the listed ones in the GeCo database it is possible to find the promotion of policies relating to participatory budgeting, civic engagement and solidarity economy, civic participation in decision-making processes relating to managing urban spaces, citizens platforms promoting participatory processes, urban regeneration of places and temporary uses, and projects to support cultural and solidarity activities. The idea of the commons, however, extends well beyond what current mapping projects have captured,[67] and so far these efforts have not provided a clear definition. What GeCo revealed, however, are key challenges faced by commons initiatives:[68] mainly economic sustainability, and legal and bureaucratic obstacles. Both issues highlight the struggle of

[65] The Community Land Trust (CLT) offers a notable commons-based ownership model. Originating in the US, it treats land as a common good through a private law trust – the CLT – that separates land from buildings. A non-profit organisation owns and manages the land to ensure affordable housing and community participation. In the EU, a leading example is the Community Land Trust Brussels (CLTB), founded in 2013 (www.cltb.be/).

[66] The Italian prototype Regulation on the commons is qualified as public policy by GeCo. However, this book argues it would be better to understand it as a legal instrument grounded in the Italian Constitution.

[67] eg, energy communities and a wide-range of repair movements may also be considered as commons. For energy communities as commons, see further M Pappalardo, 'Energy Communities and Commons. Rethinking Collective Action through Inhabited Spaces' in G Debizet et al (eds), *Local Energy Communities* (Routledge 2022). For initiatives qualified within the repair movement like repair cafès and 'Bike Kitchens' (in addition to fab labs and makers spaces that were already included in the GeCo database), see further MJ Zapata Campos et al, 'Urban Commoning Practices in the Repair Movement: Frontstaging the Backstage' (2020) 52 *Economy and Space* 1150.

[68] As it emerges from the GeCo survey, results available at: generative-commons.eu/wp-content/uploads/2020/12/Summary-of-survey-results.pdf.

commons to fit within the public/private dualism – especially regarding their relationship with public authorities, from whom support is most expected.

A. Examples of Commons Initiatives: Barcelona, Ghent, Grenoble, Amsterdam

Among the public initiatives explicitly aimed at creating a political or legal framework for commons initiatives, worth deserving a mention are the those elaborated by four cities: Barcelona (Spain); Ghent (Belgium); Grenoble (France); and Amsterdam (the Netherlands). Until today, leaving aside the case of Italian cities having adopted the regulation for the commons within the organisational model of shared administration, these cities constitute the most advanced contributions to the definition of institutional frameworks explicitly relating to the commons by the local public authorities within the EU panorama.

Barcelona started to seek a way to provide a framework for the commons as a precise political commitment of the list 'Barcelona en Comú', which in 2015 won the municipal elections for the first time. In parallel to some other policy initiatives aimed at supporting the development of a commons-oriented economy,[69] a concrete legal way to provide for institutional support of the commons was created through the definition of a programme for a participatory governance of certain assets belonging to the public (civic) heritage ('patrimoni ciutadà'),[70] in specific socio-cultural facilities. A participatory governance of certain public assets already existed back then as a specific form of civic participation (the so-called 'gestió cívica'); however, it was since the development of a new conceptual framework[71] developed in 2016 that the participatory governance of these assets was defined in a commons-oriented perspective, in the conviction that public goods and

[69] We are referring essentially to the support for a 'commons collaborative economy' within a wider Municipal Action Plan on social and solidarity economy in Barcelona: see further on that, M Bauwens and V Niaros, *Changing Societies through Urban Commons Transitions* (P2P Foundation 2017) 34 ff, and M Bauwens et al, 'Commons Economies in Action. Mutualizing Urban Provisioning Systems' in J Engle et al (eds), *Sacred Civics: Building Seven Generation Cities* (Routledge 2022) 219f. Within a commons-oriented approach was also the digital platform *Decidim*, designed for citizen participation in the design of public policies (decidim.org/).

[70] The *Programa Patrimoni Ciutadà d'Ús i Gestió Comunitària* (known as *Patrimoni Ciutadà*) was developed by the city in 2017: ajuntament.barcelona.cat/participaciociutadana/ca/patrimoni-ciutada.

[71] Published in 2016, the conceptual framework *'Comuns urbans – Patrimoni Ciutadà. Marc conceptual i propostes de línies d'acció'* can be found at: ajuntament.barcelona.cat/participaciociutadana/sites/default/files/documents/patrimoni_ciutada_marc_conceptual_v.3.0.pdf. The conceptual framework was followed by a document advancing proposals for a legal framework: ajuntament.barcelona.cat/participaciociutadana/sites/default/files/documents/comuns_urbans_patrimoni_ciutada._marc_juridic_i_propostes_normatives.pdf. For an explanation of the Barcelona commons framework in progress since 2016, see the document 'Barcelona City Council Commons Policy: Citizens Asset Programme and Community management of public resources and services' at the institutional webpage of the Barcelona municipality at: ajuntament.barcelona.cat/participaciociutadana/sites/default/files/documents/barcelona_city_council_commons_policy_citizen_assets_programme.pdf.

services can become commons by promoting new forms of public–community cooperation between local public authorities and communities. The process for reaching an overarching standardised legal framework for the shared governance of the commons, however, has stalled to date due to difficulties in the process.[72] Interestingly, the Barcelona case shows the commons emerging under the broader umbrella of citizen participation, identified by the city government as the overarching guiding concept.

The second case is the one of the city of Ghent, which has been conducting a pioneering study on the functioning of urban commons and the possibility of regulating public–commons cooperation and partnerships.[73] The study underlined on one side the huge number of already existing commons-oriented initiatives – even though not formally recognised as such – as a reflection of a very active civil society; on the other, the distinctiveness of the city's public administration in having a relatively strong supportive and facilitating role towards many among the citizens' initiatives, usually supported either officially or indirectly in different ways. However, the relation between the public administration and commoners was depicted as problematic in so far as they were not officially recognised in their distinctiveness from civic society actors – the commoners being more informal than civil society actors.[74] As a consequence, the study went further in outlining some major recommendations to the city government in order to become a 'partner city' by explicitly supporting the commons as a 'dynamic and economically functional sector'.[75] Among the long list of recommendations, what is worth noticing is that advocating for the adoption of a city regulation on the commons similar to the well-known Bologna Regulation on the commons, that would constitute the legal framework for supporting citizens' 'right to initiative' and for signing commons agreements between the city and commoners on specific commons-oriented initiatives.[76] According to that, these agreements would form a commons version of public–private partnerships, under the name of 'public–civil' or 'public–commons' agreements.[77] Notwithstanding the great hype and spread of that pioneering study, eventually the city did not follow the recommendations and did not proceed further in developing an institutionalised legal framework on

[72] For an in-depth analysis of the difficulties in this process, we may refer further to I Bianchi, 'The Commonification of the Public under New Municipalism: Commons–State Institutions in Naples and Barcelona' (2022) 60 *Urban Studies* 2116.

[73] The study, issued in 2017, was externally commissioned and carried out by Michel Bauwens and Yurek Onzia. It mapped around 500 experiences that according to the authors could have been considered as commons-oriented: see Bauwens and Onzia (n 22).

[74] On the commons as 'a challenge to traditional civil society organisations' see Bauwens and Niaros (n 69) 25 f: 'contemporary citizens are also less likely to join old style membership organizations, preferring the informality and contributory logic of the commons. In conclusion, urban commons create their own new civil society institutions, while also creating a transformative pressure on the existing CSOs' (26).

[75] ibid 47.

[76] ibid 69.

[77] ibid 67.

the commons. This, however, did not prevent commoners' initiatives to continue spreading through other means.

A third case – promising for its legal foundation and explicit commitment to the commons – is the one of Grenoble. In March 2022 the city adopted the innovative municipal resolution Principes pour une administration coopérative which establishes the first legal framework in France explicitly supporting citizens' participatory actions through the commons,[78] within a wider paradigm of 'cooperative democracy'.[79] Grounded on a solid history of cooperatives and cooperation,[80] thanks to many years of public and civic debates and initiatives on the concept of 'commons',[81] and thanks to the contribution of the group of jurists Les juristes embarqués,[82] Grenoble defined its legal framework on the commons articulated in this way: (a) the municipal resolution as the legal framework which defines the concrete principles for an *administration cooperative*;[83] (b) the 'pacte de coopération', which constitutes the legal tool institutionalising agreements on specific initiatives aimed at sharing the governance of the commons between citizens and the public authority;[84] and (c) and the 'certificat d'action citoyenne', which consists in a certificate that proves somebody's participation in citizen actions which can be used for professional purposes. Interestingly, the resolution links the notion of commons (*biens communs*) closely with public services (*service public*), in this way limiting its full autonomy. This may stem from the lack of a clear definition of commons in the resolution. All in all, the case of Grenoble is relevant because it provides for a legal framework for

[78] The resolution can be found at: share.google/nyEBzoMJA3J5pRxHX. For its annexes, see: drive.google.com/file/d/1hQQf-Aru2qQRK9feSdoLhzd12wcy3hi5/view.

[79] As outlined in the municipal Resolution, 'la démocratie coopérative consiste à proposer aux personnes d'agir concrètement en modifiant leur cadre de vie et les services publics, les considérant comme une acteurtrice à part entière, à l'initiative de solutions possibles'. According to the Resolution, the paradigm of cooperative democracy should be added as a fifth dimension of local democracy in parallel to the four other dimensions of democracy: namely 'représentative, directe, d'interpellation et participative'.

[80] Grenoble is considered as the city at the origin of the social and solidarity economy movement in France since the very first mutual aid society of glove makers was created there in 1803 (a brief history of that can be found at: www.alpesolidaires.org/actualites/grenoble-lorigine-du-mouvement-mutualiste-en-france).

[81] A list of the various initiatives that have been taking place for years in Grenoble on the commons can be found at: wiki.lescommuns.org/wiki/Grenoble?fbclid=IwAR18kyT1AdFHBBpwT3lZztU4fQEechroFNC1xxsySiUQY5dnD5xwnQy-cxo.

[82] *Les juristes embarqués* is an action-oriented research project by lawyers across disciplines, studying urban commons in France. It was led by *27ème Région* (a public policy lab: www.la27eregion.fr/), on behalf of various national and local administrations. This follows the earlier project 'Enacting the commons' (2018–20), which explored commons initiatives in Europe (see website of the project: enactingthecommons.la27eregion.fr/). The final report of *Les juristes embarqués* can be found at: www.la27eregion.fr/9261-2/.

[83] The principles defined are: cooperation; accessibility and support for empowerment; valorisation of citizens' expertise; legal innovation; cooperative administration; citizens' contribution (which is not aimed at replacing the public); and respect for the commons.

[84] The *pacte* builds on the French jurisprudential concept of occasional collaboration in the public service (*collaboration occasionnelle au service public*), where citizens are allowed to contribute to the achievement of a public service mission under public authority control and direction. Unlike that, the *pacte de coopération* allows citizens to initiate activities of general interest themselves.

commons-oriented initiatives, which are recognised in their capacity to broaden opportunities for civic participation in local democracy.

The fourth case is the one of Amsterdam, interesting to report for MeentCoop.[85] Alongside some other pilot programs, MeentCoop is the result of a collaboration between various societal actors and the municipality of Amsterdam, and constitutes an incubator for community economy and commons-oriented initiatives. This case is, however, to be read within the wider national Dutch context, where more legal initiatives started consolidating an enabling legal environment for the commons. First, a recent law[86] adopted at the national level which also enhances citizens' participation at the local level in policy implementation and evaluation and not only in a preparatory consultative phase. Second, a municipal regulation prototype – based on this law – drafted by the Association of Netherlands Municipalities (VNG) which provides municipalities with a legal tool to maximise the knowledge and experience of residents, organisations and other stakeholders by allowing them to take initiatives and take over some municipal tasks in some specific cases.[87] Third, a template of collaboration agreement between public authorities and citizens drafted as a result of a collaboration between various citizens, groups, municipal actors and the VNG which permits formalising citizens' spontaneous concrete initiatives.[88] What the Dutch case shows, in brief is, that legislation can recognise new forms of action-oriented civic participation supported by public authorities that go beyond decision-making processes. Even if this evolving legal framework has not yet made explicit reference to the commons, there is legal ground in the Netherlands to build upon.

In conclusion, the legal and policy frameworks on the commons in EU cities remain complex and evolving. The absence of clear legal definitions at national and EU levels has led to a diversity of local initiatives that declare themselves as commons-oriented and for which it is not obvious to receive support from public authorities. Not even cities like Barcelona, Ghent, Grenoble and Amsterdam have yet provided explicit definitions or solid legal frameworks for the commons. A deeper investigation would require extensive and context-based research, but for now this overview and the focus on these leading cases will suffice.

IV. Problems and Similarities Among Commons in EU Cities

Despite the complexity, a clear phenomenon with different guises is emerging across EU cities: for many that goes under the idea of 'commons', and it essentially

[85] See its website: meent.coop/.

[86] The law is titled Wet versterking participatie op decentraal niveau and entered into force on 1 January 2025.

[87] The municipal regulation prototype is available at: vng.nl/brieven/model-participatieverordening-2024.

[88] The template is available at: programmasamen.nl/covenant/.

consists of citizens' governance of certain goods of general interest through new logics which are challenging bottom-up the traditional public–private law dualism. These commons initiatives contain constitutional claims and seek institutional support or recognition: an explicit legal recognition of the commons as such, however, is so far nowhere to be seen at EU level, and also domestic levels are having difficulties in capturing by legal means the phenomenon (Italian case aside) since we are still in the early days of such a new phenomenon which is questioning us.

At this stage when the commons phenomenon is emerging more and more, however, some obstacles seem to be relatively widespread, and they could be summarised as follows: (1) the lack of legal frameworks; (2) project-based thinking; and (3) bureaucratic and economic problems.

Regarding the lack of legal frameworks in the EU – the Italian model of shared administration constituting the most advanced for its constitutional and legal ground – the law has yet to clearly define 'commons', as the concept remains unsettled and jurists struggle to fully understand and classify it. However, it may be argued that it is thanks to this lack of a clear legal framework at the EU and nation-state levels that there is more room for cities to experiment bottom-up with innovative and creative solutions: legal innovations on the shared management of the commons have, indeed, already been tried out in many cities around the EU in different ways. Notwithstanding that, the lack of clarity on a legal framework is often perceived by both the public and the citizens sides as a difficulty in dealing with the emerging phenomenon of the commons.

The second problematic aspect consists in a generalised project-based thinking and practice: without doubt, so far this approach has been experimenting with different ways to support the commons; however, the limitation of such an approach consists in the difficulty of fostering a structural support which could be replicated as a best practice in all contexts of commons–public authorities relationships, and which at its core brings us back again to the lack of a legal framework.

The last essential obstacle refers to the fact that, faced with a widespread will of citizens to participate in their communities through the commons by getting committed to activities of general interest, bureaucratic and economic problems still prevail: citizens' initiatives are, indeed, challenging the constituted legal order in so far as they are requiring a change of mentality, action, support, tools on the side of public authorities, and as a consequence they often clash with bureaucratic structures or fail to use traditional funding channels.

Alongside these persistent obstacles in the commons phenomenon, certain similarities emerge from our overview, which could help identify underlying connections among commons initiatives. The similar traits essentially boil down to the following aspects: (1) self-governance and shared governance of the commons; (2) participation; (3) initiatives of social and solidarity economy; (4) democracy; (5) the role of cities and urban policies; and (6) the reference to the Italian cities' regulation on the commons as a model to look at.

First, commons-oriented initiatives seem to take place essentially in two ways: (a) as self-governance, in so far as the community dealing with a commons is doing so in an autonomous (legal or outlawed) way; and (b) according to a shared governance with public authorities, where the leadership for this collaboration may come from both the public and the civic sides, respectively in the case where it is the public authority that wants to create a regulatory or policy framework, or where it is a grass-roots citizen initiative that asks for a public support. In both cases, the role of citizens is not replaceable in so far as they constitute the community around specific commons.

Second, all commons initiatives may be qualified as innovative forms of civic participation that go beyond a mere decision-making dimension, in so far as citizens are concretely doing something, putting into practice an action-oriented version of participation. The commons seem to constitute the label for a new form of participation that is increasingly asking to be institutionalised, and which is shifting the focus from the actual property regime of a good to its participatory governance.

The third aspect is the shared acknowledgment among many initiatives that fundamentally the commons are also about economic change: commons-oriented initiatives usually act, indeed, outside the logic of the EU internal market governed by the competition rule, but rather more in line with the idea of social economy. In this way, they aim at paving the way for a new economic model based on the principle of solidarity, which is achievable only thorough the creation of institutions founded on cooperation and mutualism among individuals: these institutions usually take the form of cooperatives, associations, foundations. This economic approach introduces *homo cooperans* – as it has been named – highlighting citizen collectives that organise to 'take matters into their own hands to address local problems'.[89] Cases like Ghent, Barcelona, Grenoble, Amsterdam (and Bologna and other Italian cities) show commons initiatives thrive in contexts with a strong, established cooperative tradition.

Fourth, with citizens central to commons governance, innovative forms of civic participation, and grass-roots solidarity design of new economic institutions, democracy itself is evolving in new directions. In this sense, the contribution of citizens to the commons has led to the qualification of democracy in new ways, so as to distinguish it from traditional forms of representative, direct, deliberative and participatory democracy. Among others this is the case, for example, of the conceptualisation of a 'contributory democracy' coming from the case of Ghent,[90] and of a 'cooperative democracy', outlined by the Grenoble

[89] Tine De Moor, 'Homo Cooperans' (Inaugural lecture, University of Utrecht, 30 August 2013) 6.

[90] 'Contributory democracy' is the term used for referring to 'a democracy of the doers' around the commons which stands in parallel to representative democracy: see Bauwens and Niaros (n 69) 23 f. See further also the debate within the French context on a *démocratie contributive* in the issue 'Démocratie contributive: une renaissance citoyenne' (2016) *La Tribune Fonda* no 232: www.fonda.asso.fr/tribunes/democratie-contributive-une-renaissance-citoyenne.

resolution,[91] both willing to capture an initiative-oriented attitude coming from citizens taking action for the general interest. This search for terms that capture bottom-up citizen initiatives toward the commons – independent of top-down public authority triggers – is a common trait among various commons experiences.

Fifth, commons initiatives seem to highlight the fundamental role of cities in experimenting in urban policies that may be considered as commons-oriented even in the absence of any explicit mention of the commons, and notwithstanding the lack of an EU or national level legal frameworks defining what the commons actually are. This book highlights cities and local governments as the key *locus* for commons initiatives, and where public authorities face diverse citizen actions and have opportunities to craft innovative local policies within their local self-government.

A last consideration should go to a curious aspect, namely the fact that many commons activities and scholars[92] look at the Bologna Regulation on the commons as the paramount achievement so far of institutionalisation of the commons within the European legal context. Attempts have also been made at translating the model of shared administration of the commons for example into the French[93] and Spanish[94] legal debates. This last aspect essentially indicates that there is widespread opinion among commons-oriented initiatives that a clear legal (and constitutional) framework would be helpful for the further development and

[91] The idea of a *démocratie coop*erative consists in 'à proposer aux personnes d'agir concrètement en modifiant leur cadre de vie et les services publics, les considérant comme un-e acteur-trice à part entière, à l'initiative de solutions possibles' (see the Grenoble Deliberation 'Principes Pour Une Administration Coopérative', 28 March 2022, above (n 78)).

[92] See, eg, Bauwens et al (n 15). They refer to the Bologna Regulation on the commons as a paradigmatic case for developing new institutional processes for public–commons partnerships (59 f and 61 ff).

[93] In the French legal debate, legal scholar Olivier Jaspar introduced *le droit administratif des biens communs* (administrative law for the commons), a new public law discipline aimed at rethinking public services and general interest services. It promotes public–commons partnerships based on cooperation, not competition. See Emile Marzolf, 'Olivier Jaspart: "Comment Les Partenariats Public-Commun Vont Réinterroger Le Droit Public"' (*Acteurpublique*, 11 March 2022). The Bologna Regulation on the commons was also translated into French by Jaspart (available at media.licdn.com/dms/document/C561FAQFmHL3ss1JrvA/feedshare-document-pdf-analyzed/0/1621115998862?e=1674691200&v=beta&t=LIJrE_TK3pv8GhbDbv8-_6PUkom9HMe3zY5F1ZqfPy8 and presented here: rpubliquepourquoifaire.unblog.fr/2019/08/30/presentation-dun-modele-de-reglement-dadministration-mise-en-commun/).

[94] In the Spanish legal debate, scholar Joaquín Tornos Mas theorised *administración compartida* (shared administration) between citizens and public authorities for commons governance. Since the principle of horizontal subsidiarity is not in the Spanish Constitution, he proposed embedding *administración compartida* into Article 9(2) of the Constitution, which states that: 'it is incumbent upon the public authorities to promote conditions which ensure that the freedom and equality of individuals and of the groups to which they belong may be real and effective, to remove the obstacles which prevent or hinder their full enjoyment, and to facilitate the participation of all citizens in political, economic, cultural and social life'. See J Tornos Mas, 'Primeros Pasos Hacia La Administración Compartida En La Administración Local de Cataluña' (*Labsus*, 2017), and J Tornos Mas, 'Bienes Comunes y Administración Compartida' in L Míguez Macho and M Almeida Cerreda (eds), *Los Retos Actuales Del Derecho Administrativo En El Estado Autonómico* (Vol 2, 2017).

institutionalisation of the phenomenon of the commons with as yet undefined boundaries. Moreover, a legal framework would help scale commons-oriented initiatives and foster solid collaboration between citizens and public authorities.

All in all, this chapter reveals a complex and diverse range of commons initiatives across the EU, where communities complement or offer alternatives to state or market services. The lack of clear legal definitions and the diversity of experiences should not be seen as a problem, but rather as a transition phase allowing both local authorities and citizens to explore innovative solutions for dealing with the 'commons challenge'.

8

Building Blocks of European Constitutional Law for the Commons Challenge

I. From Commons in Italian to Other EU Cities: Too Long a Jump?

This final chapter addresses the book's key research question by reflecting on previous discussions and shares key considerations. It adopts a European public law perspective,[1] focusing on the common constitutional principles across the 27 EU Member States as well as the evidence coming from the case of Italian cities. Additionally, it was essential to provide an analytical review of the complex picture of commons initiatives across the EU,[2] and especially of the main problems in the legal (but not only) debate,[3] and of the similarities that this book analysis has revealed.[4] Although taking the case of Italian cities as its spotlight case, the book also analysed what emerges from a wider European scenario. While Italy alone cannot define a precise European theoretical framework for EU cities to support civic participation through the commons (CPC), at the same time its strong constitutional and legal foundations make it a key contributor of a bigger EU puzzle.[5]

Such a common theoretical framework would benefit all EU cities, being key sites for experimenting with democratic innovations and for supporting new forms of citizen participation.[6] To do that, cities should be given a post-national meaning.[7] In this sense, it is possible to talk about a transnational law of cities[8]

[1] See ch 1.
[2] See ch 7, section III.
[3] See ch 7, section I and section II.
[4] See ch 7, section IV.
[5] See chs 5 and 6.
[6] See ch 2, section V.
[7] P Dann, 'Thoughts on a Methodology of European Constitutional Law' (2005) 6) *German Law Journal* 1453.
[8] On the idea of a transnational law of cities, see F Giglioni, 'L'Unione Europea per Lo Sviluppo Dei Beni Comuni' (*Labsus*, 2015), available at: www.labsus.org/2015/09/unione-europea-per-lo-sviluppo-dei-beni-comuni/.

where they can rely on a common European constitutional local government law[9] in order to find their place as political communities beyond the traditional Westphalian order.[10] The EU is, indeed, a space of legal pluralism[11] where city networks increasingly collaborate with citizens to address diverse challenges in a governance perspective. Arguably this is contributing to rethinking the public–private divide that has so far characterised state–market dualism, and that may see civil society as one of its drivers of transformation.[12] Among these emerging challenges, the commons challenge is increasingly being recognised as a puzzling phenomenon that needs to be framed and accompanied by public authorities in cities. While Italian cities have used the horizontal principle of subsidiarity as the constitutional hook to build a shared administration model that supports citizen-led commons initiatives, in contrast, the complex picture in chapter seven reveals a broader lack of legal and constitutional frameworks at both EU and national levels, where the commons phenomenon is still in an experimental, undefined phase. The shift of focus from Italian cities to other cities across the EU, therefore, constitutes a stepping-stone which aims at advancing the Italian legal contribution to the commons in the wider European legal debate still entirely in the making which as we saw presents objective difficulties for analysis. Starting from a first analysis of the Italian case, in fact, also all other EU cities can facilitate CPC by leveraging common European constitutional principles: in this sense, the lessons learnt from the Italian case can constitute only a starting point for a wider European impact on this new type of civic participation.[13]

In conclusion, the commons phenomenon represents a new form of civic participation in local democracy that challenges cities to either recognise them institutionally or allow them to self-manage outside the established legal order. EU cities are already collaborating through transnational networks or EU-funded projects,[14] sharing good practices. A common framework based on European constitutional principles – not temporary policies or projects – could offer cities a reliable foundation from which to address the commons challenge and confront diverse recurring obstacles. All in all, Italian and other EU cities constitute the *locus* for local democracy in the EU, and as such can find common ground thanks to the same European constitutional principles.

[9] G Boggero, *Constitutional Principles of Local Self-Government in Europe* (Brill 2018).

[10] See ch 3 (n 6).

[11] See ch 2 (n 147).

[12] This is claimed in H-W Micklitz, 'Rethinking the Public/Private Divide' in M Maduro et al (eds), *Transnational Law* (Cambridge University Press 2014) 271. The two other drivers of the transformation of the public–private divide are, according to the author, economy and technology.

[13] See further, C Salati, 'Città e Sussidiarietà Orizzontale: Orientamenti Dottrinali Dal Caso Italiano per l'Unione Europea' (2024) Italian Papers on Federalism.

[14] See ch 4, section II.

II. European Constitutional Principles for EU Cities to Facilitate Civic Participation Through the Commons (CPC)

The Italian case stands out for its bottom-up nature, which has gained formal recognition through Italy's legal and constitutional framework. This book studied it not only within national boundaries but in the broader transnational European context, as a pioneering model reflecting a phenomenon that is already taking place in different guises around other EU cities, as seen in chapter seven.

Key lessons from the Italian case help address the central question addressed by this book: namely, how EU cities can drive civic participation through the commons by leveraging European constitutional principles. These lessons emerge along two dimensions: internal and external. Starting from the internal dimension,[15] it is possible to refer to the innovation capacity of the Italian case within the Italian legal order, and overall are the five main lessons that can be learnt:[16] they consider: (1) the principle of horizontal subsidiarity; (2) the commons as a new form of civic participation; (3) the definition of the organisational model of shared administration; (4) the recognition of the EU law principle of solidarity by the Italian Constitutional Court; and (5) the rising role of local authorities and the emergence of the city as a legal category.

(1) The horizontal subsidiarity principle in Article 118(4) of the Italian Constitution has enabled a new relationship[17] between public and civic autonomies[18] based on the subsidiarity paradigm, which requires public authorities to support citizens' initiatives of general interest.[19] It emphasises local government's central role, closest to citizens, and fosters both institutional and societal pluralism. This principle uniquely managed to capture the commons phenomenon, granting constitutional cover to that.[20]

(2) Horizontal subsidiarity and its concept of general interest[21] shifted the commons from ownership to governance. It promotes shared governance of the commons between public authorities and citizens, in this way fostering an innovative, action-oriented civic participation – participation in doing – beyond just mere decision-making – participation in deciding:[22] this book termed it 'civic participation' through the commons (CPC).

[15] The internal dimension corresponds to what has been investigated in Part III.
[16] The considerations expressed here build upon conclusive remarks in ch 6, section IV.
[17] See ch 5, section III.C.
[18] See ch 5 (n 33).
[19] See ch 5, section III.B and section III.C.
[20] See ch 5, section IV.
[21] See ch 5, section III.B.
[22] See ch 5, section II.

(3) The innovative form of CPC in Italy, under the horizontal subsidiarity principle, is taking place through the organisational model of shared administration,[23] developed in public law and adopted by over 320 local governments since Bologna's 2014 Regulation. Using the legal tools of the regulation on the commons and collaboration pacts,[24] shared administration institutionalises de facto CPC societal practices with legal backing. Rather than a mere policy, theory or project, it is, therefore, a robust organisational model with clear normative foundations, fully legitimised constitutionally.
(4) *Shared administration* was recognised[25] by the Constitutional Court as a third space beyond state–market dualism, grounded in the EU law principle of solidarity as its archetypal constitutional principle at the supranational EU level. According to the Court, this principle, alongside EU competition law, guides public–citizen relationships aimed at the general interest beyond competition rules. The Court's decision framed the Italian case within the broader European constitutional context, offering a reference point for similar commons initiatives in other Member States.
(5) The last key lesson from the Italian case is the growing role of local authorities and the emergence of the city as a legal category. Guided by horizontal subsidiarity (Article 118(4)), local autonomy (Article 5) and regulatory autonomy (Article 117(6)) of the Italian Constitution, Italian local authorities can support bottom-up civic initiatives, acting as laboratories for civic participation.[26] Those that have adopted the shared administration model were able, in this way, to give juridical value to informal public law, recognising social practices outside mere positive law boundaries.[27] Activities like care, regeneration and shared governance of the commons gained legal legitimacy through these local efforts, despite the absence of national legislation on that. In this view, the city emerges as an emerging category within a work-in-progress 'law of cities', where democratic legitimacy arises not only from representative structures, but from institutionalised informal participation. Cities may thus be shaping a new form of democracy which is grounded on the institutionalisation of CPC thanks to horizontal subsidiarity.

These five aspects constitute the fundamental lessons that can be learnt from the Italian case on its internal dimension. However, the Italian case does not only have an internal dimension, but it has wider EU-wide appeal and impact. In fact, five other key lessons can be drawn from the wider EU context:[28] they concern (1) democracy in the EU; (2) the principle of participation; (3) the principle of subsidiarity; (4) the principle of local self-government; and (5) the rising role of cities. While the lessons from the Italian case – aside from the EU law principle

[23] See ch 6, section II.
[24] See ch 6, section II.A and section II.B.
[25] See ch 6, section III.
[26] See ch 6, section IV.
[27] See ch 6 (n 75).
[28] The external dimension corresponds to Parts I–II, and the considerations expressed here build upon what emerges from its chapters (chs 1, 2, 3 and 4).

of solidarity – are primarily grounded in Italian public and constitutional law, they offer valuable insights that can be meaningfully traced back to broader European constitutional principles. In what follows, we explore these potential connections to highlight their relevance across the European context.

(1) On democracy in the EU, this book qualified it as a distinctive system of both government and governance,[29] where non-state actors play a fundamental role in parallel to state actors, also by challenging traditional sources of law and paving the way for complementary sources of soft law. It is a type of democracy different from the one of nation states, which founds its legitimacy on both representative and participatory channels.[30] In the light of that, this book argued that it is not possible to talk of a crisis of democracy as such, but of its transformation,[31] essentially thanks to many emerging types of democratic innovations that are contributing to providing the European principle of participation with additional values.[32] In relation to this first aspect, the Italian case clearly aligns with this definition of democracy thanks to subsidiarity so that two vertical and horizontal dimensions, and shared administration can be included within democratic innovations (and its field of collaborative governance).

(2) The principle of participation foresees a right for citizens to participate in both the EU and Council of Europe (CoE) legal orders, thanks to Article 10(3) of the Treaty on European Union (TEU) and Article 1.2 of the Additional Protocol on the right to participate in the affairs of a local authority to the 1985 Charter. It was the CoE, however, that created a strict connection between the right to participate and local democracy, with the provision for a symmetrical empowerment of local authorities to enable, promote and facilitate the exercise of this right by also responding to suggestions of citizens regarding local public services.[33] Overall, the poor explanation of the content of participation makes it a European principle still allowing for great space for interpretation: in this sense, as depicted by the book the frontier of this principle constitutes an action-oriented version of it.[34] In relation to this second aspect, the Italian case was able to put in practice an innovative form of action-oriented participation – a CPC.

(3) The principle of subsidiarity in the European legal space has received greater attention from the EU than from the CoE. The EU played a key role in clarifying the principle, especially during its foundational 1990s debate, where its three roots were equally present.[35] As we argued, one of these roots – namely, the meaning of subsidiarity according to Catholic social philosophy – has been totally forgotten, therefore depriving the Treaties of an explicit recognition of the fundamental contribution that could be spontaneously given in democracy by private individuals on the basis of their self-governance.

[29] See ch 1, section IV.
[30] ibid.
[31] See ch 1, section III.
[32] See ch 2, section V.
[33] See ch 2, section IV.
[34] See ch 2, section VI.
[35] See ch 3, section II.A and ch 3, section II.C.

The book argued, however, that it is possible to find traces of this forgotten meaning of subsidiarity implicitly in the EU legal order: first, in the other EU constitutional principles of solidarity, sovereignty and participation; second, in the TEU preamble, and Article 10(3) TEU; and third in other Member States constitutions.[36] Outside the Treaties, the theoretical contribution of the European Economic and Social Committee EESC in the recognition of private actors in a governance perspective in democracy has also been given credit for an implicit valorisation of the forgotten meaning of subsidiarity. The book therefore argued that the forgotten meaning of subsidiarity is already implicit in the European constitutional tradition, and being elastic enough[37] there is no need for a treaty change: as a consequence, it is up to local governments to apply it as a harbinger of a new governance culture. A democratic reading of the EU principle of subsidiarity in both a government and governance perspective – according to a subsidiarity-as-democracy idea[38] – discloses an innovative potential for the relationship between public authorities and citizens. With relation to this third aspect, the Italian case constitutes a perfect example of constitutional recognition of this forgotten meaning of subsidiarity, therefore paving the way for other public authorities around the EU to disclose this unexplored – but intrinsic – meaning of the principle.

(4) The principle of local self-government has not been fully incorporated by the EU legal order: that is why the constitutional contribution of the CoE is fundamental in equipping EU local authorities with that.[39] This also constitutes the reason why in order to look at local authorities in the EU it is important to be aware of the multiple legal orders that have an impact on them, and as a consequence the research looked at the constitutional contribution of the wider European legal space (EU and CoE). While the EU has a more state-centric perspective, the CoE had already recognised local authorities beyond nation states' borders since its 1985 fundamental European Charter on local self-government, in this way giving an European constitutional value to institutional pluralism and more precisely to local democracy. With relation to this fourth aspect, the Italian case provides for a clear example of local authorities making use of their local self-government in supporting civic participation initiatives through the model of shared administration and its regulation.

(5) With concern to the last aspect – the rising role of cities – this book acknowledged the ongoing process of transformation of public law in the European legal space, in so far as they are emerging as political communities (*civitas*) beyond mere administrative borders (*urbs*). Their contemporary renaissance reflects a worldwide general phenomenon of urbanisation and claims their essence of human settlements with an original vocation as political communities beyond their constriction within state superstructures. This phenomenon has also been observed in the growing contribution of EU institutions through

[36] See ch 3, section II.C.
[37] See ch 3 (n 105).
[38] See ch 4, section III.
[39] See ch 3, section II.B and ch 3, section II.C.

policies and other soft-law instruments[40] relating to what is more and more defined as 'urban' or 'city/cities': this is occurring in the lack of explicit EU law competence on local authorities, which are traditionally considered within the EU bicentric structure only as passive receivers and not also as active subjects. Cities are increasingly emerging, often in networks, as laboratories of local democratic transformation through participatory practices with their inhabitants, bridging government and governance perspectives.[41] With relation to this fifth aspect, the growing conceptualisation of the idea of 'city' also within the Italian doctrinal debate shows a desire to claim its original vocation of a political community made of public authorities and citizens that together may contribute to the renewal of local democracy.

All these aspects considered, this book identified the following four European constitutional principles as key reference points forming a solid foundation for an overarching European theoretical framework applicable to other EU cities engaging with the commons:

- Participation
- Subsidiarity
- Local self-government
- Solidarity

There is still room in the Treaties to discover unexplored meanings from constitutional principles. In the light of the Italian case, such four principles prove particularly powerful. Alongside their constitutional relevance, EU soft law plays a fundamental role by proactively engaging cities from a governance perspective. While the Italian model is still evolving and not yet predominant, its widespread adoption – seen in over 320 cities implementing shared administration of the commons – demonstrates a transformative shift already under way. It is therefore the responsibility of legal scholars to provide a robust doctrinal foundation for these bottom-up innovations, guided by constitutional principles and the evolving societal landscape. Three of the four constitutional principles identified in this study of the Italian case clearly resonate with the commons phenomenon in EU cities:[42] (1) participation, increasingly realised through action-oriented civic engagement on the commons; (2) solidarity, enabling grass-roots collective actions aligned with a non-competitive economic model;[43] and (3) local

[40] See ch 4, section II.

[41] See ch 4, section IV.

[42] See ch 7, section IV, where the analysis pointed to six main emerging similarities, that could serve for future research: (1) self-governance and shared governance of the commons; (2) participation; (3) initiatives of social and solidarity economy; (4) democracy; (5) the role of cities and urban policies; and (6) the reference to the Italian cities' Regulation on the commons as a model to look at. Although based on a limited number of sources due to the challenges noted in ch 7, these similarities provide a valuable starting point to inspire and support cities as they embrace the commons challenge.

[43] M Ross, 'Solidarity – A New Constitutional Paradigm for the EU?' in M Ross and Y Borgmann-Prebil (eds), *Promoting Solidarity in the European Union* (Oxford University Press 2010). See also, ch 3 (nn 86–87).

self-government, reflecting the active role of cities as political communities collaborating with citizens in the search for new solutions. Although subsidiarity in its horizontal dimension did not explicitly emerge across EU cities because rooted in the Italian context, this does not mean it should not also be considered as a potential future reference point for other EU cities.

In conclusion, EU cities can facilitate CPC by leveraging the common European constitutional principles of participation, local self-government, subsidiarity and solidarity. This can be argued not only on the basis of the inspiring Italian case – which stands as a compelling example because of its high-level institutionalisation – but from what emerged from the comparative overview of commons-related cases in chapter seven. The following image captures visually this book's central argument and its answers to the main research question.

Figure 2 Building blocks of European constitutional law for EU cities to face the commons challenge (author's elaboration)

III. Civic Participation Through the Commons (CPC) in EU Cities: First Building Blocks for a Common Theoretical Framework

All in all, these four European constitutional principles are essential reference points for EU cities to drive civic participation through the commons. They form the first essential European constitutional law building blocks of a work-in-progress theoretical framework, that is needed to strengthen EU cities' capacity to deal with the commons challenge. Other principles could be added to the picture, but only thanks to further research. As the legal understanding of the commons phenomenon evolves, this framework provides cities with concrete guidance – being at the forefront of dealing with this phenomenon. Even in the absence of national legislation, this framework empowers cities to develop their own organisational models, regulations and policies. While local legal context remains important, this framework can act as a crucial enabler for innovation – despite its abstract nature and varying local realities. Without it, EU cities would keep on lacking the legal clarity and direction necessary to support grass-roots civic participation through the commons. Local democracy, in the end, is where the commons phenomenon is most visible.

In conclusion, an overarching theoretical framework is essential to equip EU cities with clear constitutional and legal tools for addressing the challenges of the commons. Commons-based initiatives are growing rapidly across Europe, demanding institutional recognition and support. A common framework made of building blocks of European constitutional principles strengthens these initiatives without imposing uniformity. It reflects not abstract theory, but patterns already emerging across cities. The Italian case offers concrete proof that these principles can effectively drive civic participation through the commons, setting a clear path forward for cities across the EU.

Conclusion

Findings

This book identified key building blocks of European constitutional principles that EU cities can leverage to drive civic participation through the commons (CPC), drawing extensively from the pioneering experience of Italian cities. Part I explored the evolving boundaries of democracy and participation; Part II examined the role of subsidiarity and local self-government in strengthening local democracy, as well as the growing recognition of cities as autonomous legal subjects in a rapidly urbanising world. Part III analysed how Italian cities are already applying these principles to support the commons. Part IV offered a general overview of the commons debate and initiatives across EU cities, ultimately answering the book's research question.

Chapter one set the scene entering the European legal space by defining democracy in the EU according to forms and levels. It renounced the narrative of democratic crisis, showing instead that democracy is thriving at the local level through participatory practices that extend democratic legitimacy beyond representative models. Consequently, the concept of governance was introduced to highlight the distinctive nature of EU democracy – an integrated system of government and governance in which both representation and participation actively shape democratic transformation.

Chapter two examined the principle of participation in the European legal space, tracing its foundations at the intersection of legal and political scholarship and highlighting the constitutional contributions of both the EU and the Council of Europe (CoE) legal orders. While the EU contribution focuses on participation at the supranational level, the CoE played a pivotal role in establishing the constitutional link between civic participation and local democracy through its 1985 European Charter on local self-government. Building on this foundation, the chapter demonstrated the widespread and growing wave of democratic innovations emerging at the local level across the EU, often in the absence of normative provisions on them. These developments show an emerging shift towards participatory practices with an increasingly action-oriented dimension, pushing participation beyond decision-making.

Chapter three examined the local level of democracy in the European legal space, identifying subsidiarity and local self-government as foundational principles present in both CoE and EU legal orders. The EU has significantly shaped the principle of subsidiarity, while the CoE has firmly established local self-government as a European constitutional standard, offering a key reference for local authorities often under-recognised in the EU's bicentric legal framework. Revisiting the EU's 1990s subsidiarity debate, the chapter recovered what it called the forgotten meaning of subsidiarity: a horizontal interpretation of this principle, rooted in Catholic social philosophy, which affirms the duty of public authorities to support citizens acting on matters of general interest. This meaning is embedded in European constitutional tradition and some hints of that are traceable in the EU Treaties. The chapter demonstrated that local governments, being closest to citizens, are best positioned to implement subsidiarity according to this additional meaning.

Chapter four identified a shift from 'local' to 'urban,' marked by the city's rise as an emerging autonomous subject beyond traditional administrative state structures. This trend, supported by both academic work and EU institutional action through soft-law instruments, presents a new challenge for European public law. In this way, the city as such is reawakening its original vocation of human settlement before its constriction within states' superstructures. In doing so, cities are reclaiming their foundational role as laboratories for democracy transformations, where participatory demands increasingly emerge beyond representative channels. In this context, the forgotten meaning of subsidiarity re-emerges as a core European principle guiding cities as political communities.

Chapter five and chapter six presented the case of over 320 Italian cities that have used constitutional and legal tools to support civic participation through the commons (CPC). Chapter five presented the constitutional roots of Italian cities' model of shared administration of the commons. CPC represents a concrete form of participation that goes beyond decision-making to also include concrete action. This was enabled by the constitutional principle of horizontal subsidiarity in Article 118(4) of the Italian Constitution, which obliges public authorities to support citizens' initiatives in the general interest. This principle provided constitutional legitimacy to the commons by aligning their social relevance with the notion of general interest.

Chapter six then analysed the administrative implications of the shared administration model, enabled by a prototype municipal regulation and the collaboration pact tool, which has expanded across Italian cities since Bologna's pioneering role in 2014. Shared administration redefined the citizen–state relationship through a horizontal and collaborative dynamic, with local authorities playing a central role. The Italian Constitutional Court further reinforced this model by linking it to the EU principle of solidarity, presenting it as a valid alternative to the competition-based market logic. The explicit link between EU solidarity and shared administration (and implicitly with the commons) marks a milestone in the European constitutional debate on the commons, laying a solid foundation for future democratic innovation. Chapter six also confirmed the growing recognition of cities as autonomous legal actors in Italy, aligning with broader trends in European public law. This evolution stems from local governments' active commitment to formally integrating grass-roots social practices – referred to as informal public law. Among these, civic participation through the commons has secured institutional backing via shared administration, firmly grounded in the principle of horizontal subsidiarity.

Chapter seven provided a comprehensive overview of the commons in the EU, highlighting the challenges of a debate in the making – ranging from definitional and linguistic barriers to interdisciplinary complexity. It affirmed that the commons constitute a resource whose governance is shared by a community according to a set of rules in a third space between the state–market dualism. While a unified legal framework on the commons is still absent at the EU level, relevant legal elements exist in areas such as property, governance, state aid, public–private partnerships, the social dimension of the EU, services of general interest, and human rights. In parallel to that, the chapter emphasised that insights can already be drawn from commons-based initiatives emerging across EU cities. It identified shared problems – a lack of legal recognition, project-based thinking, and bureaucratic and economic constraints – and similarities, including their shared or self-governance, their connection with participation, their ties to the social and solidarity economy, their democratic nature, and the central role of cities and urban policies in enhancing them. The Italian experience was referenced as a leading example. Overall, the chapter showed EU cities as ongoing laboratories for the commons.

Chapter eight forms the core of the book, drawing the contours of a theoretical framework made of European constitutional principles that cities across the EU can leverage for facilitating CPC. It also showed how the Italian case contributes directly to that, being the pioneer case within the EU. It demonstrated that the principles of subsidiarity, participation, local self-government, and solidarity – rooted in European constitutional traditions – serve as essential building blocks that EU cities can leverage in order to drive CPC. EU soft law was also highlighted for its supportive role in urban governance and its relevance to commons-based approaches. In addition to these four principles, the Italian model of shared administration was praised for its creative legal approach to the commons challenge. The chapter concluded that EU cities can effectively drive and facilitate CPC by leveraging these four principles and experimenting with their own organisational models.

The Way Forward

The case of Italian cities is only a small part of a much bigger puzzle that still needs to be pieced together. Without any doubt, however, it constitutes a pioneering case worth a spotlight in the analysis for having – first in the EU – outlined a constitutional and legal framework supporting the commons. In doing so, it constitutes only the beginning of what appears to be a long-term innovation in the relationship between citizens and public authorities. This book has contributed by laying some foundational building blocks that should be taken into account for the future construction of an overarching European theoretical framework. This should be composed of constitutional and legal pieces at different levels of government that cities could use as a higher cover for supporting commons-oriented initiatives. The commons challenge, in fact, is much wider than the Italian case, and targets local democracy in cities around the whole EU and beyond that. As a consequence, two main aspects are the desirable next research steps: (1) a comparative legal study on the commons in EU Member States; and (2) a comparative legal study trying to validate the building blocks of European constitutional law identified in this book in all other EU Member States.

(1) The first aspect could be investigated by a comparative work on the commons in the legal orders of the 27 EU Member States. This comparative work should ideally be organised and carried out by a team of national experts willing to understand to what extent the commons are already institutionalised or traceable in their legal orders, and which are the ongoing experiments carried out. Since, as we have seen, the commons lie at the intersection between public and private, it would be better to have two national experts from each country, able to provide for both perspectives on the commons, namely a public law perspective as well as a private one. Such research would contribute to filling the existing gap on an overall legal picture on the commons in the EU.
(2) The second aspect could also be explored by a collective work involving one national expert from each EU Member State. The aim would be to validate the European constitutional principles of subsidiarity, local self-government, participation, and solidarity as ideal reference points for other cities in all the 27 EU Member States to elaborate at the local level – and according to their national legal orders – their own organisational models to drive CPC. This type of research on the one hand would validate the findings from this book; on the other, it would complement our findings with the identification of other building blocks of European constitutional law that could serve for facing the commons challenge.

These two aspects constitute to date open questions that suggest new paths for future research. In parallel to the contribution of the scholarship, however, it is important to state that desirable steps could also come from public authorities within the European legal space, and more precisely from cities themselves. In fact, no lack of constitutional or legal framework prohibits cities from experimenting in new ways in order to face the commons challenge. On the opposite, local authorities' regulations have the advantage of constituting potential pioneering bottom-up experiments that may pave the way for a long-term systemic change.

All things considered, these aspects constitute the research agenda for the future development of a more comprehensive European theoretical framework for EU cities facing the commons challenge. All of that demonstrates that the four building blocks identified by this book are only the beginning, and more paths still need to be explored. The overall long-term ambition is to unleash the creative potential of EU cities in facilitating active citizens exercising an innovative form of civic participation through the commons. Cities are, in fact, composing themselves around new institutionalisation processes together with their inhabitants: it will take a lot of practice to implement this ideal vision.

REFERENCES

Literature

Addink, H, *Good Governance: Concept and Context* (Oxford University Press 2019).

Aguado i Cudolà, V, 'Nuevas Formas de Participación Ciudadana. En Especial, La Gestión y Administración Compartida' [2023] *Anuario del Gobierno Local* 235.

Aichholzer, G and Rose, G, 'Experience with Digital Tools in Different Types of E-Participation' in L Hennen et al (eds), *European E-Democracy in Practice* (Springer Open 2020).

Albanese, A, 'Il principio di sussidiarietà orizzontale: autonomia sociale e compiti pubblici' (2002) 1 *Diritto Pubblico* 51.

Albanese, RA, 'Usi Civici e Beni Comuni Urbani. Tra Presente e Passato, Tra Pubblico e Privato' in RA Albanese et al (eds), *Gestire i Beni Comuni Urbani Modelli e Prospettive* (Rubbettino 2020).

Alber, E and Salati, C, 'Coupling Social Innovation and Local Government: Shared Administration in Commons Governance' in K Kössler et al (eds), *Public Participation in Local Governance: An Urban–Rural Perspective* (Palgrave Macmillan 2025).

Alber, E and Valdesalici, A, 'Framing Subnational "Institutional Innovation" and "Participatory Democracy" in Italy: Some Findings on Current Structures, Procedures and Dynamics' in F Palermo and E Alber (eds), *Federalism as Decision-Making* (Brill Nijhoff 2015).

Alemanno, A, 'Beyond Consultations. Reimagining European Participatory Democracy' (Carnegie Europe, HEC Paris Research Paper, 2018).

—— 'Europe's Democracy Challenge: Citizen Participation in and Beyond Elections' (2020) 21 *German Law Journal* 35.

—— 'Levelling the EU Participatory Playing Field: A Legal and Policy Analysis of the Commission's Public Consultations in Light of the Principle of Political Equality' (2020) 26 *European Law Journal* 114.

—— 'Unboxing the Conference on the Future of Europe' (2021) HEC Paris Research Series.

Alemanno, A and Organ, J, 'The Case for Citizen Participation in the European Union: A Theoretical Perspective on EU Participatory Democracy' in J Organ and A Alemanno (eds), *Citizen Participation in Democratic Europe: What Next for the EU?* (ECPR Press/Rowman & Littlefield Publishers 2021).

Alessi, NP, *A Global Law of Diversity: Evolving Models and Concepts* (Routledge 2024).

Alessi, NP and Salati, C, 'Federalism beyond Government: Thinking Outside the (Institutional) Box through the Commons' (forthcoming 2026).

Allegretti, G, 'Giustizia Sociale, Inclusività e Altre Sfide Aperte per Il Futuro Dei Processi Partecipativi Europei' in U Allegretti (ed), *Democrazia partecipativa: esperienze e prospettive in Italia e in Europa* (Firenze University Press 2010).

Allegretti, U, 'Basi Giuridiche Della Democrazia Partecipativa in Italia: Alcuni Orientamenti' (2006) 3 *Democrazia e Diritto* 151.

Allegretti, U (ed), *Democrazia partecipativa: esperienze e prospettive in Italia e in Europa* (Firenze University Press 2010).

—— 'Democrazia Partecipativa: Un Contributo Alla Democratizzazione Della Democrazia' in U Allegretti (ed), *Democrazia partecipativa: esperienze e prospettive in Italia e in Europa* (Firenze University Press 2010).

—— 'Democrazia Partecipativa' (2011) *Enciclopedia del Diritto* 295.

—— 'La democrazia partecipativa in Italia e in Europa' (2011) 1 *Rivista dell'Associazione Italiana dei Costituzionalisti* 4.

—— 'Participatory Democracy in Multi-Level States' in C Fraenkel-Haeberle et al (eds), *Citizen Participation in Multi-Level Democracies* (Brill 2015).
—— 'La Partecipazione Come "Utopia Realistica"' in A Valastro (ed), *Le Regole Locali Della Democrazia Partecipativa. Tendenze e Prospettive Dei Regolamenti Comunali* (Jovene 2016).
Ansell, C and Gash, A, 'Collaborative Governance in Theory and Practice' (2008) 18 *Journal of Public Administration Research and Theory* 543.
Antonini, L, *Sussidiarietà fiscale: La frontiera della democrazia* (Guerini 2005).
Arban, E, 'Re-Centralizing Subsidiarity: Interpretations by the Italian Constitutional Court' (2015) 25 *Regional & Federal Studies* 129.
—— 'Constitutional Law, Federalism and the City as a Unique Socio-Economic and Political Space' in E Hirsch Ballin et al (eds), *European Yearbook of Constitutional Law 2020: The City in Constitutional Law* (2020).
—— 'City, State: Reflecting on Cities in (Comparative) Constitutional Law' (2021) 19 *ICON* 343.
—— 'An Intellectual History of Federalism: The City and the "Unit" Question' in E Arban (ed), *Cities in Federal Constitutional Theory* (Oxford University Press 2022).
—— *Cities in Federal Constitutional Theory* (Oxford University Press 2022).
Arena, G, 'Introduzione All'amministrazione Condivisa' (1997) *Studi Parlamentari e Di Politica Costituzionale.*
—— 'Il principio di sussidiarietà orizzontale nell'art. 118, u.c. della Costituzione' (*Astrid Online*, 2003).
—— 'User, Customers, Allies: New Perspectives in Relations Between Citizens and Public Administrations' in G Arena and M Chiti (eds), *Public Administration, Competitiveness and Sustainable Development* (Firenze University Press 2003).
—— *Cittadini Attivi* (Laterza 2006).
—— 'Immigrazione e Cittadinanze' in R Acciai and F Giglioni (eds), *Poteri Pubblici e Laicità Delle Istituzioni: Studi in Onore Di Sergio Lariccia* (Aracne editrice 2007).
—— 'Le Diverse Finalità Della Trasparenza Amministrativa' in F Merloni (ed), *La Trasparenza Amministrativa* (Giuffrè 2008).
—— 'Beni Comuni. Un Nuovo Punto Di Vista' (*Labsus*, 2010).
—— 'Le Città Come Beni Comuni' (*Labsus*, 2013).
—— 'La Cittadinanza Attiva Nella Costituzione' in F Cortese et al (eds), *Dallo Status Di Cittadino Ai Diritti Di Cittadinanza* (Editoriale Scientifica 2014).
—— 'Un Regolamento per La Cura Condivisa Dei Beni Comuni' (*Labsus*, 2014).
—— 'Democrazia Partecipativa e Amministrazione Condivisa' in A Valastro (ed), *Le Regole Locali Della Democrazia Partecipativa: Tendenze e Prospettive Dei Regolamenti Comunali* (Jovene 2016).
—— 'Amministrazione e Società. Il Nuovo Cittadino' (2017) 1 *Rivista Trimestrale di Diritto Pubblico* 43.
—— 'La "Società Della Cura" e Il Valore Politico Dei Piccoli Gesti Quotidiani' (*Labsus*, 2018).
—— *I Custodi Della Bellezza* (Touring 2020).
—— 'Sussidiarietà Orizzontale Ed Enti Del Terzo Settore' in A Fici et al (eds), *I Rapporti Tra Pubbliche Amministrazioni Ed Enti Del Terzo Settore. Dopo La Sentenza Della Corte Costituzionale n. 131 Del 2020* (Editoriale Scientifica 2020).
Arena, G and Bombardelli, M (eds), *L'Amministrazione Condivisa* (Editoriale Scientifica 2022).
Arena, G and Bonasora, P, 'Il Vertice Di Labsus Cambia per Fare Spazio a Nuove Energie!' (*Labsus*, 2021).
Arena, G and Iaione, C, *L'Italia Dei Beni Comuni* (Carocci 2012).
Arnstein, SR, 'A Ladder of Citizen Participation' (1969) 35 *Journal of the American Planning Association* 216.
Asenbaum, H, 'Rethinking Democratic Innovations: A Look through the Kaleidoscope of Democratic Theory' (2021) 20 *Political Studies Review* 680.
Auby, JB, 'Droit de La Ville. An Introduction' (2013) 5 *Italian Journal of Public Law* 302.
—— *Droit de la Ville: Du Fonctionnement Juridique des Villes au Droit à la Ville* (LexisNexis 2013).
Aust, HP and Nijman, JE (eds), *Research Handbook on International Law and Cities* (Edward Elgar Publishing 2021).

Avbelj, M, 'The Theory of Principled Legal Pluralism' in M Avbelj (ed), *The European Union under Transnational Law* (Hart Publishing 2018).
Bächtiger, A et al (eds), *The Oxford Handbook of Deliberative Democracy* (Oxford University Press 2018).
Bailey, S and Mattei, U, 'Social Movements as Constituent Power: The Italian Struggle for the Commons' (2013) 20 *Indiana Journal of Global Legal Studies* 965.
Barber, BR, *Strong Democracy* (University of California Press 1984).
—— 'Three Challenges to Reinventing Democracy' in PQ Hirst and S Khilnani (eds), *Reinventing Democracy* (Blackwell Publishers 1996).
—— *If Mayors Ruled the World: Dysfunctional Nations, Rising Cities* (Yale University Press 2013).
Barber, NW, 'Subsidiarity in the Draft Constitution' (2005) 11 *European Public Law* 197.
—— 'The Limited Modesty of Subsidiarity' (2005) 11 *European Law Journal* 308.
Bartl, M, 'The Way We Do Europe: Subsidiarity and the *Substantive* Democratic Deficit' (2015) 21 *European Law Journal* 23.
Bartoletti, R and Faccioli, F, 'Public Engagement, Local Polities, Civic Collaborations' (2016) *Social Media + Society* 7.
Bauman, Z, *Europe: An Unfinished Adventure* (Polity 2004).
Bauwens, M et al, 'Commons Economies in Action. Mutualizing Urban Provisioning Systems' in J Engle et al (eds), *Sacred Civics. Building Seven Generation Cities* (Routledge 2022).
—— *Peer to Peer: The Commons Manifesto* (University of Westminster Press 2019).
Bauwens, M and Niaros, V, *Changing Societies through Urban Commons Transitions* (P2P Foundation 2017).
Bauwens, M and Onzia, Y, *A Commons Transition Plan for the City of Ghent* (City of Ghent and P2P Foundation 2017).
Benvenuti F, 'Il Ruolo Dell'amministrazione Nello Stato Democratico Contemporaneo' in G Marongiu and G Candido De Martin (eds), *Democrazia e Amministrazione. In Ricordo Di Vittorio Bachelet* (Giuffrè Editore 1992).
—— *Il Nuovo Cittadino: Tra Libertà Garantita e Libertà Attiva* (Marsilio 1994).
Berge, E, 'Protected Areas and Traditional Commons: Values and Institutions' (2005) 60 *Norsk Geografisk Tidsskrift/Norwegian Journal of Geography* 72.
Berman, HJ, 'The Western Legal Tradition in a Millennial Perspective: Past and Future' (2000) 60 *Louisiana Law Review* 739.
—— *Law and Revolution, II: The Impact of the Protestant Reformations on the Western Legal Tradition* (Belknap Press 2006).
Bertacchini, E et al, 'Defining Cultural Commons' in E Bertacchini et al (eds), *Cultural Commons: A New Perspective on the Production and Evolution of Cultures* (Edward Elgar Publishing 2012).
Besselink, LFM, Albers, HSJ and Eijsbouts, WT, 'Subsidiarity in Non-Federal Contexts: The Netherlands and the European Union', Report Prepared for the XVI FIDE Conference in Rome (1994).
Bessette, JM, 'Deliberative Democracy: The Majority Principle in American Government' in RA Goldwin and WA Schambra (eds), *How Democratic Is the Constitution?* (AEI Press 1980).
Bherer, L et al, 'The Participatory Democracy Turn: An Introduction' (2016) 12 *Journal of Civil Society* 225.
Bianchi, I, 'The Commonification of the Public under New Municipalism: Commons–State Institutions in Naples and Barcelona' (2022) 60 *Urban Studies* 2116.
Bifulco, R, 'Democrazia deliberativa, partecipativa e rappresentativa: tre diverse forme di democrazia' in U Allegretti (ed), *La democrazia partecipativa in Italia e in Europa* (Firenze University Press 2010).
Bin, R, 'Contro La Governance: La Partecipazione Tra Fatto e Diritto' in G Arena and F Cortese (eds), *Per Governare Insieme: Il Federalismo Come Metodo* (Cedam 2011).
—— 'Cose e Idee. Per Un Consolidamento Della Teoria Delle Fonti' (2019) 1 *Diritto Costituzionale* 11.
Blank, Y, 'The City and the World' (2006) 44 *Columbia Journal of Transnational Law* 875.
—— 'Federalism, Subsidiarity, and the Role of Local Governments in an Age of Global Multilevel Governance' (2010) *Fordham Urban Law Journal* 509.
—— 'Démocratie contributive: une renaissance citoyenne' (2016) *La Tribune Fonda* no 232.

Blokker, P, 'Constitutional Mobilization and Contestation in the Transnational Sphere' (2018) 45(S1) *Journal of Law and Society* 52.
Blomgren Amsler, L, 'Collaborative Governance: Integrating Management, Politics, and Law' (2016) 76 *Public Administration Review* 700.
Bloomberg, M, 'City Century. Why Municipalities Are the Key to Fighting Climate Change' (October 2015) *Foreign Affairs* 116.
Bobbio, L, 'Invece Dello Stato: Reti' (2005) 34 *Parolechiave* 33.
—— 'Dilemmi Della Democrazia Partecipativa' (2006) 4 *Democrazia a Diritto* 11.
—— *Il futuro della democrazia* (Corriere della Sera 2010 reprint of 1984 edition).
Boggero, G, 'La Carta Europea Dell'autonomia Locale Nella Giurisprudenza Degli Stati Europei' (2015) 43 (5–6) *Le Regioni* 1077.
—— *Constitutional Principles of Local Self-Government in Europe* (Brill 2018).
Bohman, J and Rehg, W (eds), *Deliberative Democracy: Essays on Reason and Politics* (MIT Press 1997).
Bollier, D, *Think Like a Commoner: A Short Introduction to the Life of the Commons* (New Society Publishers 2011).
Bollier, D and Helfrich, S, *The Wealth of the Commons. A World beyond Market and State* (The Commons Strategy Group 2013).
Bombardelli, M, 'La Cura Dei Beni Comuni: Esperienze e Prospettive' (2018) 5 *Giornale Di Diritto Amministrativo* 559.
Borgonovo, Re D, *Le quattro stelle della Costituzione. Per una cittadinanza responsabile* (Il Margine 2013).
Bostan, A, 'Transnational Law – A New System of Law?' (2021) 11 *Juridical Tribune* 332.
Bovis, CH, *EU Public Procurement Law* (Edward Elgar Publishing 2012).
Brezovnik, B et al (eds), *Local Self-Government in Europe* (Lex Localis 2021).
Brunazzo, M, 'Istituzionalizzare La Partecipazione? Le Leggi Sulla Partecipazione in Italia' (2017) 3 *Istituzioni Del Federalismo* 837.
Bruni, L and Zamagni, S, *Civil Economy: Another Idea of the Market* (Agenda Publishing 2016).
Burini, C and Sforzi, J, 'Imprese di comunità e beni comuni. Un fenomeno in evoluzione' (Euricse 2020).
Bussu, S, 'Collaborative Governance: Between Invited and Invented Spaces' in S Elstub and O Escobar (eds), *Handbook of Democratic Innovation and Governance* (Edward Elgar Publishing 2019).
Cacciari, M, *La città* (Pazzini Editore 2021).
Cahill, M, 'Subsidiarity as the Preference for Proximity' (2021) 66 *American Journal of Jurisprudence* 129.
Cahill, M and O'Sullivan, G, 'Subsidiarity and the City: The Case for Mutual Strengthening' in E Arban (ed), *Cities in Federal Constitutional Theory* (Oxford University Press 2022).
Calliess, C, 'Europe as Transnational Law – The Transnationalization of Values by European Law' (2009) 10) *German Law Journal* 1367.
Camerlengo, Q, 'Città e Cittadini: Uno Spazio per i Beni Comuni?' in B Biscotti et al (eds), *Città, Cittadini, Conflitti* (Giappichelli 2020).
Cameron, F, 'Widening and Deepening' in F Cameron (ed), *The Future of European Integration and Enlargement* (Routledge 2004).
Capone, N, 'Urbanistica e Beni Comuni Di Uso Civico e Collettivo. Considerazioni Preliminari' in F De Notaris (ed), *Avere Memoria, Costruire Il Futuro* (La scuola di Pitagora 2020).
Caprotti, F et al, 'Beyond the Smart City: A Typology of Platform Urbanism' (2022) 4 *Urban Transformations* 1.
Caranta, R, 'Participation into Administrative Procedures: Achievements and Problems' (2010) 2 *Italian Journal of Public Law* 311.
Carlotto, I, 'I Beni Comuni e i Regolamenti per l'amministrazione Condivisa' in R Realdon (ed), *La Sussidiarietà Orizzontale Nel Titolo V Della Costituzione e La Sussidiarietà Generativa* (Cedam 2018).
Carney, FC (trans), *The Politics of Johannes Althusius* (Beacon Press 1964).
Cassese, S, 'L'aquila e le mosche. Principio di sussidiarietà e diritti amministrativi nell'area europea' (1995) 118 *Il Foro Italiano* 373.
—— 'L'arena Pubblica. Nuovi Paradigmi per Lo Stato' (2001) 3 *Rivista Trimestrale di Diritto Pubblico* 601.

—— 'The Administrative State in Europe' in A von Bogdandy et al (eds), *The Max Planck Handbooks in European Public Law: The Administrative State* (Oxford University Press 2017).
—— 'Identità e Funzioni Delle Riviste Pubblicistiche' (2021) 4 *Forum Di Quaderni Costituzionali* 26.
Castells, M, *Rupture: The Crisis of Liberal Democracy* (Polity Press 2018).
Cavallo Perin, R, 'Beyond the Municipality: The City, Its Rights and Its Rites' (2013) 5 *Italian Journal of Public Law* 307.
Cavallo Perin, R et al (eds), *Attualità e Necessità Del Pensiero Di Santi Romano* (Editoriale Scientifica 2019).
Cerulli Irelli, V, 'L'amministrazione Condivisa Nel Sistema Del Diritto Amministrativo' in G Arena and M Bombardelli (eds), *L'amministrazione Condivisa* (Editoriale Scientifica 2022).
—— 'Sussidiarietà (Diritto Amministrativo)' (2003) *Enciclopedia Giuridica*, Treccani.
Cerulli Irelli, V and Cameli, R, 'Il Principio di Sussidiarietà Orizzontale nei Lavori dell'Assemblea Costituente' (*Astrid Online*).
Cerulli Irelli, V and De Lucia, L, 'Beni Comuni e Diritti Collettivi' (2014) 1 *Politica del Diritto* 3.
Chalmers, D and Tomkins, A (eds), 'Soft Law' in D Chalmers and A Tomkins, *European Union Public Law* (Cambridge University Press 2007).
Cheneval, F, '*Demoicratic* Self-Government in the European Union's Polycentric System: Theoretical Remarks' in J van Zeben and A Bobić (eds), *Polycentricity in the European Union* (Cambridge University Press 2019).
Cheneval, F and Schimmelfennig, F, 'The Case for Demoicracy in the European Union' (2013) 51 *Journal of Common Market Studies* 334.
Chiti, M, 'La Rigenerazione Di Spazi e Beni Pubblici: Una Nuova Funzione Amministrative?' in F Di Lascio and F Giglioni (eds), *La Rigenerazione Di Beni e Spazi Urbani. Contributo al Diritto Delle Città* (Il Mulino 2017).
Christiansen, T and Piattoni, S (eds), *Informal Governance in the European Union* (Edward Elgar Publishing 2003).
Chwalisz, C, 'The Pandemic Has Pushed Citizen Panels Online' *Nature* (12 January 2021).
Ciaffi, D, 'Sharing the Commons as a "New Top" of Arnstein's Ladder of Participation' (2019) 45 *Built Environment* 162.
Ciaffi, D and de Groot, T, *From the Netherlands the Idea of Public–Civic Partnership as a Declination of Sharing Administration* (Labsus, 2021).
Cirillo, R and De Tullio, MF (eds), *Healing Culture, Reclaiming Commons, Fostering Care: A Proposal for EU Cultural Policies* (Italian Institute for the Future 2021).
Claes, M, 'How Common Are the Values of the European Union?' (2019) 15 *Croatian Yearbook of European Law & Policy* VII.
Constant, B, *The Liberty of Ancients Compared with That of Moderns* (1819).
Cornella, S, 'Beni Comuni e Disciplina Europea Sugli Aiuti Di Stato' in M Bombardelli (ed), *Prendersi Cura Dei Beni Comuni per Uscire Dalla Crisi* (Editoriale Scientifica 2016).
Cortese, F, 'Dalle Valli Di Pesca Ai Beni Comuni: La Cassazione Rilegge Lo Statuto Dei Beni Pubblici?' (2011) 11 *Giornale Di Diritto Amministrativo* 1170.
—— 'What Are Common Goods (Beni Comuni)? Pictures from the Italian Debate' (2017) 11(2) *Polemos* 417.
—— 'I Beni Mutanti. Fisiologia e Sfide Del Dibattito Sui Beni Comuni' (2018) 1 *Munera* 13.
—— 'Il Nuovo Diritto Delle Città: Alla Ricerca Di Un Legittimo Spazio Operativo' in GF Ferrari (ed), *Smart City: L'evoluzione Di Un'idea* (Mimesis 2020).
—— 'Che Cosa Succede in Città?' (2024) 3 *Munus*.
Cotturri, G, 'Storia del principio di sussidiarietà in Costituzione' in G Arena and G Cotturri (eds), *Il Valore Aggiunto: Come la Sussidiarietà Può Cambiare l'Italia* (Carocci 2010).
Craig, P, 'Subsidiarity: A Political and Legal Analysis' (2012) 50(S1) *Journal of Common Market Studies* 72.
Crouch, C, *Post-Democracy After the Crises* (Polity 2020).
Cuesta Lopez, V, 'The Lisbon Treaty's Provisions on Democratic Principles: A Legal Framework for Participatory Democracy' (2010) 16 *European Public Law* 123.

Cunningham, F, *Theories of Democracy: A Critical Introduction* (Routledge 2002).
Curi, U, 'Alle radici dell'idea di città' in F Pizzolato et al (eds), *La città e la partecipazione tra diritto e politica* (Giappichelli 2019).
D'Atena, A, 'Il principio di sussidiarietà nella Costituzione italiana' [1997] *Rivista Italiana di Diritto Pubblico Comunitario* 603.
—— 'Costituzione e principio di sussidiarietà' (2001) 1 *Quaderni Costituzionali* 13.
—— 'Sussidiarietà e proporzionalità nelle dinamiche multilivello e nelle relazioni pubblico-privato' (2022) 4 *Federalismi.it.*
Dahl, RA, *Democracy and Its Critics* (Yale University Press 1989).
—— 'The Problem of Civic Competence' (1992) 3(4) *Journal of Democracy* 45.
—— 'A Democratic Dilemma: System Effectiveness versus Citizen Participation' (1994) 109 *Political Science Quarterly* 23.
Dani, M and Palermo, F, 'Della Governance e Di Altri Demoni (Un Dialogo)' (2003) 4 *Quaderni Costituzionali* 785.
Dann, P, 'Thoughts on a Methodology of European Constitutional Law' (2005) 6 *German Law Journal* 1453.
De Moor, T, 'Homo Cooperans' (Inaugural lecture, University of Utrecht, 30 August 2013).
De Tullio, MF, 'Commons towards New Participatory Institutions. The Neapolitan Experience' in P Gielen and N Dockx (eds), *Exploring Commonism: A New Aesthetics of the Real* (Valiz 2018).
De Visser, M, 'The Future Is Urban: The Progressive Renaissance of The City in EU Law' (2020) 7 *Journal of International and Comparative Law* 389.
De Visser, M et al, 'Introduction: The City as a Multifaceted and Dynamic Constitutional Entity' in E Hirsch Ballin et al (eds), *European Yearbook of Constitutional Law 2020: The City in Constitutional Law* (TMC Asser Press 2020).
—— 'Constitutionalizing Cities: Realizing Government Agendas or Sites for Denizen Engagement?' in A Flynn et al (eds), *Cities and the Constitution: Giving Local Governments in Canada the Power they Need* (McGill-Queen's University Press 2024).
De Witte, B, 'Article 4(2) TEU as a Protection of the Institutional Diversity of the Member States' (2021) 27 *European Public Law* 559.
Deleixhe, M, 'Conclusion: Is the Governance of the Commons a Model for a New Global Governance?' in S Cogolati and J Wouters (eds), *The Commons and a New Global Governance* (2018).
Della Cananea, G, 'Is European Constitutionalism Really "Multilevel"?' (2010) 70 *Heidelberg Journal of International Law* 283.
—— 'Transnational Public Law in Europe' in MP Maduro, K Tuori and Sankari S (eds), *Transnational Law: Rethinking European Law and Legal Thinking* (Cambridge University Press 2014).
—— 'Jean-Bernard Auby e Lo Ius Publicum Europeum' in G Della Cananea and J Ziller (eds), *Il Nuovo Diritto Pubblico Europeo: Scritti in Onore Di Jean-Bernard Auby* (Giappichelli 2019).
Della Porta, D, *Can Democracy Be Saved? Participation, Deliberation and Social Movements* (Polity 2013).
Dickovick, JT, 'Municipalization as Central Government Strategy: Central–Regional–Local Politics in Peru, Brazil, and South Africa' (2009) 37 *Publius: The Journal of Federalism* 1.
Donati, D, *Il Paradigma Sussidiario: Interpretazioni, Estensione, Garanzie* (Il Mulino 2014).
Drew, J, *Reforming Local Government* (Springer 2020).
Drew, J and Grant, B, 'Subsidiarity: More than a Principle of Decentralization – A View from Local Government' (2017) 47 *Publius: Journal of Federalism* 522.
Dryzek, JS et al, 'The Crisis of Democracy and the Science of Deliberation' (2019) 363 *Science* 1144.
Duret, P, 'La sussidiarietà "orizzontale": le radici e le suggestioni di un concetto' (2000) 1 *Jus Online.*
Đurman, P, 'Participation in Public Administration Revisited: Delimiting, Categorizing and Evaluating Administrative Participation' (2020) 20 *Croatian and Comparative Public Administration* 79.
Ehrlich, E, *Fundamental Principles of the Sociology of Law* (Harvard University Press 1936).
Elazar, DJ, *Exploring Federalism* (University of Alabama Press 1987).
Elia, M, 'International Conference of Urban Commons' (2021) 21 *Global Jurist* 483.
Eliantonio, M et al (eds), *EU Soft Law in the Member States: Theoretical Findings and Empirical Evidence* (Bloomsbury Publishing 2021).

Elster, J (ed), *Deliberative Democracy* (Cambridge University Press 1998).
Elstub, S and Escobar O, 'Defining and Typologising Democratic Innovations' in S Elstub and O Escobar (eds), *Handbook of Democratic Innovation and Governance* (Edward Elgar Publishing 2019).
Ercan, SA and Gagnon, JP, 'The Crisis of Democracy Which Crisis? Which Democracy?' (2014) 1(2) *Democratic Theory* 1.
Escobar, O and Elstub, S, 'Forms of Mini-Publics: An Introduction to Deliberative Innovations in Democratic Practice' (New Democracy, Research and Development Note 4, 2017)
Etty, T et al, 'Legal, Regulatory, and Governance Innovation in Transnational Environmental Law' (2022) 11 *Transnational Environmental Law* 223.
Etzioni, A, 'The Third Sector and Domestic Missions' (1973) 33 *Public Administration Review* 314.
Fennell, LA, 'Ostrom's Law: Property Rights in the Commons' (2011) 5 *International Journal of the Commons* 9.
Ferri, D, 'L'Unione Europea Sulla Strada Della Democrazia Partecipativa?' (2011) 2 *Istituzioni del Federalismo* 298.
—— 'European Citizens … Mind the Gap! Some Reflections on Participatory Democracy in the EU' (2013) 5(3) *Perspectives on Federalism* 56.
Ferri, D and Cortese, F (eds), *The EU Social Market Economy and the Law* (Routledge 2019).
Finck, M, 'Challenging the Subnational Dimension of Subsidiarity in EU Law' (2015) 8 *European Journal of Legal Studies* 5.
—— 'Fragmentation as an Agent of Integration: Subnational Authorities in EU Law' (2017) 15 *ICON* 1119.
Floridia, A, 'Participatory Democracy versus Deliberative Democracy: Elements for a Possible Theoretical Genealogy. Two Histories, Some Intersections' 7th ECPR General Conference Sciences Po (Bordeaux, 4–7 September 2013).
—— 'The Origins of the Deliberative Turn' in A Bächtiger et al (eds), *The Oxford Handbook of Deliberative Democracy* (Oxford University Press 2018).
Florida, R, *The New Urban Crisis* (Basic Books 2017).
Føllesdal, A, 'Survey Article: Subsidiarity' (1998) 6 *Journal of Political Philosophy* 190.
—— *Subsidiarity* (Cambridge University Press 2025).
Follesdal, A and Hix, S, 'Why There is a Democratic Deficit in the EU: A Response to Majone and Moravcsik' (2006) 44 *Journal of Common Market Studies* 533.
Foster, SR, 'Collective Action and the Urban Commons' (2011) 87 *Notre Dame Law Review* 57.
Foster, SR and Iaione, C, 'The City as a Commons' (2016) 34 *Yale Law & Policy Review* 281.
—— 'Ostrom in the City. Design Principles and Practices for the Urban Commons' in B Hudson et al (eds), *Routledge Handbook of the Study of the Commons* (Routledge 2019).
—— *Co-Cities* (MIT Press 2022).
Foster, SR and Swiney, CF, *The Cambridge Handbook of Commons Research Innovations* (Cambridge University Press 2022).
Fraenkel-Haeberle, C et al, *Citizen Participation in Multi-Level Democracies* (Brill-Nijhoff 2015).
Frankenberg, G, 'Democracy' in M Rosenfeld and A Sajó (eds), *The Oxford Handbook of Comparative Constitutional Law* (Oxford University Press 2012).
Frosini, TE, 'Sussidiarietà (Principio Di) (Dir.Cost.)' (2008) *Enciclopedia del Diritto* 1134.
Frug, GE, 'The City as a Legal Concept' (1980) 93 *Harvard Law Review* 1057.
—— 'Empowering Cities in a Federal System' (1987) 19 *The Urban Lawyer* 553.
Frug, GE and Barron, DJ, 'International Local Government Law' (2006) 38 *The Urban Lawyer* 1.
Fukuyama, F, 'Social Capital, Civil Society and Development' (2001) 22 *Third World Quarterly* 7.
—— 'Against Identity Politics: The New Tribalism and the Crisis of Democracy' (2018) 97(5) *Foreign Affairs* 90.
Gamper, A, 'Direct Democracy' in (2019) *Max Planck Encyclopedia of Comparative Constitutional Law (MPECCoL)*.
Ganuza, E and Baiocchi, G, 'The Long Journey of Participatory Budgeting' in S Elstub and O Escobar (eds), *Handbook of Democratic Innovation and Governance* (Edward Elgar Publishing 2019).
Gaspari, F, 'Città intelligenti e intervento pubblico' (2019) 98 *Il diritto dell'economia* 71.

Genio, G, 'Gli usi civici nella legge n. 168 del 2017 sui domini collettivi: sintonie e distonie attraverso la giurisprudenza costituzionale e il dibattito in sede costituente' (2018) *Federalismi.It*.

Giglioni, F, 'Sussidiarietà Orizzontale e Terzo Settore' (*Astrid Online*, 2002).

—— 'Alla Ricerca Della Sussidiarietà Orizzontale in Europa' in D Donati and A Paci (eds), *Sussidiarietà e Concorrenza* (Il Mulino 2010).

—— 'La Sussidiarietà Orizzontale Nella Giurisprudenza' in G Arena and G Cotturri (eds), *Il Valore Aggiunto: Come La Sussidiarietà Può Cambiare l'Italia* (Carocci 2010).

—— 'Subsidiary Cooperation: A New Type of Relationship between Public and Private Bodies Supported by the EU Law' (2010) 2 *Rivista Italiana di Diritto Pubblico Comunitario* 485.

—— 'L'Unione Europea per Lo Sviluppo Dei Beni Comuni' (*Labsus*, 2015).

—— 'Beni Comuni e Autonomie Nella Prospettiva Europea: Città e Cittadinanze' in M Bombardelli (ed), *Prendersi Cura Dei Beni Comuni per Uscire Dalla Crisi* (Editoriale Scientifica 2016).

—— 'Forme Di Cittadinanza Legittimate Dal Principio Di Sussidiarietà' (2016) 2 *Diritto e Società* 305.

—— 'I Regolamenti Comunali per La Gestione Dei Beni Comuni Urbani Come Laboratorio per Un Nuovo Diritto Delle Città' (2016) 2 *Munus* 290.

—— 'Order without Law in the Experience of Italian Cities' (2017) 9 *Italian Journal of Public Law* 291.

—— 'Il Diritto Pubblico Informale Alla Base Della Riscoperta Delle Città Come Ordinamento Giuridico' (2018) 2 *Rivista Giuridica Dell'edilizia* 3.

—— 'Le Città Come Ordinamento Giuridico' (2018) 1 *Istituzioni Del Federalismo* 29.

—— 'Verso Un Diritto Delle Città. Le Città Oltre Il Comune' in E Carloni and F Cortese (eds), *Diritto Delle Autonomie Territoriali* (Cedam 2020).

—— 'Forme e Strumenti Dell'amministrazione Condivisa' in G Arena and M Bombardelli (eds), *L'Amministrazione Condivisa* (Editoriale Scientifica 2022).

Giglioni, F and Nervi, A, *Gli Accordi Delle Pubbliche Amministrazioni* (Edizioni Scientifiche Italiane 2019).

Gilbert, N, *Transformation of the Welfare State: The Silent Surrender of Public Responsibility* (Oxford University Press 2002).

Gilbert, N and Gilbert, B, *The Enabling State: Modern Welfare Capitalism in America* (Oxford University Press 1989).

Giordano, FM, 'Subsidiarity, a Transformative Principle for the Future of European Democracy' (2021) 4 *De Europa* 99.

Gios, G, 'Beni Collettivi o Beni Comuni? Una Lettura Della Distinzione Tra Profili Dominicali e Modelli Di Gestione in Base Alla Teoria Economica' in M Bombardelli (ed), *Prendersi Cura Dei Beni Comuni per Uscire Dalla Crisi* (Editoriale Scientifica 2016).

Gori, L, 'La Disciplina del volontariato individuale, ovvero dell'applicazione diretta dell'art.118, ultimo comma, Cost.' (2018) 1 *Associazione Italiana Dei Costituzionalisti* 1.

—— 'La "Saga" Della Sussidiarietà Orizzontale. La Tortuosa Vicenda Dei Rapporti Fra Terzo Settore e P.A.' *Federalismi.It* (2020).

—— 'Sentenza 131/2020: Sta Nascendo Un Diritto Costituzionale Del Terzo Settore' (2020) *Impresa Sociale*.

—— 'Terzo Settore Come Protagonista Dell'attuazione Della Costituzione' in S Pellizzari and C Borzaga (eds), *Terzo Settore e Pubblica Amministrazione: La Svolta Della Corte Costituzionale* (Euricse 2020).

—— *Terzo Settore e Costituzione* (Giappichelli 2022).

Gotti, G, 'La Sussidiarietà Orizzontale Nello Spazio Costituzionale Europeo' (2025) *Associazione Italiana dei Costituzionalisti*.

Granat, K, 'The Subsidiarity Principle in the EU Treaties' in K Granat, *The Principle of Subsidiarity and its Enforcement in the EU Legal Order: The Role of National Parliaments in the Early Warning System* (Hart Publishing 2018).

Grimm, D, 'Types of Constitutions' in M Rosenfeld and A Sajó (eds), *The Oxford Handbook of Comparative Constitutional Law* (Oxford University Press 2012).

Grossi, P, *Le Comunità Intermedie Tra Moderno e Post-Moderno* (Marinetti 2015).

Gussen, B, *Axial Shift City Subsidiarity and the World System in the 21st Century* (Palgrave Macmillan 2019).
Hage, J et al (eds), 'Sources of Law' in *Introduction to Law* (Springer International Publishing 2017).
Halmai, G, 'Does Illiberal Democracy Exist?' in G Amato, B Barbisan and C Pinelli (eds), *Rule of Law vs Majoritarian Democracy* (Hart Publishing 2021).
Hardin, G, 'The Tragedy of the Commons' (1968) 162 *Science* 1244.
Harris, C, 'Mini-Publics: Design Choices and Legitimacy' in S Elstub and O Escobar (eds), *Handbook of Democratic Innovation and Governance* (Edward Elgar Publishing 2019).
Harvey, D, 'The Right to the City' (2003) 27 *International Journal of Urban and Regional Research* 939.
Heinelt, H, *Handbook on Participatory Governance* (Edward Elgar Publishing 2018).
Hendriks, F, 'Democratic Innovation beyond Deliberative Reflection: The Plebiscitary Rebound and the Advent of Action-Oriented Democracy' (2019) 26 *Democratization* 444.
Hendriks, F et al, 'European Subnational Democracy: Comparative Reflections and Conclusions' in J Loughlin, F Hendriks and A Lidström (eds), *The Oxford Handbook of Local and Regional Democracy in Europe* (Oxford University Press 2012).
Hennen L, et al, *European E-Democracy in Practice* (Springer Open 2020).
Hèritier, A (ed), *Common Goods: Reinventing European and International Governance* (Rowman & Littlefield Publishers 2002).
Hess C, 'Mapping the New Commons' (Paper, 12th Biennial Conference of the International Association for the Study of the Commons, Governing Shared Resources: Connecting Local Experience to Global Challenges, 14–18 July 2008).
—— 'The Unfolding of the Knowledge Commons' (2012) 8(1) *St Antony's International Review* 13.
Hillion, C, 'The Copenhagen Criteria and their Progeny' in C Hillion (ed), *EU Enlargement: A Legal Approach* (Hart Publishing 2004).
Himsworth, CMG, *The European Charter of Local Self-Government: A Treaty for Local Democracy* (Edinburgh University Press 2015).
Hirsch Ballin, E et al (eds), *European Yearbook of Constitutional Law 2020: The City in Constitutional Law* (Springer 2020).
Hirschl, R, *City, State: Constitutionalism and the Megacity* (Oxford University Press 2020).
—— 'Constitutional Design and the Urban/Rural Divide' (2022) 16 *Law & Ethics of Human Rights* 1.
Hoeksma, J, 'Replacing the Westphalian System' (2020) The Federal Trust.
Hooghe, L and Marks, G, 'Types of Multi-Level Governance' (2001) 5-11 European Integration Online Papers.
Hörcher, F, *The Political Philosophy of the European City: From Polis, through City-State, to Megalopolis?* (Lexington Books 2021).
Hudson, B et al, *Routledge Handbook of the Study of the Commons* (Routledge 2019).
Huntington, SP, *Political Order in Changing Societies* (Yale University Press 1968).
—— 'Democracy's Third Wave' (1991) 2 *Journal of Democracy* 12.
Iaione, C, *La Città Come Bene Comune* (Labsus, 2011).
—— 'Città e Beni Comuni' in G Arena and C Iaione (eds), *L'Italia Dei Beni Comuni* (Carocci 2012).
—— 'La Città Come Bene Comune' (2013) 1 *Aedon* 31.
—— 'The CO-City: Sharing, Collaborating, Cooperating, and Commoning in the City' (2016) 75 *American Journal of Economics and Sociology* 415.
—— 'The Right to the Co-City' (2017) 15 *Italian Journal of Public Law* 80.
Iaione, C et al, 'Participatory Governance of Culture and Cultural Heritage: Policy, Legal, Economic Insights From Italy' (2022) 4 *Frontiers in Sustainable Cities.*
Iaione, C and de Nictolis, E, 'The Role of Law in Relation to the New Urban Agenda and the European Urban Agenda' in NM Davidson and G Tewari (eds), *Law and the New Urban Agenda* (Routledge 2020).
—— 'The City as a Commons Reloaded: From the Urban Commons to Co-Cities Empirical Evidence on the Bologna Regulation' in SR Foster and CF Swiney (eds), *The Cambridge Handbook of Commons Research Innovations* (Cambridge University Press 2022).

Iaione, C, Pais, I and de Nictolis, E, 'Valutare: La Valutazione Dei Patti Di Collaborazione' in R Paltrinieri (ed), *Culture e pratiche di partecipazione* (FrancoAngeli 2020).
Ioriatti, E, 'Common Contexts of Meaning in the European Legal Setting: Opening Pandora's Box?' (2022) 36 *International Journal for the Semiotics of Law* 275.
Ivanyna, M and Shah, A, 'How Close Is Your Government to Its People? Worldwide Indicators on Localization and Decentralization' (2012) World Bank Policy Research Working Paper No 6138.
Jacobs, J, *The Death and Life of Great American Cities* (Vintage Books 1961).
Jakab, A, 'What Can Constitutional Law Do Against the Erosion of Democracy and the Rule of Law?' 2019-15 MPIL Research Paper Series.
Jäske, M and Setälä, M, 'Referendums and Citizens' Initiatives' in S Elstub and O Escobar (eds), *Handbook of Democratic Innovation and Governance* (Edward Elgar Publishing 2019).
John, P, *Local Governance in Western Europe* (SAGE Publications Ltd 2001).
Kaufman, AS, 'Human Nature and Participatory Democracy' (1960) 3 *NOMOS: American Society for Political and Legal Philosophy* 266.
Kelemen, RD, 'Europe's Other Democratic Deficit: National Authoritarianism in Europe's Democratic Union' (2017) 52(SI2) *Government and Opposition* 211.
Kellerbauer, M, Klamert, M and Tomkin, J (eds), *The EU Treaties and the Charter of Fundamental Rights: A Commentary* (Oxford University Press 2019).
Kersting, N et al, *Local Governance Reform in Global Perspective* (VS Verlag für Sozialwissenschaften 2009).
Keymolen, E and Voorwinden, A, 'Can We Negotiate? Trust and the Rule of Law in the Smart City Paradigm' (2019) 34 *International Review of Law, Computers & Technology* 233.
King, L, 'Cities, Subsidiarity, and Federalism' in JE Fleming and JT Levy (eds), *Federalism and Subsidiarity* (New York University Press 2014).
Kioupkiolis, A, 'Transforming City Government: Italian Variants on Urban Commoning' (2022) 44(3) *Administrative Theory & Praxis* 186.
Kirchmair, L, 'International Law and Public Administration: The European Charter of Local Self-Government' (2015) 3 *Pro Publico* Bono 124.
Kjaer, AM, *Governance* (Wiley 2004).
Klamert, M and Kochenov, D, 'Article 2 TEU' in M Kellerbauer, M Klamert and J Tomkin (eds), *The EU Treaties and the Charter of Fundamental Rights: A Commentary* (Oxford University Press 2019).
Klijn, EH, 'Trust in Governance Networks: Looking for Conditions for Innovative Solutions and Outcomes' in SP Osborne (ed), *The New Public Governance? Emerging Perspectives on the Theory and Practice of Public Governance* (Routledge 2010).
Kochenov, D, *EU Enlargement and the Failure of Conditionality: Pre-Accession Conditionality in the Fields of Democracy and the Rule of Law* (Kluwer Law International 2008).
—— 'Europe's Crisis of Values' (2014) 48 *Revista Catalana de Dret Públic* 106.
—— 'The Acquis and Its Principles: The Enforcement of the "Law" versus the Enforcement of "Values" in the European Union' in A Jakab and D Kochenov (eds), *The Enforcement of EU Law and Values* (Oxford University Press 2017).
Kohler-Koch, B and Rittberger, B, 'Review Article: The "Governance Turn" in EU Studies' (2006) 44 *Journal of Common Market Studies Annual Review* 27.
Kooiman, J (ed), *Modern Governance: New Government–Society Interactions* (Sage 1993).
Kössler, K and Kress, A, 'European Cities Between Self-Government and Subordination: Their Role as Policy-Takers and Policy-Makers' in E Hirsch Ballin et al (eds), *European Yearbook of Constitutional Law 2020: The City in Constitutional Law* (Springer 2020).
Kriesi, H, 'Is There a Crisis of Democracy in Europe?' (2020) 61 *Polit Vierteljahresschr* 237.
Kuhn, T, *The Structure of Scientific Revolutions* (University of Chicago Press 1962).
Kutay, A, 'Limits of Participatory Democracy in European Governance' (2015) 21 *European Law Journal* 803.
La Porta, S, *L'organizzazione Delle Libertà Sociali* (Giuffrè 2004).
Ladeur, K-H, 'European Law as Transnational Law – Europe Has to Be Conceived as an Heterarchical Network and Not as a Superstate!' (2009) 10 *German Law Journal* 1357.
Ladner, A et al (eds), *Patterns of Local Autonomy in Europe* (Palgrave Macmillan 2019).

Ladner, A, Keuffer, N and Bastianen, A, *Local Autonomy Index in the EU, Council of Europe and OECD countries (1990–2020), Release 2.0* (European Commission 2021).

Landemore, H, *Open Democracy: Reinventing Popular Rule for the Twenty-First Century* (Princeton University Press 2020).

Landry, C, *The Creative City: A Toolkit for Urban Innovators* (Earthscan 2008).

Laws, D and Forester, J, *Conflict, Improvisation, Governance: Street Level Practices for Urban Democracy* (Routledge 2015).

Lefebvre, H, 'Le Droit à La Ville' (1967) 6 *L'Homme et La Société* 29.

——*Il diritto alla città* (Ombre Corte 2013).

Leino, P, 'Disruptive Democracy: Keeping EU Citizens in a Box' in I Govaere et al (eds), *Critical Reflections on Constitutional Democracy in the European Union* (Hart Publishing 2019).

Leipzig Charter and the Urban Agenda for the EU (18 September 2020).

Lember, V et al, 'Engaging Citizens in Policy Making: The Potential and Challenges of e-Participation' in T Randma-Liiv and V Lember (eds), *Engaging Citizens in Policy Making: E-Participation Practices in Europe* (Edward Elgar Publishing 2022).

Lewanski, R, 'Institutionalizing Deliberative Democracy: The "Tuscany Laboratory"' (2013) 9 *Journal of Public Deliberation* Article 10.

Lijphart, A, *Patterns of Democracy: Government Forms and Performance in Thirty-Six Countries* (Yale University Press 2012).

Lille Action Programme, adopted at the Informal Council of Ministers responsible for Urban Development (Lille, 3 November 2000).

Longo, E, 'Local Governments and Metropolitan Cities' in E Arban et al (eds), *Federalism and Constitutional Law: The Italian Contribution to Comparative Regionalism* (Routledge 2021).

Loorbach, D, et al, 'Sustainability Transitions Research: Transforming Science and Practice for Societal Change' (2017) 42 *Annual Review of Environment and Resources* 599.

López Pulido, JP, *Perspectiva Cognitiva y Nudge Público: La Actuación Conductual de Los Poderes Públicos* (Editorial Aranzadi 2023).

Luciani, M, 'Forme di governo' (2010) *Enciclopedia del Diritto.*

Luther, J, 'Il principio di sussidiarietà: un "principio speranza" per il diritto costituzionale comune europeo?' (1996) 119 *Il Foro Italiano* 184.

—— 'La sussidiarietà come principio sussidiario del diritto pubblico comune europeo' in D Ciaffi and FM Giordano (eds), *Storia, percorsi e politiche della sussidiarietà. Le nuove prospettive in Italia e in Europa* (Il Mulino 2020).

Macdonald, G, *Sussidiarietà Orizzontale: Cittadini Attivi Nella Cura Dei Beni Comuni* (Aracne editrice 2018).

Macpherson, CB, *The Life and Times of Liberal Democracy* (Oxford University Press 1977).

Magnusson, W, *Politics of Urbanism: Seeing Like a City* (Routledge 2011).

Manin, B, *The Principles of Representative Government* (Cambridge University Press 1997).

Mansbridge, JJ, *Beyond Adversary Democracy* (University of Chicago Press 1983).

Marella, MR, 'The Commons as a Legal Concept' (2016) 28 *Law Critique* 61.

Marks, G, 'Structural Policy in the European Community' in AM Sbragia (ed), *Europolitics: Institutions and Policymaking in the 'New' European Community* (The Brookings Institution 1992).

Marks, G et al, 'European Integration from the 1980s: State Centric v. Multilevel Governance' (1996) 34 *Journal of Common Market Studies* 341.

Martinico, G, 'Federalism, Regionalism and the Principle of Subsidiarity' in E Arban et al (eds), *Federalism and Constitutional Law: The Italian Contribution to Comparative Regionalism* (Routledge 2021).

—— 'Taming National Identity: A Systematic Understanding of Article 4.2 TEU' (2021) 27 *European Public Law* 447.

Marzolf, E, 'Olivier Jaspart: "Comment Les Partenariats Public-Commun Vont Réinterroger Le Droit Public"' (*Acteurpublique*, 11 March 2022).

Massa Pinto, I, 'Il principio di sussidiarietà nel progetto di trattato che istituisce una Costituzione per l'Europa' (2003) II *Diritto Pubblico Comparato ed Europeo* 1220.

——*Il principio di sussidiarietà: profili storici e costituzionali* (Jovene 2003).

Mattei, U, *Beni comuni. Un manifesto* (Laterza 2011).
Mattei, U, et al, *Invertire la rotta: idee per una riforma della proprietà pubblica* (Il Mulino 2007).
Mattei, U and Quarta, A, 'Right to the City or Urban Commoning? Thoughts on the Generative Transformation of Property Law' (2015) 1 *Italian Law Journal* 303.
McGinnis, M (ed), *Polycentricity and Local Public Economies: Readings from the Workshop in Political Theory and Policy Analysis* (University of Michigan Press 1999).
McGinnis, MD and Ostrom, E, 'Reflections on Vincent Ostrom, Public Administration, and Polycentricity' (2012) 72 *Public Administration Review* 15.
Medda, R, *Il Governo Locale Delle Aree Urbane in Italia* (Edizioni Scientifiche Italiane 2022).
Mendes, J, 'Participation and the Role of Law after Lisbon: A Legal View on Article 11 TEU' (2011) 48(6) *Common Market Law Review* 1849.
Mény, Y, 'De La Démocratie En Europe: Old Concepts and New Challenges' (2003) 41 *Journal of Common Market Studies* 1.
—— 'Conclusion: A Voyage to the Unknown' (2012) 50(S1) *Journal of Common Market Studies* 154.
Merkel, W and Kneip, S, *Democracy and Crisis: Challenges in Turbulent Times* (Springer 2018).
Merloni, F, 'Le Autonomie Nella Costituzione Repubblicana' (2010) 108(3) *Astrid Rassegna.*
Micciarelli, G, 'Le Teorie Dei Beni Comuni al Banco Di Prova Del Diritto La Soglia Di Un Nuovo Immaginario Istituzionale' (2014) 1 *Politica & Società* 123.
Micciché, C, *Beni comuni: risorse per lo sviluppo sostenibile* (Editoriale Scientifica 2018).
Michels, A, 'Innovations in Democratic Governance: How Does Citizen Participation Contribute to a Better Democracy?' (2011) 77 *International Review of Administrative Sciences* 275.
Michiara, P, 'I Patti Di Collaborazione e Il Regolamento per La Cura e La Rigenerazione Dei Beni Comuni Urbani. L'esperienza Del Comune Di Bologna' (2016) 2 *Aedon.*
Micklitz H-W, 'Rethinking the Public/Private Divide' in M Maduro et al (eds), *Transnational Law* (Cambridge University Press 2014).
Millon-Delson, C, *Le principe de subsidiarité* (Presses Universitaires de France 1993). Italian translation *Il principio di sussidiarietà* (Giuffrè Editore 2003).
Modugno, F, 'E' Possibile Parlare Ancora Di Un Sistema Delle Fonti?' (2008) *Associazione Italiana dei Costituzionalisti* 2.
Moreno, C et al, 'Introducing the "15-Minute City": Sustainability, Resilience and Place Identity in Future Post-Pandemic Cities' (2021) 4 *Smart Cities* 93.
Morison, J and Harkens, A, 'Principle of Participation' (2017) *Max Planck Encyclopedia of Comparative Constitutional Law (MPECCoL).*
Morozov, E and Bria, F, *Rethinking the Smart City: Democratizing Urban Technologies* (Rosa Luxemburg Stiftung 2018).
Mueller, FH, 'The Principle of Subsidiarity in the Christian Tradition' (1943) 4 *American Catholic Sociological Review* 144.
Mumford, L, *The City in History* (Harcourt Brace Jovanovich Inc 1961).
Muzi, L, 'L'amministrazione Condivisa Dei Beni Comuni Urbani: Il Ruolo Dei Privati Nell'ottica Del Principio Di Sussidiarietà Orizzontale' in F Di Lascio and F Giglioni (eds), *La Rigenerazione Di Beni e Spazi Urbani* (Il Mulino 2017).
Nesi, G, 'The Shifting Status of Cities in International Law? A Review, Several Questions and a Straight Answer' (2021) 30 *Italian Yearbook of International Law Online* 15.
Nesti, G, 'Defining and Assessing the Transformational Nature of Smart City Governance: Insights from Four European Cases' (2020) 86 *International Review of Administrative Sciences* 29.
Nicholls, W and Vermeulen, F, 'Rights *through* the City: The Urban Basis of Immigrant Rights Struggles in Paris and Amsterdam' in MP Smith and M McQuarrie (eds), *Remaking Urban Citizenship: Organizations, Institutions, and the Right to the City* (Transactions Publishers 2012).
Nicola, F, 'Invisible Cities in Europe' (2012) 35 *Fordham International Law Journal* 1282.
Nicolaïdis, K, 'Conclusion: The Federal Vision Beyond the Federal State' in K Nicolaïdis and R Howse (eds), *The Federal Vision: Legitimacy and Levels of Governance in the United States and the European Union* (Oxford University Press 2001).

Nicolaïdis, K, 'The New Constitution as European "Demoi-Cracy"?' (2004) 7(1) *Critical Review of International Social and Political Philosophy* 76.
Nicolaïdis, K, 'European Demoicracy and Its Crisis' (2013) 51 *Journal of Common Market Studies* 351.
Nicolaïdis, K, 'The Idea of European Demoicracy' in J Dickson and P Eleftheriadis (eds), *Philosophical Foundations of European Union Law* (Oxford University Press 2012).
Nicolaïdis, K and van Zeben, J, 'Polycentric Subsidiarity' in J van Zeben and A Bobić (eds), *Polycentricity in the European Union* (Cambridge University Press 2019).
Nicolini, M, 'Theoretical Framework and Constitutional Implications: Participatory Democracy as Decision-Making in Multilayered Italy' in F Palermo and E Alber (eds), *Federalism as Decision-Making* (Brill-Nijhoff 2015).
Nicotina, A, 'A Procedural Idea of Environmental Democracy: The "Débat Public" Paradigm within the EU Framework' (2021) 14(2) *Review of European Administrative Law* 85.
Nigro, M, 'Il nodo della partecipazione' [1980] *Rivista Trimestrale di Diritto e Procedura Civile* 225.
Nijkamp, P and Cohen-Blankshtain, G, 'Opportunities and Pitfalls of Local E-Democracy' in U Allegretti (ed), *Democrazia partecipativa: esperienze e prospettive in Italia e in Europa* (Firenze University Press 2010).
Oomen, B and Baumgärtel, M, 'Frontier Cities: The Rise of Local Authorities as an Opportunity for International Human Rights Law' (2018) 29 *European Journal of International Law* 607.
Osborne, SP, 'The New Public Governance?' (2006) 8 *Public Management Review* 377.
——*The New Public Governance? Emerging Perspectives on the Theory and Practice of Public Governance* (Routledge 2010).
Osborne, SP et al, 'Co-Production and the Co-Creation of Value in Public Services: A Suitable Case for Treatment?' (2016) 18(5) *Public Management Review* 639.
Ostrom, E, *Governing the Commons: The Evolution of Institutions for Collective Action* (Cambridge University Press 1990).
—— 'Crossing the Great Divide: Coproduction, Synergy, and Development' (1996) 24 *World Development* 1073.
Ostrom, V, 'Faustian Bargains' (1996) 7 *Constitutional Political Economy* 303.
——*The Meaning of Democracy and the Vulnerability of Democracies: A Response to Tocqueville's Challenge* (University of Michigan Press 1997).
——*The Meaning of American Federalism: Constituting a Self-Governing Society* (Institute for Contemporary Studies 1991).
——'Polycentricity' in MD McGinnis (ed), *Polycentricity and Local Public Economies: Readings from the Workshop in Political Theory and Policy Analysis* (University of Michigan Press 1999).
Ostrom, V et al, 'The Organization of Government in Metropolitan Areas: A Theoretical Inquiry' (1961) 55 *American Political Science Review* 831.
Ozzola, F, 'Dal Dire al Fare. La Sussidiarietà Orizzontale in Pratica' in G Arena and G Cotturri (eds), *Il Valore Aggiunto: Come La Sussidiarietà Può Salvare l'Italia* (Carocci 2010).
Pace, A, 'Violazione della "libertà sociale" o, piuttosto, restrizione della "libertà individuale"?' (1998) 2 *Giurisprudenza Costituzionale* 584.
Palermo, F, *La forma di Stato dell'Unione Europea* (Cedam 2005).
——'Internazionalizzazione Del Diritto Costituzionale e Costituzionalizzazione Del Diritto Internazionale Delle Differenze' (2009) European Diversity and Autonomy Papers no 2.
—— 'Participation, Federalism, and Pluralism: Challenges to Decision Making and Responses by Constitutionalism' in C Fraenkel-Haeberle et al (eds), *Citizen Participation in Multi-Level Democracies* (Brill 2015).
—— 'Partecipazione come fonte di legittimazione? Nuovi processi decisionali e Sfide per il sistema delle fonti' in S Catalano et al (eds), *Processi decisionali e fonti del diritto* (Edizioni Scientifiche Italiane 2022).
Palermo, F and Kössler, K, *Comparative Federalism: Constitutional Arrangements and Case Law* (Hart Publishing 2017).
Panara, C, *The Sub-National Dimension of the EU: A Legal Study of Multilevel Governance* (Springer 2015).

——'The Enforceability of Subsidiarity in the EU and the Ethos of Cooperative Federalism' (2016) 22 *European Public Law* 305.
——'Subsidiarity v Autonomy in the EU' (2022) 28 *European Public Law* 269.
Panara, C and Varney, M, *Local Government in Europe: The 'Fourth Level' in the EU Multilayered System of Governance* (Routledge 2013).
Papisca, A, 'Relevance of Human Rights in the Glocal Space of Politics: How to Enlarge Democratic Practice beyond State Boundaries and Build up a Peaceful World Order' in K de Feyter et al (eds), *The Local Relevance of Human Rights* (Cambridge University Press 2011).
Pappalardo, M, 'Energy Communities and Commons. Rethinking Collective Action through Inhabited Spaces' in G Debizet et al (eds), *Local Energy Communities* (Routledge 2022).
Pascapè, F, 'Usi Collettivi Urbani e Rapporto Tra Il Membro Della Comunità e La Pubblica Amministrazione Locale Nell'esperienza Gestionale Del Comune Di Napoli' in R Albanese et al (eds), *Gestire i Beni Comuni Urbani. Modelli e Prospettive: Atti Del Convegno Di Torino, 27–28 Febbraio 2019* (Rubbettino 2020).
Pastori, G, 'Sussidiarietà e diritto alla salute' (2002) 1 *Diritto Pubblico* 85.
——'L'insegnamento di un maestro' (2017) 1 *Rivista Trimestrale Di Diritto Pubblico* 143.
Pateman, C, *Participation and Democratic Theory* (Cambridge University Press 1970).
——'Participatory Democracy Revisited' (2012) 10 *Perspectives on Politics* 7.
Pavani, G, 'From Smart to Sharing? Presente e Futuro Delle Città (al Di Là Delle Etichette)' (2019) 4 *Istituzioni Del Federalismo* 849.
——'European Sharing and Collaborative Cities: The Italian Way' (2022) 28 *European Public Law* 79.
Pazos-Vidal, S, *Subsidiarity and EU Multilevel Governance: Actors, Networks and Agendas* (Routledge 2019).
Pech, L, 'The Rule of Law as a Well-Established and Well-Defined Principle of EU Law' (2022) 14 *Hague Journal on the Rule of Law* 107.
Peers, S et al (eds), *The EU Charter of Fundamental Rights: A Commentary* (Bloomsbury Publishing 2021).
Pellizzari, S, 'Il Principio Di Sussidiarietà Orizzontale Nella Giurisprudenza Del Giudice Amministrativo: Problemi Di Giustiziabilità e Prospettive Di Attuazione' (2011) 3 *Istituzioni Del Federalismo* 593.
Pellizzari, S and Borzaga, C, *Terzo Settore e Pubblica Amministrazione. La Svolta Della Corte Costituzionale* (Euricse 2020).
Perlo, N, 'Le Principe de Subsidiarité Horizontale: Un Renouvellement de La Relation Entre l'Administration et Les Citoyens. Étude Comparée Franco-Italienne' (2014) 66 *Revue internationale de droit comparé* 983.
Pernice I, 'Multilevel Constitutionalism and the Crisis of Democracy in Europe' (2015) 11 *European Constitutional Law Review* 541.
Peters, B, 'Towards the Europeanization of Participation? Reflecting on the Functions and Beneficiaries of Participation in EU Environmental Law' in C Fraenkel-Haeberle et al (eds), *Citizen Participation in Multi-Level Democracies* (Brill 2015).
Peterson, J, 'Subsidiarity: A Definition to Suit Any Vision?' (1994) 47 *Parliamentary Affairs* 116.
Petkova, B, 'Federalism in 2030' (2022) Graz Law Working Paper Series No 1.
Piattoni, S, *The Theory of Multi-Level Governance* (Oxford University Press 2010).
Pizzolato, F, 'Il Civismo e Le Autonomie Territoriali' in F Bassanini et al (eds), *Il Mostro Effimero. Democrazia, Economia e Corpi Intermedi* (Il Mulino 2019).
Pizzolato, F et al (eds), *La Città e La Partecipazione Tra Diritto e Politica* (Giappichelli 2019).
——*La Città Oltre Lo Stato* (Giappichelli 2021).
Polanyi, M, *The Logic of Liberty* (University of Chicago Press 1951).
Police, A, 'Le Autonomie Pubbliche Come Ordinamenti Giuridici' in R Cavallo Perin et al (eds), *Attualità e Necessità Del Pensiero Di Santi Romano* (Editoriale Scientifica 2019).
Popelier, P, 'Subnational Multilevel Constitutionalism' (2014) 6(2) *Perspectives on Federalism* 1.
——*Dynamic Federalism: A New Theory for Cohesion and Regional Autonomy* (Routledge 2021).

Poplawska, E, 'The Principle of Subsidiarity under the 1997 Constitution of Poland' [1997] *Saint Louis-Warsaw Transatlantic Law Journal* 107.
Pratchett, L and Krimmer, R, 'The Coming of E-Democracy' (2005) 1(3) *International Journal of Electronic Government Research* 1.
Putnam, R, *Making Democracy Work* (Princeton University Press 1993).
Quarta, A, 'Beni Comuni, Uso Collettivo e Interessi Generali: Un Percorso Giurisprudenziale' (2019) 3 *Rassegna Di Diritto Civile* 933.
Quarta, A and Ferrando, T, 'Italian Property Outlaws: From the Theory of the Commons to the Praxis of Occupation' (2015) 15 *Global Jurist* 261.
Rajan, R, *The Third Pillar: How Markets and the State Leave the Community Behind* (Penguin 2019).
Ranchordás, S, 'Smart Cities, Artificial Intelligence and Public Law: An Unchained Melody' in A Quintavalla and J Temperman (eds), *Artificial Intelligence and Human Rights* (Oxford University Press 2023).
Raspadori, F, 'La partecipazione dei cittadini all'Unione Europea e lo spettro della democrazia' (2022) *Federalismi.it*.
Ratti, C and Claudel, M, *The City of Tomorrow: Sensors, Networks, Hackers, and the Future of Urban Life* (Yale University Press 2016).
—— *La città di domani: Come le reti stanno cambiando il futuro urbano* (Einaudi 2017).
Rescigno, U, 'Principio Di Sussidiarietà Orizzontale e Diritti Sociali' (2002) 1 *Diritto Pubblico* 5.
Rieiro, A, 'The Commons and the Social and Solidarity Economy' in *Encyclopedia of the Social and Solidarity Economy* (Edward Elgar Publishing in partnership with United Nations Inter-Agency Task Force on Social and Solidarity Economy (UNTFSSE) 2023).
Rigolot, C, 'Transdisciplinarity as a Discipline and a Way of Being: Complementarities and Creative Tensions' (2020) 7 *Humanities and Social Sciences Communications* 100.
Rocca, E, 'The City, Between *Innen* and *Aussen*: The Revolution of the Horizontal Subsidiarity Principle in Italy' (2017) 5 *Birkbeck Law Review* 135.
Rodotà, S, 'Linee guida per un nuovo codice dei beni pubblici' in U Mattei et al (eds), *Invertire la rotta: idee per una riforma della proprietà pubblica* (Il Mulino 2007).
—— *Iperdemocrazia: Come Cambia La Sovranità Democratica Con il Web* (Laterza 2013).
—— *Solidarietà: Un'utopia Necessaria* (Laterza 2014).
—— *Vivere La Democrazia* (Laterza 2018).
Rosboch, M, *Le Comunità Intermedie e l'avventura Costituzionale* (Heritage Club 2017).
Rosenfeld, M, 'Comparative Constitutional Analysis in United States Adjudication and Scholarship' in M Rosenfeld and A Sajó (eds), *The Oxford Handbook of Comparative Constitutional Law* (Oxford University Press 2012).
Rosenfeld, M and Sajó, A (eds), *The Oxford Handbook of Comparative Constitutional Law* (Oxford University Press 2012).
Ross, M, 'Solidarity – A New Constitutional Paradigm for the EU?' in M Ross and Y Borgmann-Prebil (eds), *Promoting Solidarity in the European Union* (Oxford University Press 2010).
—— 'Transnational Solidarity: A Transformative Narrative for the EU and Its Citizens?' (2020) 56 *Acta Politica* 220.
Rossi, E, Il Fondamento Del Terzo Settore è Nella Costituzione. Prime Osservazioni Sulla Sentenza n. 131 Del 2020 Della Corte Costituzionale' (2020) 3 *Forum Di Quaderni Costituzionali* 53.
Rossi, E and Gori, L (eds), *Ridefinire Il Volontariato* (2020).
Russack, S, 'EU Parliamentary Democracy: How Representative?' in S Blockmans and S Russack (eds), *Representative Democracy in the EU: Recovering Legitimacy* (Rowman & Littlefield Publishers 2019).
Sacchetti, S and Salvatori, G, '"Shared Administration" as a New Relationship between the Public Sector and the Social Economy' (2023) 126 Euricse Working Paper Series.
Salati, C, 'La Libertà Dei Cittadini Attivi Oltre Lo Stato: Prime Considerazioni Sull'amministrazione Condivisa in Unione Europea' in F Pizzolato et al (eds), *La Città Oltre Lo Stato* (Giappichelli 2022).
—— 'L'Amministrazione Condivisa come Innovvazione Democratica' (Labsus, 2025).
—— 'The Forgotten Meaning of the EU Principle of Subsidiarity – Horizontal Subsidiarity in Italian Local Governments' (2023) Diversity Governance Papers.

——'Città e Sussidiarietà Orizzontale: Orientamenti Dottrinali Dal Caso Italiano per l'Unione Europea' (2024) Italian Papers on Federalism.

Salati, C and Arban, E, 'Sussidiarietà, pluralismo e autonomie: un canale aggiuntivo alla partecipazione' in S Salati and E Alber (eds), *Partecipazione e innovazioni democratiche in Italia. Una prospettiva multidisciplinare e multilivello* (forthcoming 2026).

Salvatore, A (ed), *Maurice Hauriou. La Teoria Dell'istituzione e Della Fondazione* (Quodlibet 2019).

Sassen, S, 'The Global City: Introducing a Concepts' (2005) 11(2) *Brown Journal of World Affairs* 27.

Saunders, C and Arban, E, 'Federalism and Local Governments' in E Arban (ed), *Cities in Federal Constitutional Theory* (Oxford University Press 2022).

Scheppele, KL et al, 'EU Values Are Law, after All: Enforcing EU Values through Systemic Infringement Actions by the European Commission and the Member States of the European Union' (2021) 39 *Yearbook of European Law* 3.

Schnettger, A, 'Article 4(2) TEU as a Vehicle for National Constitutional Identity in the Shared European Legal System' in C Calliess and G van der Schyff (eds), *Constitutional Identity in a Europe of Multilevel Constitutionalism* (Cambridge University Press 2019).

Schragger, R, 'Conclusion: The City in the Future of Federalism' in E Arban (ed), *Cities in Federal Constitutional Theory* (Oxford University Press 2022).

Schumpeter, JA, *Capitalism, Socialism and Democracy* (Geo Allen & Unwin 1943).

Sellers, JM and Lindström, A, 'Decentralization, Local Government, and the Welfare State' (2007) 20 *Governance* 609.

Sen, A, 'Individual Freedom as Social Commitment' (Winter/Spring 1998/99) 25(4)–26(1) *India International Centre Quarterly* 53.

Sennett, R, 'The Open City' (Urban Age, LSE Cities, 2006).

Servillo, L et al, 'Small and Medium-Sized Towns in Europe: Conceptual, Methodological and Policy Issues' (2017) 108 *Tijdschrift Voor Economische En Sociale Geografie* 365.

Sgueo, G, *The Practice of Democracy: A Selection of Civic Engagement Initiatives* (Study, European Parliament 2020).

Shaw, J and Štiks, I, 'The Constitutionalisation of Cities and the Future of Global Society' (2021) *Identities* 295.

Shore, C, '"European Governance" or Governmentality? The European Commission and the Future of Democratic Government' (2011) 17 *European Law Journal* 287.

Simonati, A, 'The (Draft) European Charter of the Commons – Between Opportunities and Challenges' (2018) 16(2) *Central European Public Administration Review* 91.

Smith, G, *Democratic Innovations: Designing Institutions for Citizen Participation* (Cambridge University Press 2009).

Snyder, F, 'The Effectiveness of European Community Law: Institutions, Processes, Tools and Techniques' (1993) 56 *Modern Law Review* 19.

Sommermann, K-P, 'Citizen Participation in Multi-Level Democracies: An Introduction' in C Fraenkel-Haeberle et al (eds), *Citizen Participation in Multi-Level Democracies* (Brill-Nijhoff 2015).

Sørensen, E et al, 'Political Boundary Spanning: Politicians at the Interface between Collaborative Governance and Representative Democracy' (2020) 39 *Policy and Society* 530.

Spanò, M, 'Private Law Arrangements for the Commons: A New Comparative Perspective' in F Girard and C Frison (eds), *The Commons, Plant Breeding and Agricultural Research* (Routledge 2018).

Stefan, O et al, 'EU Soft Law in the EU Legal Order: A Literature Review' (2019) King's College London Law School Research Paper (forthcoming).

Stephan, M et al, 'An Introduction to Polycentricity and Governance' in A Thiel et al (eds), *Governing Complexity: Analyzing and Applying Polycentricity* (Cambridge University Press 2019).

Stephenson, P, 'Twenty Years of Multi-Level Governance: "Where Does It Come From? What Is It? Where Is It Going?"' (2013) 20 *Journal of European Public Policy* 817.

Steytler, N, 'Comparative Conclusions' in N Steytler (ed), *Local Government and Metropolitan Regions in Federal Systems* (McGill-Queen's University Press 2009).

Steytler, N (ed), *Local Government and Metropolitan Regions in Federal Systems* (McGill-Queen's University Press 2009).
—— *The Forum of Federations Handbook on Local Government in Federal Systems* (Palgrave Macmillan 2024).
Swiney, CF, 'The Urbanization of International Law and International Relations: The Rising Soft Power of Cities in Global Governance' (2020) 41 *Michigan Journal of International Law* 227.
Talamanca, M, *Istituzioni di diritto romano* (Giuffrè 1990).
Tamanaha, BZ, 'Understanding Legal Pluralism: Past to Present, Local to Global' (2008) 30(3) *Sydney Law Review* 375.
Tiberi, G, 'La Dimensione Costituzionale Del Terzo Settore' (*Astrid Online*, 2008).
Toniatti, R et al (eds), *An Ever More Complex Union: The Regional Variable as the Missing Link in the EU Constitution?* (Nomos 2004).
Tornos Mas, J, 'Bienes Comunes y Administración Compartida' in L Míguez Macho and M Almeida Cerreda (eds), *Los Retos Actuales Del Derecho Administrativo En El Estado Autonómico* (Vol 2, 2017).
Tornos Mas, J, 'Primeros Pasos Hacia La Administración Compartida En La Administración Local de Cataluña' (*Labsus*, 2017).
Tosato, E, 'Sul principio di sussidiarietà dell'intervento statale' in *Nuova Antologia* (1959) (Now in *Persona, Società Intermedie e Stato*, Giuffrè Editore, Milano, 1989).
Trettel, M, *La democrazia partecipativa negli ordinamenti composti: Studio di diritto comparato sull'incidenza della tradizione giuridica nelle democratic innovations* (Edizioni Scientifiche Italiane 2020).
—— 'Democratic Innovations in (Subnational) Constitution-Making: The Institutionalized Case(s) of the Italian Provinces of Trento and Bolzano'. *Innovation: The European Journal of Social Science Research*, 2021.
—— 'Rethinking Participatory Democracy through Federalism: Citizen Participation, Power-Sharing and Decision-Making Processes' in NP Alessi and M Trettel (eds), *Federalism and the Law of Diversity* (Brill Nijhoff 2025).
Tuori, K, 'Transnational Law: On Legal Hybrids and Legal Perspectivism' in MP Maduro, K Tuori and S Sankari (eds), *Transnational Law: Rethinking European Law and Legal Thinking* (Cambridge University Press 2014).
Valastro, A, 'La Democrazia Partecipativa Alla Prova Dei Territori: Il Ruolo Delle Amministrazioni Locali Nell'epoca Delle Fragilità' in A Valastro (ed), *Le Regole Locali Della Democrazia Partecipativa. Tendenze e Prospettive Dei Regolamenti Comunali* (Jovene 2016).
—— 'La Democrazia Partecipativa Alla Prova Dei Territori: Tendenze e Prospettive Dei Regolamenti Comunali' (2016) 3 *Osservatorio Sulle Fonti* 14.
—— 'La Partecipazione Alla Prova Dei Territori: Dal "Decidere" al "Fare"' (*Labsus*, 2016).
Van Deth, JW, 'A Conceptual Map of Political Participation' (2014) 49 *Acta Politica* 349.
Van Laerhoven, F and Barnes, C, 'Facilitated Self-Governance of the Commons' in B Hudson et al (eds), *Routledge Handbook of the Study of the Commons* (Routledge 2019).
Van Zeben, J, 'Local Governments as Subjects and Objects of EU Law: Legitimate Limits?' in S Bardutzky and E Fahey (eds), *Framing the Subjects and Objects of Contemporary EU Law* (Edward Elgar Publishing 2017).
—— 'Polycentric Features of the European Union' in J van Zeben and A Bobić (eds), *Polycentricity in the European Union* (Cambridge University Press 2019).
—— 'Policentricity' in B Hudson et al (eds), *Routledge Handbook of the Study of the Commons* (Routledge 2019).
—— 'Polycentricity as a Theory of Governance' in J van Zeben and A Bobić (eds), *Polycentricity in the European Union* (Cambridge University Press 2019).
van Zeben, J and Bobić, A (eds), *Polycentricity in the European Union* (Cambridge University Press 2019).
—— 'Conclusions – Pathways to Polycentricity' in J van Zeben and A Bobić (eds), *Polycentricity in the European Union* (Cambridge University Press 2019).

——'The Potential of a Polycentric European Union' in J van Zeben and A Bobić (eds), *Polycentricity in the European Union* (Cambridge University Press 2019).

Vanni, MB, 'Understanding the commons: the reception of Elinor Ostrom's work in Italian legal scholarship' [2014] *Ius Publicum* 1.

Violini, L, 'Il principio di sussidiarietà' in G Vittadini (ed), *Sussidiarietà. La riforma possibile* (Milano 1998).

Vivero-Pol, JL et al, *Routledge Handbook of Food as a Commons* (Routledge 2019).

Vodyanitskaya, E, 'Local Government' (2016) *Max Planck Encyclopedia of Comparative Constitutional Law (MPECCoL)*.

Von Bogdandy, A, 'Founding Principles of EU Law: A Theoretical and Doctrinal Sketch' (2010) 16 *European Law Journal* 106.

—— 'The Transformation of European Law: The Reformed Concept and Its Quest for Comparison' 2016-14 MPIL Research Paper Series.

——'The Idea of European Public Law Today' 2017-4 MPIL Research Paper Series.

—— 'European Democracy: A Reconstruction through Dismantling Misconceptions' (2022) MPIL Research Paper Series.

Von Bogdandy, A and Bast, J (eds), *Principles of European Constitutional Law* (Hart Publishing 2009).

Wagner, RE, 'Self-Governance, Polycentrism, and Federalism: Recurring Themes in Vincent Ostrom's Scholarly Oeuvre' (2005) 57 *Journal of Economic Behaviour & Organization* 173.

Weiler, JHH et al, 'European Democracy and its Critique' (1995) 18 *West European Politics* 4.

Weinstock, D, 'Cities and Federalism' in JE Fleming and JT Levy (eds), *Federalism and Subsidiarity* (New York University Press 2014).

Westerman, P, 'From Houses to Ships: Governance as a Form of Law' (2018) 14(4) *Le Libellio* 5.

Wilke, M and Wallace, H, 'Subsidiarity Approaches to Power Sharing in the European Community' (1990) RIIA Discussion Paper No 27.

Zapata Campos, MJ et al, 'Urban Commoning Practices in the Repair Movement: Frontstaging the Backstage' (2020) 52 *Economy and Space* 1150.

Zielonka, J, 'The Remaking of the EU's Borders and the Images of European Architecture' (2017) 39 *Journal of European Integration* 641.

Literature (Electronic)

Fattori, T, *Public-Commons Partnership and the Commonification of that which is Public* (2007): commonsblog.files.wordpress.com/2007/10/fattori-commonification-of-that-which-is-public.pdf.

Holemans, D, *Introducing the Partner State: Public-Civil Partnerships for a Better City* (21 June 2019): www.nesta.org.uk/blog/introducing-partner-state-public-civil-partnerships-better-city/).

Kimmel J et al, *Urban Commons Shared Spaces* (Commons Network and raumlaborberlin 2018): www.commonsnetwork.org/wp-content/uploads/2018/11/SharedSpacesCommonsNetwork.pdf.

Quarta, A and Vercellone, A, 'The Rise of Urban Commons in Europe' (Blogdroiteuropeen, 20 January 2021): blogdroiteuropeen.com/2021/01/20/the-rise-of-urban-commons-in-the-europe-by-alessandra-quarta-and-antonio-vercellone/.

Rodotà, S, 'Constituting the Commons in the Context of State, Law and Politics' in *Economics and the Common(s): From Seed Form to Core Paradigm* (2013): boellblog.org/wp-content/uploads/2013/10/ECC-Rodota-keynote.pdf).

Vercellone, C et al, 'Managing the Commons in the Knowledge Economy' (d-cent Project, 2015): shs.hal.science/halshs-01180341.

Others (Selection)

Labsus, Annual report (2024): www.labsus.org/rapporto-labsus-2024/.

Labsus, Prototype of municipal regulation on commons 2025 (English version) www.labsus.org/wp-content/uploads/2024/06/June.2024.REGULATION-ON-COLLABORATION-BETWEEN-CITIZENS-AND-ADMINISTRATIONS-FOR-THE-CARE-OF-COMMON-GOODS-1.pdf.

Labsus, Prototype of municipal regulation on commons 2025 (Italian version) www.labsus.org/wp-content/uploads/2024/06/febbraio.2025.PROTOTIPO-LABSUS.-REGOLAMENTO-SULLA-COLLABORAZIONE-TRA-CITTADINI-E-AMMINISTRAZIONI.pdf.

Municipality of Barcelona 'Comuns urbans – Patrimoni Ciutadà. Marc conceptual i propostes de línies d'acció' (2016) ajuntament.barcelona.cat/participaciociutadana/sites/default/files/documents/patrimoni_ciutada_marc_conceptual_v.3.0.pdf.

Municipality of Barcelona Programa Patrimoni Ciutadà d'Ús i Gestió Comunitària (2017) ajuntament.barcelona.cat/participaciociutadana/ca/patrimoni-ciutada.

Municipality of Bologna, Regolamento generale sulle forme di collaborazione tra soggetti civici e Amministrazione per la cura dei beni comuni urbani e lo svolgimento di attività di interesse generale (2023) www.comune.bologna.it/amministrazione/documenti-e-dati/regolamenti/regolamento-collaborazione-soggetti-civici-amministrazione-beni-comuni-urbani.

Municipality of Grenoble, resolution Principes pour une administration cooperative (2022): share.google/nyEBzoMJA3J5pRxHX.

INDEX

www.ingramcontent.com/pod-product-compliance
Ingram Content Group UK Ltd.
Pitfield, Milton Keynes, MK11 3LW, UK
UKHW020813290926
15470UKWH00003B/1136

9 781509 989669